PERSONAL PROPERTY
OF
DAVID & DANIEL
DULMAGE

Vera M. Kemp

0116

David Dulmage

Economics for Canadians

Economics for Canadians

HELEN BUCKLEY
Economic Consultant

KENNETH BUCKLEY
Professor of Economics
University of Saskatchewan

TORONTO

THE MACMILLAN COMPANY OF CANADA LIMITED

PRINTED IN CANADA BY THE BRYANT PRESS LIMITED

Preface

This book is designed to meet the demand for an introductory course in economics and was written specifically for the Canadian reader. The elements of economics are, of course, not limited in their application to any single country, but the illustration of economic principles requires an institutional setting. Our objective was to make that setting a Canadian one, to describe the main features and problems of the Canadian economy, and to introduce elements of economic theory as a means of studying and interpreting our system and others like it. Finally, we wished to discuss briefly alternative economic systems; this has been done in the last chapter.

The need for such a book is clear enough. Until a generation ago economics as an academic discipline was left to the universities, possibly because of the intrinsic difficulty of the subject matter but also because the economic issues discussed within the body politic were few in number and of long standing. But all this has changed with the emergence of the welfare state. Over the past generation a greater role in economic decision-making has been assigned to governments, with the result that economic issues have become topics of everyday political and social discussion. Since the vast majority of the population does not go to university, it was inevitable in a liberal democracy like ours that the study of economics should spread into the secondary schools. There are many Canadians who want to understand the economic approach to social problems and its application to major issues in their own country.

The authors gratefully acknowledge the comments and criticism of Dr. A. E. Safarian of the University of Saskatchewan and Mr. Ian J. Wilson of Saskatchewan Teachers College, Saskatoon, who read portions of the text. They are also indebted to Miss Margaret Buckley who typed the manuscript. For the selection of photographs, the preparation of charts and the task of seeing the manuscript through publication the authors wish to thank Miss Gladys E. Neale, Miss Winifred Eayrs and Mrs. Jane Hill of The Macmillan Company of Canada, and Mr. Robert Kunz, the artist.

H. L. B.
K. A. H. B.

September 1960

Contents

Tables, Charts and Graphs

PART I

Chapter 1

Introduction

We cannot expect to understand what economics is until we have studied the subject. But we can readily see why we study it. Economics is defined as "the study of man's activity in using scarce resources to satisfy wants". If the means of satisfying human wants were not scarce, there would be no economic problems and no need to study economics. The scarce means are the basic economic resources — a country's labour force, its natural resources and machinery and equipment — that are used to produce goods and services. If these resources were not scarce we could produce enough to satisfy everybody's wants. So we find the root of the economic problem in scarcity.

The nature of the economic problem is easily recognized in one's own family. The wants of every member of the family are definite and clear enough. The scarcity of means — the family income — is clear too! No matter what the family income we all want more of something: more travel, books, plays, more or better automobiles, more and better clothes, houses, and food. The solution to this problem is a greater income.

Economists look, not at a single family, but at all families and at whole countries and they find the same problem. The total wants in Canada, or in any country, far exceed the productive capacity available to satisfy them. And so we study the process of production and the way in which goods and services are *shared* among the population. By studying these processes we attempt to understand how the economic system works and if and how it could be made to work better.

Each of us looks at the economic system from two points of view: as a self-interested individual and as a citizen in a democracy.

As individuals we want to understand our own personal economic experience. Although jobs and money are far from being the whole of life most of us are greatly interested in these matters. It is not only that we want more of the things money will buy. In our kind of society the individual's standing in the community is influenced by his economic status. His opportunities, which may determine the whole direction of his life, depend in large part upon the income of his parents. And scarcely anyone is immune to the effects of unemployment or inflation. Simply to understand our own place and prospects within the economic system is one reason why we study economics.

As citizens in a democracy we have another reason. Political parties divide on issues of economic policies and ask for our support. It is our responsibility, as voters, to have some understanding of the issues. The difficulty of judging economic policies is complicated by a multitude of biased advisers. Not only politicians but all the agencies which influence public opinion urge upon us conflicting versions of right and wrong.

We must recognize that the agencies of propaganda are likely to promote policies of benefit to themselves. Political parties, interested in promoting their own power, may succeed in misleading us. But if some politicians talk economic nonsense — and get away with it — that is a reflection on us. In a democracy we get the kind of politicians and the kind of government we deserve. Consequently, it is a mistake to blame the government when we suffer economic ills. The fault is always our own.

The student of economics also learns that the economic system is not a machine.

There are no experts who know what levers to push or pull to make the economy run well. The economy is a social organization, made up of human beings. The economic decisions of our political representatives affect all of us for good or ill. Virtually every policy which benefits some of us will harm others. So the economic issues of the day turn out to be ethical issues. As citizens, we need to know where we stand.

Economic problems are never simple and, because the problems are also ethical ones, the same answer will not satisfy everyone. No one can tell the individual voter what he should support. He has to make his own choice on the basis of whatever knowledge he has. The study of economics does not provide the answers. It does provide a method of thought and a framework of knowledge essential to an informed judgment. But the individual must still choose among conflicting policies the ones that appear to him to be more right and less wrong than the alternatives.

For these reasons we study the institutions and agencies and the processes of our economy. We begin with the end result: the performance of the economic system. How fully does it satisfy our wants? This is the question of wealth and welfare, the subject of Chapter 2.

Chapter 2

National Income and Economic Welfare

1. INTRODUCTION

Our Level of Living

Canada is a wealthy country. Compared with most of the world's population the average Canadian lives in luxury and takes for granted a level of living far above the aspirations of the vast majority of humanity. We do not know that he is happier or wiser than the average Asian or African but certainly he is richer in material comforts.

Consider food. Few Canadians have to worry about getting enough to eat. Almost all Canadians have three meals a day and most Canadian families can afford the kind and variety of foods that make up a well-balanced diet. In many countries the standard diet leans heavily on the cheaper foods — cereals or root crops — and often on a single dish, such as rice or beans or fish. There are still places where people, day by day, actually do go hungry. There are still places where the failure of a single crop can bring whole districts perilously close to starvation.

More and better food is only a part of our high level of living. A modest house in Canada is a marvel of luxury compared with the Arab's tent or the adobe hut of the Mexican farmer. And we have so many other things that Arabs and Mexicans (and much of the world) do without. Electric stoves and refrigerators, washing machines and radios are standard equipment in Canada, at least in the cities, and most Canadian families have cars and television sets. In Europe these things are not so common, and in much of the world they are owned, if at all, by the rich. Hospitals and

schools, movies, books and libraries: these are a few of the other things which Canadians take for granted. They cannot be counted part of the level of living in places where they are not generally available. In many countries almost everything beyond the bare essentials of living is a luxury.

Problems in Economic Welfare

Consideration of these national differences raises the question: "Why?". Why poverty and even hunger for so many while a few fortunate nations are adding to their comfort with each passing year? What makes some nations wealthy while others remain poor? This is the question that inspired Adam Smith's *The Wealth of Nations*; and although this book, which marks the beginning of modern economics, was written nearly 200 years ago, its central problem is as fresh and interesting as ever. To understand our economic welfare we must first know the reason for the "wealth of nations".

The second problem in economic welfare is to explain the differences in wealth *within* a country. The individual's level of living does not only depend upon the place in which he happens to live. There are sheiks and maharajahs of great wealth in the poorest countries and families existing on a bare minimum of food and clothes and shelter even in the richest countries. Within Canada people do not all live equally well. We have our rich and our poor. This raises the second question of economic welfare: the question of shares in national wealth.

In the study of economic welfare there is

Information Service of India

Outdoor fruit-selling in India. Canada's per capita income is more than twenty times that of India.

a third major problem: the fact that our level of living *changes*. At times jobs are plentiful, farmers have markets for their crops and Canadians in general are prosperous. But there are also times when jobs and incomes melt away and many Canadians find their level of living reduced. So great is the contrast between good years and bad years that this periodic lowering of living standards is sometimes called the number one economic problem for countries like Canada. Although we do not have the problem of mass poverty, we are still confronted, from time to time, with widespread economic distress.

Income is a Measure of Welfare

These three problems in economic welfare will occupy our attention throughout this chapter and, indeed, throughout much of this book. We want to look at all the things that affect our level of living as a nation and as individuals. Alternatively, because income is a good measure of the level of living, we can ask: what makes our *incomes* large or small, and why do incomes fluctuate through time?

If we want to compare the economic welfare of two families living in the same city, the first thing we do is compare their incomes. This will show us how much each family can buy. We will not know precisely how they stand because one family may be larger than the other and need more income. One might get more for each dollar by careful budgeting, or it might save on fruits and vegetables by growing these at home. Still another consideration is that one of the families might care more than the other for leisure pursuits that require little or no money. Nevertheless, in spite of these differences, the incomes of the two families will tell us more about their levels of living than any other single measure.

Now if we want to compare economic welfare between two countries what we

Dominion Stores Limited

A modern supermarket illustrates one aspect of Canada's higher level of living.

must do is compare *their* incomes. What is the income of a country?

The National Income

The national income is the sum of all the different incomes earned (in a year) by everyone in the country. There are the wages and salaries paid out to cooks, carpenters, teachers and all other employees. Wages and salaries are the largest part of the total national income. Then there are payments made to people for the use of their property in production: rent for land, interest on loans, and profits on business investments. These earnings, which are called investment income, are added to wages and salaries to give the grand total— the national income.

National Income and Production

Incomes are paid out in the form of money. But a family's real income is not the amount of money it happens to earn. You can see this by imagining that there were no food or clothes or anything else to buy in the stores: the family's money would be worthless! A family's *real income* is made up of the food, clothes, and other goods and services that money will buy.

Similarly, if we look at the country as a whole, we can see that the *real* national income is not the money going out as income. It is the grand total of all the goods and services produced in that year. The real national income depends upon how much is produced.

Now let us consider the problem of *measuring* the national income. What we want to know is the total quantity of goods and services that have been produced. One way of measuring national income, therefore, would be to add up the value of the thousands upon thousands of goods and services of every kind produced during the

Toronto Real Estate Board

A second problem in economic welfare: to explain why some Canadians . . .

City of Toronto Planning Board

. . . live less well than others.

year. But national income may be measured in another way. As goods and services are produced and sold, money payments go out to everyone who worked (or whose property was used) in production. And if we add these money income payments we have a measure of the total value of production. They come to the same thing.

To see why, suppose we know the value of all the bread produced in Canada last year. This would cover all the costs of producing bread, including wages and salaries and the cost of the raw materials. Obviously, then, the value of the bread covers all the incomes in the bread industry. But also, since it includes the value of the *flour* used, it covers incomes in the flour-milling industry, and incomes of farmers whose wheat went into Canadian bread! (Incomes from wheat and flour sold abroad are not reflected in the output of the bread industry but they can be picked up separately.)

If we add the value of all the *finished* goods and services produced during the year, we get a sum which is equal to all the incomes paid out in every industry. Similarly, if we add the money income payments, we show both the total income earned and the total value of production. Therefore, to say that Canada's national income is $23 billion means that $23 billion in income went out to Canadians, and also that $23 billion worth of bread, hats, cars, and goods and services of every kind became available for us to buy.

So it is that countries which *produce* abundantly (compared to their populations) are countries with high levels of national income. Countries with less output are, of course, the countries with lower incomes.

Using the concept of national income we can restate the three problems in economic welfare. The first problem is the *size* of the national income. What makes the income of a country high or low? The second is the *distribution* of that income among the people who created it. How do we share the results of production? The third problem is to explain the *changes* in national income. Why does the national income fluctuate?

2. THE SIZE OF THE NATIONAL INCOME

Rich Countries and Poor Countries

Measures of production and national income can be used to make rough comparisons of economic welfare among people in different countries. Some figures are given in Table 1 below. Income is not a perfect measure of welfare, even for families in the same city, and we should keep in mind that comparisons among countries are even less precise because living conditions vary greatly. The Ceylonese family, for example, does not need to spend on winter clothes or central heating. Further, the different incomes in Table 1 are all expressed in Canadian dollars and a dollar may buy more in some countries than in others. To illustrate the difficulty, take per capita income in India. At the official rate of exchange (approximately five rupees to the dollar) an income of 300 rupees is expressed as 60 Canadian

dollars. But if five rupees buy more in India than a dollar buys in Canada, which is quite possible, then incomes in India are somewhat higher than our figures show.

Now let us look at Table 1. Here we

TABLE 1
Per Capita Income in Nine Countries, 1957 **(in Canadian dollars)**

United States...	2094
Canada..	1437
United Kingdom...	940
France...	832
Turkey...	378
Japan..	248
Brazil...	155
Egypt...	107
India..	60

Source: Statistical Yearbook, United Nations, 1958.

have incomes in nine countries in many different parts of the world. The national income of each has been divided by its total population to show the average income per person.

What differences in living standards these figures must reflect! The gap between the richest country and the poorest is almost unbelievable. India, for example, has a per capita income which is less than 3 per cent of America's and roughly 4 per cent of

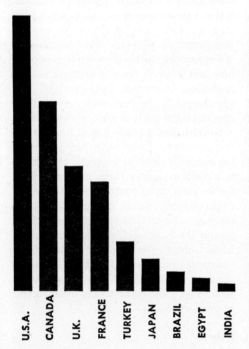

U.S.A. CANADA U.K. FRANCE TURKEY JAPAN BRAZIL EGYPT INDIA

Canada's. Income in Brazil is well above India's but still only one-tenth of the Canadian income. There is also a considerable range of incomes within the group of so-called wealthy nations. Per capita income in the United States is almost 50 per cent higher than in Canada and the difference is larger still between Canada and France.

If *all* countries were included in the table only a few would appear at or above the level of France. (In addition to the three countries listed there would be Australia and New Zealand and the countries of northwestern Europe.) These economically

favoured countries account for a small fraction of the world's population. Taken together they include 400 million people, which is only 14 per cent of the 2800 million people in the world!

How much lower are the incomes of the rest of the world can be judged from the six remaining countries in Table 1. The income level in Brazil is probably higher than the average for Central and South America; the level in Egypt can be taken to represent much of Africa. Among the Asian countries, which contain half the world's population, Japan and Turkey are relatively advanced. The extreme poverty indicated by India's income is likely to be more typical. High incomes, then, are the privilege of a few, and their economic success is not easily copied. In the world today all countries are working to raise living standards, yet the difference between rich and poor remains great and continues to grow. Incomes are rising, slowly, in the underdeveloped countries but much more rapidly in those nations which are already rich.

The Level of Production

Now we turn to the question "why?". Why average incomes of $100 in one country, $2000 in another? Why does Canada stand so high on the income scale? We have seen that income and production are measures of the same thing: a high national income means a large quantity of goods and services produced. To discover why national income is high or low we must turn to production.

The Economic Resources of a Farm

For a start, let us take a small production unit — a single farm — and see what determines the size of its output. Actually there are several factors. One, obviously, is the *land*. The farmer's crop will depend upon how many acres of land he has and, also, on the *kind* of land, upon its fertility and whether it is flat and easy to work.

A second factor is *labour*. The farmer may work alone or with the help of his family or he may hire farm workers. The number of people working, how long and hard they work, and how much skill and knowledge they possess all influence the size of the crop.

A third factor is the machinery the farmer uses. The wheat farmer with a tractor and combine can produce much more than another farmer, similarly situated, who uses an old-fashioned threshing outfit. This third factor is called *capital*. It includes, besides machinery, the buildings on the farm, the farm trucks and farm tools, and livestock of all kinds.

Land, labour, and capital are called the *factors of production*. These factors of production and the technology they reflect explain why the farm's output is large or small. Technology covers such things as the farmer's knowledge of farming methods, and the skills which are learned through education and experience. Technology is also reflected in the kinds of capital employed.

The Economic Resources of the Nation

The output of a single farm depends upon the amounts and kinds of land, labour, and capital that are used on the farm. The output of the nation as a whole depends upon the same factors: land, labour, and capital. Technology is not treated as a separate factor of production because the technology of production cannot be separated from the other three factors. In a sense, the technology is "in them".

Land

Land as a factor of production is not only farm land but all natural resources. That is, the term "land" is defined to include all the mineral, forest and water resources of a country as well as its farm and other land. And as with the farm land, we are concerned with the quality as well as the quantity of these resources.

We call these resources "natural resources" because they are provided by Nature. They were not produced by man. They are simply there as part of our physical environment. What parts of Nature can be used as resources in production depends upon our

knowledge. In other words, it depends upon our technology. The Sudbury nickel deposits were not economic resources two hundred years ago because the Indians did not know how to use nickel. And many elements in our physical environment that are not used today will become economic resources in the future as technology develops.

Different countries are by no means equal in the natural resources they possess, and there are few so well endowed as Canada. It is our good fortune to possess millions of acres of farm land and forests and an abundance of minerals and water-power. We are doubly fortunate to have a population that is small relative to these natural resources. Contrast China, which has approximately the same land area as Canada, but thirty times as many people to feed!

Nevertheless, Canada's wealth in natural resources is far from being the only reason for our high national income. Differences in natural resources alone cannot account for the great variations in output from country to country. Some, such as Switzerland, manage to have relatively high levels of living on the basis of few natural resources, while others (Malaya, for example, or Indonesia), much richer in natural resources, are near the bottom of the income scale. And so we must go on to the other factors of production.

Labour

A country's labour force includes every person who contributes to production in any way. It covers the store manager as well as the miner, the scientist and poet as well as the farmer. All are working to satisfy somebody's wants, and are therefore contributing to the total output of goods and services. The size of that total output depends upon the number of people working, and also on their quality as workers. By quality is meant their health and energy and their skill and knowledge. The knowledge used in production is, of course, technology.

With labour, as with natural resources,

Information Service of India

Harvesting rice by hand in India. The amount each worker can produce is relatively small.

National Film Board Photo

This Saskatchewan farmer uses three combines and harvests more than 2,000 acres of wheat.

there are very great differences from one country to another. Canada's working population, which numbers around six million, is small compared with more than 100 million in India. But of course it is not just the number of persons in the labour force that matters. Probably Canada's greatest strength in production lies with the quality of her labour force. Consider first the tremendous variety of skills our different workers possess: carpenters, mechanics, doctors, engineers, physicists — it would take pages to list them all. Some of these skills are the result of years of specialized training, but all are more easily acquired because every Canadian receives some education. Then, too, there is our capacity for work, the result of high standards of nutrition, public health, and medical services.

The labour force in poorer countries is handicapped in two ways: by lack of education and by the effects of malnutrition and disease. Where the vast majority of the labour force cannot read or write, or where large numbers suffer from malaria, dysentery or inadequate nutrition, the West's industrial techniques cannot be copied overnight. The process of improving the quality of the labour force in those countries will be slow and expensive.

Capital

Capital, the third factor of production, covers all the factory, office and other buildings, structures such as railways, dams, and roads; machinery and equipment; as well as stock-piles of raw materials and partly finished goods. These things are produced by man for the single purpose of increasing his further production. Just as the primitive fisherman makes a net to catch more fish, we produce capital of many kinds to increase our production of other things. The time the fisherman spends making a net is well repaid: he can then catch so many more fish. In much the same way, we find that the cost of making machines to make the goods we want is well repaid in greater production. Capital enables us to produce so much more *per person*.

The stock of capital available for use in production varies greatly from one part of the world to another. Canadian farmers, for example, have the combine, the tractor, and electricity on the farm, while farmers in the poorest countries have little beyond a simple plough and hand tools to aid their labour. For power they use the mule, the water-buffalo — or even human power. In almost every field of production Canadians work with highly developed, specialized machinery and equipment and this is another reason for our high productivity.

Size of the National Income

An experienced and efficient farmer who works a good-sized piece of land with a large quantity of capital produces a large output. Accordingly, his income is high. In the same way, a highly skilled and healthy labour force working with an abundance of capital and natural resources per worker produces a large national output — and a high income per capita. It is in this way that we can answer the question: what makes a country rich or poor? The answer lies in the *combination* of all the factors of production. The particular combination we find in Canada spells large output and a high national income. Other combinations result in lower output and lower incomes. In most of the poorer countries the labour force is large but lacking in skills; the development of natural resources is limited to those in which only a simple technology is required; capital is scarce and the amount of capital used per worker is very small. When we contrast our resources, our labour force, our capital and our technology, we can understand our high level of income.

3. SHARES IN THE NATIONAL INCOME

A vital question for every family is the size of its share in the national income. A high national income does not mean that all Canadians live like kings. A few are millionaires but most of us are considerably less wealthy and many Canadians have barely enough to live on. Our national income is divided in such a way that some Canadians have high incomes, some have low incomes, and some are in between. To explain the distribution of national income would take us well beyond the scope of the present chapter, but we can begin by describing it more fully. Let us look at the actual incomes of Canadians. What is the average income? How far do incomes range above and below that average? How many Canadians can be called "rich", and how do they compare in numbers with the poor?

The Average Income

Average income received by Canadians is somewhat higher than the $1437 shown in Table 1, which is income *per capita*. Income per capita is the national income divided by the total population (men, women and children), many of whom do not actually receive any income at all. In this section we look at the incomes received by individuals. Unfortunately, we cannot look at the incomes of *all* Canadians because statistics on farm income are not available; but apart from that limitation our figures will tell us a great deal about the distribution of income in Canada.

In 1957 the average non-farm income "received" in Canada was $2800. To find this average income we took the total of all the income going out and divided by the total number of income receivers. If total income was actually distributed in this way — an equal share for each individual — then each individual would have got $2800. But income is not divided evenly. A better way of finding an "average" income is to take the half-way point on the income scale. This is called the median income: half of all incomes received are *greater* than this income and half are *less*. In 1957 the median income in Canada was $2350. (The median is below the average because a few very high incomes pull the average up.) If we could include the 800,000 Canadians who make their living on farms our median income would be lower still. In 1955 the average farm income was only half the level of the average non-farm income.

Inequality of Incomes

An income of $2350 cannot be called a large income, at least not in Canada. And since one-half the non-farm income receivers got *less*, you can see that there are a great many Canadians with low incomes. High incomes, on the other hand, are reserved for a very small company. In 1957 less than 2 per cent of income receivers had incomes of $10,000 or more! These are the basic facts of income distribution in Canada. Not only do incomes vary greatly — from low to high — but low incomes are numerous and high incomes rare.

For more detailed information on income distribution we go to Table 2. Here our income receivers are grouped by income classes: the percentage with incomes of less than $1000, the percentage between $1000 and $2000, and so on. The table also shows

INCOME GROUP	PER CENT OF INDIVIDUALS	PER CENT OF INCOME
UNDER $2000	👤👤👤👤👤👤👤👤	💰💰💰
$5000 AND OVER	👤👤👤	💰💰💰💰💰💰

Each symbol represents 5% of total.

how much of the total income went to each group. To illustrate, let us look at the first group, individuals with incomes under $1000. In numbers, they account for 25 per cent of all individual income receivers (column 2); their combined incomes, however, were less than 5 per cent of all the income paid out to individuals (column 3).

TABLE 2

Distribution of Incomes of Canadian Individuals, 1957

(excludes farm population and farm income)

(1)	(2)	(3)
	Per Cent of All	Per Cent of Total Income
Income Group	Individuals	Received
Under $1000......	25.2	4.8
$1000 to $1999......	18.2	9.5
$2000 to $2999......	18.4	16.1
$3000 to $3999......	15.9	19.6
$4000 to $4999......	10.3	16.2
$5000 to $9999......	10.3	23.2
$10,000 and over......	1.7	10.6
Total....................	100.0	100.0

Source: *Distribution of Non-farm Incomes in Canada by Size, 1957, D.B.S.*

In 1957, one-half of all non-farm income receivers were below $2350, the median income. In Table 2 we see that 25 per cent were actually below $1000. Another 25 per cent, then, were between $1000 and $2350. Of the remaining 50 per cent the vast majority received less than $5000. Above the $5000 mark we find the small group (10 per cent of the total) with incomes from $5000 to $10,000, and the very few (2 per cent of the total) who received $10,000 or more. Clearly, the number of Canadians who have low incomes greatly exceeds the number who can be called wealthy.

The best measure of inequality is column 3, which shows how the total income is divided. We see that a relatively small share — approximately 15 per cent — went to the two lowest income groups. Yet the number of individuals in the two groups was well over 40 per cent of all income receivers!

At the other extreme, individuals at the top of the scale received a much greater than proportionate share. One-third of all income in 1957 went to the 12 per cent whose incomes exceeded $5000, and over 10 per cent of all income went to the fortunate few at the very top.

Where to draw the line between low incomes and incomes that provide a reasonable level of living is a difficult question, but incomes of $1000 — or even $2000 — must certainly be counted low. It is disturbing to see how low some incomes are in Canada. Of course, we have been looking at incomes of *individuals*. Incomes of Canadian *families* are higher because, in many families, there is more than one individual receiving income. In Table 2, the majority of individuals in the lowest income group were not heads of families but relatives of the head. Further, a survey of family income would exclude individuals who are not part of a family, and these are often the individuals — the young and the very old — with the lowest earning power.

Family incomes, then, are higher but the fact of inequality remains. When we study family incomes (Chapter 6) we shall find that the pattern of family income in Canada follows the pattern we have found for individuals. The way our national income is shared results in high incomes for a few — whether individuals or families — medium incomes for many, and low incomes for a great many more.

This unequal sharing of the national income is found in every country, not only in Canada. Indeed, much greater extremes of wealth and poverty are found elsewhere. The gulf which separates the oil-rich sheik from the nomad herdsman of the Arabian desert has no parallel in Canada. Nevertheless, the differences among Canadians are large enough. Can we approve a system that gives so much to so few, that leaves so little for a great many fellow citizens? And why does our system apportion incomes in this unequal fashion? These are questions that we must leave for later chapters.

4. FLUCTUATIONS IN NATIONAL INCOME

Prosperity and Depression

In underdeveloped countries the chief economic problem is the low level of national income. Somehow those countries must produce more. They must produce enormously greater quantities of goods and services. But in Canada, as in other countries which have managed to achieve high levels of income, another problem arises: the problem of *keeping* income high. Our incomes should be as high as possible not just some of the time but at all times. But for all our ability to produce we have not yet discovered how to make high incomes stable.

In some years all available economic resources, including labour, are fully employed. This means that total production (or income) is as high as possible and we have "prosperity". But there are also times when resources are unemployed and run to waste. Workers are out of jobs; plant and equipment are idle. This makes production lower, less income is paid out, and national income falls. If the decline is not too great or long-lived it is called a "recession"; a prolonged period of hard times is called a "depression".

Recession in the 1950's

To illustrate what can happen let us look at some recent history. The year 1956 was a good year for Canadians. Most of them had jobs and the few without (only 2 per cent of the labour force) were mainly seasonal and other workers moving from one job to another. Production and incomes had been rising, with two minor interruptions, for more than a decade and reached an all-time high in 1956. No clouds were visible on the economic horizon, at least as far as most of us could see. Yet by mid-winter of 1957-8 half a million Canadians were unemployed. By March, 1958 the number had increased to 600,000 — one-tenth of the labour force. Prosperity had given way to recession.

Even a mild recession affects the economic well-being of a great many people. In this case, most of the 600,000 Canadians without jobs had been drawing wages the year before; now they had to rely on the much lower incomes provided by unemployment insurance benefits. For these and other Canadians with lower incomes the end of prosperity was real enough. Yet we cannot call it a depression. The incomes of most of the population were well maintained and,

Toronto Star Syndicate

Relief-camp strikers on a hunger march in British Columbia, 1935.

even more important, large-scale unemployment did not last long. To see what depression means we must go back to the grim record of the 1930's.

Depression in the 1930's

In the thirties mass unemployment lasted for more than a decade. In the worst year 20 per cent of the labour force was unemployed and many more held only part-time jobs. Thousands of Canadian families lived on "relief", a subsistence allowance which barely covered the cost of groceries and the poorest kind of shelter. The jobs that men and women needed so desperately simply did not exist. A restless army of unemployed men moved back and forth across the country seeking work, and high-school students faced the prospect of waiting years to find a steady job.

The depression of the thirties was probably the worst in our history but it was not the first. A major depression one hundred years ago was one of the reasons the Fathers of Confederation pressed for the union of the colonies of British North America. After Confederation there were major depressions in the 1870's and the 1890's; another occurred just before World War I, another in the early 1920's, and then

the great depression of the 1930's. There have also been a great many minor depressions, such as the recession of 1957-8.

Must We Have Depressions?

In the light of past history the alternation of good and bad times — prosperity and depression — appears to be an inevitable part of our economic system. Our economy may run at full capacity, as in 1956, yet the next year experience large-scale unemployment. But why should employment and production be reduced? Why cannot Canada go on *increasing* her output of goods and services year after year?

These are questions we cannot answer here. We shall come back to them in a later chapter (Chapter 8) when we examine the reasons for prosperity and depression. It seems likely that periodic loss of income will continue to be a major problem in the economic welfare of Canada for some time to come. However, there are some grounds for hoping that the next depression, if not averted, can be made less severe. We can have this hope because economists know more about the causes of depressions than they used to, and governments are committed to try to maintain high levels of income and employment.

QUESTIONS FOR DISCUSSION

1. We have said that income is a good measure of economic welfare, whether we are comparing the welfare of two families in the same city, or of people in different countries. But income is not a perfect measure. Explain why comparisons of income do not tell us *exactly* how the level of living differs between two families, and between two countries.

2. India's second Five Year Plan, announced in 1956, is designed to raise living standards for millions of Indians. The Plan called for expansion in the steel industry, for more hydro-electric power, and for other additions to India's capital resources. From what you have learned about the *three* factors of production, can you suggest other projects which would help to achieve the goal of raising national income?

3. Through the Colombo Plan, which was launched in 1950, Canada is contributing to the economic development of several countries in south-east Asia. The largest grants have been made to India, Pakistan and Ceylon. Canadian funds have been used in developmental works (such as irrigation, hydro-electric projects, transportation equipment, and the Indian atomic reactor) and in technical training. By 1957 more than 600 Asians had received training in Canada and roughly 100 Canadians, experts in various fields, had been sent to Colombo Plan countries. The total cost to Canadians, from 1950 to April, 1958, was $197 million, approximately $12 for each man, woman and child in Canada. The annual cost works out to $1.50 per capita.

As a class project, see if you can obtain more information about the Colombo Plan. (Reports of the Consultative Committee of the Colombo Plan may be had by writing to the Queen's Printer, Ottawa.) Have brief reports written on the economic problems in the various recipient countries, and let the class discuss the adequacy of the aid forthcoming from advanced countries.

4. If we compare the distribution of income in Canada with the distribution of income in the United States, we find somewhat *more* inequality in Canada. What does this tell us about our lowest incomes? For example, the share of total income going to the lowest-income groups must be (higher) (lower) in Canada? What can we say about our highest incomes?

5. In 1957, the median income for non-farm income receivers in Canada was $2350. As we have seen, a great many Canadians received less than $1000, a very small percentage received more than $10,000. The *reasons* for such large differences will be given in later chapters. Can you anticipate what some of the reasons might be?

Class discussion topic: Should "something be done" to lessen the inequality of income distribution, or can you defend the degree of inequality that exists?

6. In Section I we learned that per capita income in Canada is the second highest in the world. This is an enviable achievement, but it does not mean there are no problems left to solve. What is the chief problem concerning the level of national income in Canada?

Chapter 3

The Economic System

1. INTRODUCTION

The different incomes of rich countries and poor countries, as we have seen, reflect differences in the factors of production. Yet the high productivity of Canadian workers cannot be explained solely by their skills and energy and the relatively large amounts of capital and natural resources they have to work with. High productivity is also a result of the way in which production is organized.

Walk into an automobile assembly plant and you will see thousands of individual workers, each with a limited specialized job. They are engaged not in the production of

Ford Motor Company of Canada

Car bodies move through the final trim line. Elsewhere, the frames are being readied, engines and transmissions hooked up, instrument panels put together. These and other sub-assembly processes are all co-ordinated to produce the modern car.

automobiles but only in the final stage of automobile production. If you were to take any part of an automobile, say a headlight, and trace its life history, you would meet thousands of other workers in other industries, many of them in other countries. You would find them in mining, in fabrication, in finance, in transportation, and in a host of other industries, all contributing in some way to the output of automobile headlights. Even less complex industries, such as agriculture, are specialized and depend upon a variety of other specialized industries for machinery and equipment, fuels and other supplies.

If we travel abroad and visit less developed economies or, in imagination, travel backwards in time to Canada's early settlements, the incredible specialization of production in the Canada of today comes clearly home to us. In Section 2 we see how far specialization has been carried and why it raises our level of living.

Need for a System

In Section 3 we turn to the problem of directing economic activity. A highly specialized economy does not run itself. It is not enough to have a labour force producing things. They must produce the right things, and in the right amounts. In Canada, that means they must produce the goods and services that people want: particular kinds of food, clothes, houses, and a host of other things besides.

Here we find the heart of the economic problem. While our wants are boundless, there are very definite limits to our economic resources. Even in well endowed countries like Canada, there is not the land, labour and capital to produce enough to satisfy everyone's wants completely. So in some manner we must decide *what* things to produce, and how much of each. We need a *system* to guide production.

We must also have some way of determining who gets what, and how much. That is, we need a system for dividing up the national product: a method of settling the *income* each person will get.

Every economy, even the most primitive, needs some kind of a system to guide production and to distribute incomes. The two chief types in the world today are the Russian, where economic activity is guided by the State, and our own. In Canada, as in most western democracies, we rely mainly on a price system. At one time we left the job of directing the economy almost entirely to the price system but in recent years we have assigned a large role to government. Although we are still a long way from the other extreme where the government makes all the decisions, it seems best to call ours a *mixed* enterprise system. This means we use *both* the price system and government control. The price system is described briefly in Section 3 and the role of government in Section 4.

2. SPECIALIZATION, EXCHANGE AND MONEY

Direct Production

There are places in the world where each family looks after most of its own needs. They grow or gather food for themselves, they build their own houses, and make their own clothes. This is called direct production. In Canada the early settlers were obliged to satisfy many of their wants

directly. Crops and animals provided food and clothing, and, from the materials at hand, the family made furniture, kitchen utensils, and the simple tools their work required.

With direct production there is much work and little to show for it. The pioneer family worked from dawn to dusk and

Embassy of Indonesia, Ottawa

The Indonesian farmer supplies much of his own food, although he too may specialize.

earned little beyond the bare necessities of living. Fortunately, there is another and better way of organizing production.

Specialization

As soon as the pioneer farmer could produce a crop for sale — a small surplus of wheat or oats or cheese beyond the needs of his own family — the door was opened to a higher standard of living. With cash in his pocket he could obtain tea or shoes or any one of a hundred things that could not be produced on the farm. And as time went by the typical Canadian farmer produced more and more of the marketable crops, less and less of his own family's needs. In short, he specialized.

In the modern world specialization has been carried so far that few traces of direct production remain. The typical Canadian works at one particular job and with his pay cheque buys the things he needs from others. The farmer produces more for himself than the rest of us but he too is usually a specialized producer, growing wheat but buying his bread in town, or raising pigs and getting his pork chops from the butcher.

Specialization takes many forms. Specialization in the production of *services* by doctors, barbers, mechanics and musicians is a division of labour of a simple and obvious kind. But in the production of *commodities* the division of labour is carried much further and becomes very complex. Most commodities come through a long succession of stages from raw materials to finished product, and at each stage the process of production may be subdivided into a multitude of separate operations. In making a pair of shoes, for example, there are ninety operations; a man's coat requires one hundred and fifty. To make a strip of steel into a spring leaf for an automobile spring involves thirteen operations! With specialized production each worker is confined to a narrow range of tasks. Accordingly, the contribution of any one worker to the final product is very small.

Another form of specialization is geographic. In different parts of Canada production is concentrated on the things which the region can do easily and best. Wheat, therefore, is the chief product of our prairies; base metals and pulp and paper are the predominant industries on the Canadian shield. Specialization occurs also between countries. For obvious reasons Canadians do not grow coffee or bananas, and the countries which produce them in abundance are less suited to growing wheat. Throughout the world most regions have some advantage in producing something, and specialization has become world-wide.

Advantages of Specialization

The chief result of specialization is a tremendous expansion of output. If each family or even each province attempted to be a self-sufficient economy, the total output would be a mere trickle compared to the flood of goods and services actually turned out each year. There are several reasons why specialization makes a larger output possible.

For one, the man with a special talent, say for carpentry or welding, can concentrate on the single job that he can do best. The community reaps the benefit of his talent by keeping him at one job. Others, without special talents, can acquire great skill through practice. Whether skills are natural or acquired, skilled workers are more productive than unskilled and the society which takes advantage of their skills can produce more goods and services.

Specialization increases efficiency in another way. It saves time. The specialized worker does the same job, usually in the same place, throughout the day. He is not switching from gardening to house building to shoe repairing as he would have to do in an economy where each family produced only for itself.

Specialization also saves tools. The construction worker does not need the full line of tools required to build a house; each worker — the carpenter, the plasterer, the plumber — needs only his own specialized tools.

Another advantage of specialization is that it encourages mechanization. When a job is split up into a series of separate, simple operations it becomes easier to invent mechanical aids. For this reason division of labour is a spur to invention.

Exchange

The man who specializes in making shoes cannot eat his product, and the man who raises pigs has more pork than he can eat. People (or regions) who produce one thing must be able to *trade* their surplus products for others. And so the organization of a modern economy depends upon *both* specialization and exchange. This raises a new problem: *how* are the products of different specialists to be exchanged?

Barter

One way is by direct exchange, which is called barter. A shoemaker could trade one pair of shoes for some bread, another for meat, and still others for all the other things he wanted. To get his bread, however, he could not go to *any* baker. He would have to shop around until he found a baker who needed shoes. The same is true with meat and everything else he wanted to buy. Then there is still the problem of deciding what is equal value for different products. How many loaves of bread should be exchanged for a pair of shoes, for a pound of steak, for a box of apples? Clearly barter is a clumsy, time-wasting way of doing business. When we think of the thousands upon thousands of things exchanged each day, we realize that our economy would never work with barter. There has to be a better way of trading. And, of course, there is.

Money

The use of *money* makes exchange easy. The shoemaker sells his product to anyone who can pay money and uses this money income to buy the many things he wants. Money also solves the problem of comparing values. Instead of saying a pair of shoes is worth 50 loaves of bread, we say bread is worth 20 cents a loaf and shoes $10 a pair. Thus we can measure the value of all goods in money terms. The same is true of services. A carpenter's wage is $2.50 an hour, a doctor's fee is $10 a call. Everything that is bought and sold has a *price*, which is simply a way of expressing its exchange value in terms of money.

Burdens of Specialization

Specialization, exchange, and money are interdependent and form the basis of the highly efficient production machine which the modern world has evolved. Together they make possible a spectacular volume of output. Without them no community can rise beyond a bare subsistence level of living.

Nevertheless, there is a debit side. Consider the deadly monotony of many jobs in specialized production. The assembly-line worker who repeats one simple operation over and over for seven hours a day knows little of the satisfaction of the craftsman. He also misses the variety that lightened the job for the jack-of-all trades. Another disadvantage of specialization is the increased dependence on remote forces beyond our control. The auto worker in Ontario may find himself out of work because a crop failure on the prairies reduced the demand for cars. And his narrow, specialized training makes it hard for him to find another job. There are, too, many complications which go with the use of money: particularly the problems of inflation and deflation which we examine in later chapters.

These unpleasant features of modern life are by-products of our way of organizing the economy. However, as our pioneer ancestors could tell us, there were many unpleasant features in their simple, less specialized way of life — not the least of these was poverty. Only our way of organizing production can provide the level of living we know today and, no matter what our economic difficulties, we will never abandon specialization.

3. THE PRICE SYSTEM

Planning Production

As this book is written, some six million Canadians are working at a great variety of jobs from one end of the country to the other. How do they manage to produce the things which buyers want? Take a large city like Toronto. Somehow the stores and restaurants have food to feed over a million people every day, and there are always enough clothes, furniture, dishes, cars and other products to satisfy the demands of people with the money to buy them. This does not just happen. The coffee, for example, was grown in Brazil and had to be transported thousands of miles, then ground, packaged and distributed in the right amounts among hundreds of stores. Everything in the stores got there through the efforts of dozens or hundreds or, with some products, even thousands of individual producers. Although there does not seem to be any over-all "planning", the stores keep stocked with all the things Toronto people want to buy.

To illustrate the problem, think of the city's milk supply which moves daily from hundreds of separate farms into the dairies, and from the dairies to the city's households. If Toronto uses six million quarts a week, the local dairy farmers must produce six million quarts a week and not five million or seven million or some other amount. But what prevents farmers from suddenly increasing their herds and producing too much milk — or switching to pigs and producing too little milk? These things do not happen. The right amount of milk continues to come in! Clearly, the production of milk is *planned*. And since all products appear in approximately the right amounts there must be some system to show individ-

Ontario Milk Producer

This dairy farm north of Toronto is one of many needed to supply milk daily to a million city dwellers.

ual producers what to make — and how much.

In Russia the planning is done by the government. Production goals are set for meat and milk, tractors, houses, and so on, and each production unit — collective farm or factory — is assigned a quota. We will see later (Chapter 17) that this kind of plan-

Hunting Survey Corporation Limited

The price system does the planning which makes sure that the right amount of milk reaches Toronto daily.

ning is difficult and that it has a number of disadvantages. But more important is the fundamental difference in objectives. With State planning the production goals are chosen by the central planners. In Canada the aim is to produce what people want.

The Profit System

How is production planned under the very different conditions of our economic system? Here production must conform with the wishes of the consumers, yet decisions in production are left to countless individual producers! The task seems impossible. Since no government agency arranges for the production of wheat or tractors or the many other commodities we want, how is it done? How is it, in our illustration, that hundreds of dairy farmers keep on supplying the right amount of milk to the people of Toronto?

The system rests on the fact that every producer is in business to make *profits*. He earns a profit by producing efficiently the products that people want and for which they will pay a profitable price. If too little of anything is produced the price (and there-

fore profits) will rise, and this encourages greater production. If too much is produced, price and profits will fall, which leads to less production. Thus the quantity produced is brought into harmony with the wishes of consumers.

Consumers are the ones who "plan" production because they determine what is profitable to produce. They show what they want every time they go shopping. The system does not take account of *all* their wants since wants must be made known by actual purchases. The average person cannot vote for the production of expensive sports cars because he does not have the money to buy one. But when he is actually *buying* he is showing his preferences: for hamburger or pork chops, for nylon shirts or broadcloth, for a magazine or a book. To the extent of his income, then, each consumer commands the activity of producers. While producers are free to decide what to make — and how much — they can only profit by producing what consumers will buy.

Sometimes producers make mistakes. Let us say that Company A has produced too many tractors. Then Company A will make

Ford Motor Company of Canada

Despite the money, time and thought that went into its design and publicity, the Edsel failed to sell. The Ford Motor Company was forced to discontinue its production.

losses instead of profits and, if its production is too far out of line, it may go out of business altogether. Thus the profit system checks a misuse of resources, such as the production of too many tractors. Because resources are scarce, society cannot afford to waste them. On the other hand, when the problem is a shortage of tractors, the possibility of making greater profits will soon lead producers to fill the gap.

Role of Prices

What we have called the "profit system" is simply a system of guiding production. It is also known as the "price system" because prices play such an important part. Indeed, so important that Part 3 of this book is devoted to the study of prices. "Free" prices keep producers posted on what is profitable.

Prices are "free" when no one person or company or government board sets the prices on things we buy. The store manager who stamps 89 cents on a pound of coffee did not decide that price alone, nor did the manufacturer, nor even the grower. Since the coffee must be *sold*, its price also depends upon what people will pay. And so we say that such prices are decided freely by the actions of all buyers and sellers.

Here is how free prices work. Suppose farmers begin selling more eggs than Toronto people want to use. What would happen? With eggs piling up in their refrigerators the stores would cut the price of eggs to tempt people to buy more. This lower price would discourage farmers from producing so many eggs; it would be a sign that they could make greater profits by changing to some other product. Thus the surplus of eggs would be corrected.

Similarly, if the problem were a shortage of eggs, the stores would raise the price — which would discourage some of their customers from buying. The higher price would act as a signal to farmers to make larger deliveries to enjoy the greater profits available in the egg business. Thus the shortage of eggs would be corrected.

Whenever a change is needed in production, whether it is more eggs or fewer eggs or more or less of anything, *price changes* point the way that producers should follow. Thus no one has to tell individual producers what to do. The job of guiding production is done by prices.

Incomes in a Price System

Every community must have a system to direct production. And every community must also have a system to share the results of production. In Canada the price system performs the second as well as the first of these tasks.

Each productive service has its price. The carpenter's wage, the corporation president's salary, the rent the landowner receives for the use of his land: all these are prices. And they are decided in much the same way as any other price. No government planning board decides the wage for a carpenter. Like other prices, wages depend partly on what buyers (that is, employers) are willing to pay, partly on what sellers (that is, the carpenters) are willing to take. This wage is also the *income* of carpenters. Thus the process of pricing the services of the carpenter, the corporation president or the landowner determines how each will share in the national income.

In the last section of this chapter — and in later chapters — we will bring in other factors which affect the distribution of income. Nevertheless, in spite of labour unions, minimum wages and other social legislation, the price system sets the basic pattern of earnings. High prices are paid for any service valued by the community and supplied by relatively few people (for example, movie stars, top executives, doctors). Low prices are assigned to unskilled labour and other services that are supplied by a multitude of people.

Advantages of a Price System

First and foremost, production is geared to the wants of consumers. And since we are *all* consumers we all have a voice in planning production. We do not all have an equal voice but, within the limits set by incomes, everybody votes. The things we want — and can buy — are the things that get made.

Secondly, resources are directed to their best use. The farmer, for example, uses his land for the crop that is in greatest demand because that is the one that pays the most. Producers are also under pressure to use resources efficiently and, as a result, the costs of production tend to be as low as possible.

A third advantage is that a price system can work *automatically*. Whenever there is reason for a change in production (more eggs, for example, or fewer eggs), the price will change and bring about the appropriate action by producers.

These are powerful recommendations. Nevertheless, we no longer rely, as we were once inclined to do, on the price system alone. More and more, in all the western democracies, governments help to guide economic activity. Reasons for this shift to greater government direction and control are sketched briefly in the following section.

4. ROLE OF THE GOVERNMENT

If this book had been written fifty or even thirty years ago, this section would be scarcely needed because then the two-fold job of planning production and determining incomes was left almost entirely to the price system. Why has part of the job been turned over to government?

There are several reasons. First, there are problems that a price system is powerless to solve. For example, in a price system there is great inequality of incomes and, as time passes, this problem gets worse instead of better. Fifty years ago people accepted the inequality. Today, however, Canadians want to do something about it. We are also trying to prevent depressions, control inflation, and remedy other economic evils. Canadians, acting through their governments, have undertaken to improve many areas of economic life where the price system failed to achieve satisfactory results.

Another reason for using the government has been the decline of competition in our economy. When the consumer can pick and choose among a great many different sellers *all* sellers are bound to make prices as attractive as possible. Fifty years ago, in a world of small-scale production units, there was a great deal of competition. Today, in an age of large and powerful corporations, sellers can more easily combine and agree to fix prices. Then the consumer must pay higher prices to them all. Government action is needed to give consumers the protection they used to get from a competitive price system.

Over the years we have found more and more places in the economy where governments can be useful. Now let us see more precisely what governments do.

Community Services

There is one segment of the economy where governments have been active for many years. Roads and bridges, street lights and sewers, the post office and similar services have long been supplied by governments. We call them "community services" because they are provided by governments and the benefits are shared by the community as a whole.

Redistributing Incomes

A price system determines automatically the incomes people earn but there is no special merit in the result. In other words, a price system is not necessarily the *best* way of deciding how much income each person should receive. An obvious shortcoming is that a price system does not assure that everyone will earn enough to live on! It determines what the services of a carpenter are worth in the market but *not* what happens to the carpenter if age or sickness prevents him from working. The very old, the handicapped and chronically ill, the widow with young children are among those unable to work at all or who work so little that they cannot live on what they earn. Their incomes must be provided outside of the price system.

We also criticize the distribution of income in a price system on the grounds of excessive inequality. Canadians find it morally repugnant that many individuals should earn $500 a year while a few earn a hundred times that amount. It is not difficult to accept differences in income that reflect differences in *effort*, but many high incomes are a product of accident or luck: being born to parents who leave a vast fortune, for example, or having a voice like Bing Crosby's. If we exclude these extreme cases there are still a great many individuals who owe their higher incomes to better opportunities of one kind or another. The young man whose parents could afford to give him a university education or capital to launch him in the business world is likely to have a higher income than his less fortunate contemporaries. Even greater effort on their part cannot eliminate the disadvantage created by the difference in opportunities.

This is not to say that Canadians favour complete equality of incomes. There must be economic rewards for hard work, difficult jobs, and the bearing of unusual risks. But Canadians have accepted the goal of greater equality of opportunities. This is reflected in the development of a variety of government policies. One of the earliest was the provision of primary and secondary schools at the public expense. More recently the emphasis has shifted to direct income payments such as family allowances and universal old-age pensions. Policies of this kind *redistribute* income because the taxes to finance them bear more heavily on individuals with middle and high incomes. Through these and many similar policies governments change the pattern of income which the price system decrees.

Economic Stability

Another important function of government is to avoid, if possible, the worst of economic disasters: mass unemployment and runaway inflation. A generation ago Canadians regarded fluctuations in the level of employment and prices as necessary evils. Today we expect something to be done and we look to the government to do it. How governments attempt to maintain stability of employment, income, and prices is the subject of Chapters 8 and 11. The attempt to achieve economic stability through government action is another admission that a price system *alone* cannot produce the results we want. Hence, we choose to use the government as well as the price system to direct economic activity.

Making the Price System Work

If an economic system is to work in the best interests of everybody it must put consumers first — because everybody, whether farmer, wage earner, or business man, is a consumer. At one time, the price system met this test reasonably well. By and large, consumers' wants directed production and consumers bought their goods and services at the lowest possible prices. Our modern price system cannot guarantee these results to the same degree. When a few large firms dominate an industry, consumers may be obliged to pay higher prices. Profits are then greater than necessary and sellers gain at the expense of buyers.

To protect consumers Canadian governments limit the power of big business firms. The lines of attack include regulation of rates and public ownership in "public utility" industries (such as railroads, electric light and power, and urban transportation). There are also laws against monopoly practices to assure the benefits of competition in other industries. These several methods are described more fully in later chapters. We should note that anti-monopoly laws are not a modification of the price system. Rather they are an attempt to restore the competitive conditions which are essential if the price system is to serve consumers efficiently.

QUESTIONS FOR DISCUSSION

1. A good many North Americans in recent years have tried their hands at unfamiliar tasks, such as making furniture or boats, building summer cottages, and so on. From what you know of the disadvantages of specialization, suggest some reasons for the popularity of "do-it-yourself". (The advantages of specialization can be used to describe its limitations.)

2. Name the two chief difficulties of exchanging goods by barter, and show how each is solved by the use of money. (Let members of the class bring anything they are willing to trade and have a practical demonstration of the inefficiency of barter.)

3. (a) Make a list of things you use every day. Examining each one, try to imagine the various stages and specialties involved in its production. (For example, an ordinary pencil would involve the wood industry, lead-mining, rubber-growing and processing, and services from the transportation industry, finance, insurance, and wholesale and retail trade — in addition to the pencil industry itself.) How many separate industries do you have on your list? Now consider the job of getting the right things in the right places in the right amounts — assuming that you alone had to do the job of planning.

(b) In describing our own economy, we say that production is *planned*, although no one does the planning! How does a farmer decide whether to grow wheat or corn or raise cattle? How does the manufacturer decide whether to produce 1000 or 10,000 tractors? Explain why we say that production is geared to the wants of consumers.

4. In any economy, some things are produced in large quantity, some things in small quantity. In Canada, for example, the output of Fords and Chevrolets is relatively large, of Cadillacs very small. Why? Can you relate this to what you read in Chapter 2 about the distribution of income?

5. The inequality of Canadian incomes is partly a result of the price system for the price system tells us that some services in production are worth more than others. What are the conditions that give a particular service a high price? A low price? Give five examples of both kinds of service.

6. What does it mean to say that the government "redistributes" income? Explain *how* and give some of the reasons *why*. What are the other major roles of government in a mixed economy?

Chapter 4

Forms of Business Organization

We study economics to understand the big booming confusion of economic life that goes on around us. The first three chapters set the stage. Now we turn to the major agents or institutions that provide the action of economic life: the business and production units that mobilize economic resources (Chapter 4); the labour unions (Chapter 5); the consuming units or households and families for whom, in the final analysis, all production is organized (Chapter 6). We have to understand these major agents in the economy before going on to the economic process itself because the way things get done depends, to a large extent, upon the character of the actors.

RELATIVE NUMBERS (in percentages) OF THE DIFFERENT KINDS OF BUSINESS FIRMS

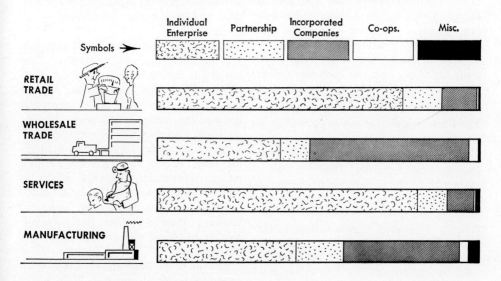

1. UNINCORPORATED BUSINESS

Of the five main types of business organization the private corporation is by far the most important. In numbers, however, the corporation ranks a very poor second. There are many more small business firms owned by single persons. These are called *individual enterprises* and, along with *partnerships*, they make up what is called the "unincorporated business sector" of the economy.

The Individual Enterprise

The individual enterprise is a one-man show. A single individual puts up the money, takes all the profit (or bears all the losses) and usually runs the business him- self. The proprietor may or may not have other people working for him, but so long as he is the sole owner his firm is an indi- vidual enterprise.

The small independent grocery is a good example. Most confectionery and variety stores are individual enterprises, as are most barber shops, filling stations, garages and restaurants. In addition, there are the self- employed, such as trappers and fishermen, as well as doctors, lawyers and other pro- fessional workers. There are also many individual enterprises in the construction industry. Last, but not least, there is the farmer. Every Canadian farm is a business firm and almost all of them are organized as individual enterprises. Indeed, agriculture is the stronghold of the individual form of business organization. Of the total income earned in 1956 by unincorporated business firms of every kind over 40 per cent was earned by farm operators. The service in- dustries accounted for 18 per cent, retail trade for 17 per cent and business firms in the construction industry for 9 per cent of the total.

The Partnership

A very similar kind of business organiza- tion is formed when two or more persons go into business together. This is called a partnership. The partnership has served in a great variety of industries in the past but its usefulness today is much more limited. It is rarely found in manufacturing or even in trade. The partnership survives chiefly in the entertainment business — for example, "Wayne and Shuster" — and in the pro- fessions, where it is often used by lawyers, accountants, doctors, and other profes- sional workers.

Getting Started

You may have thought of going into busi- ness yourself some day. The easiest way to do so is to become the proprietor of an individual enterprise. With a few thousand dollars you buy a small store and you are in business. It is as simple as that. If you have a partner, you would have a lawyer draw up a partnership contract. The contract would state how the business is to be run, what each partner is to do and the salary each will receive, how the profit, if any, is to be shared, and so on. When both partners sign the contract the business is a going concern.

Raising Capital

Getting started in business is no guarantee of success. In almost any business a prime necessity is the ability to *borrow money*. As we shall see in Chapter 9, the typical firm needs short-term credit to purchase stock and to finance part of its own credit sales. It may also need long-term loans to finance expansion, such as adding to the store or buying new equipment. Few firms can meet the costs of expansion entirely out of profits. It is here that we find the most serious weakness of the unincorporated busi- ness. It cannot borrow money easily. Let us see why.

First of all, the unincorporated enterprise is a "personal" business. In the eyes of the law it has no existence independent of its owner. This means, for example, that the business cannot be sued. It also means that the business cannot owe money. If there are losses, therefore, the owner is held per- sonally responsible. He can be made to pay the debts of the business from his own pocket. That is, his personal as well as his business assets may be seized by his credi- tors. This characteristic is called "unlimited liability": there is no limit on the owner's liability to people who can legally demand payment.

The life of an unincorporated business is linked to the life of its owner. If the owner dies or retires the business comes to an end. The prospective investor may hesitate to tie up his money in a business whose success or failure depends upon a single owner or a few partners. Not only their business ability but their luck and their health are also important. As a general rule the unincor- porated business is also handicapped by its small size, and by the fact that its name and prospects are relatively unknown.

For all these reasons unincorporated enterprise finds it difficult to borrow money. Investors turn elsewhere to find safer uses for their money, and the credit needs of unincorporated business go begging.

The partnership is better equipped to raise capital than the individual enterprise because it does have more than one owner. Two or more partners can contribute savings to the firm and more capital can be obtained by taking in more partners. But the number of partners is limited if only because each partner will want to take part in all major decisions. It becomes a case of too many cooks ruining the broth. Consequently, the partnership cannot raise very large sums of money.

Advantages and Disadvantages of Unincorporated Enterprise

One of the chief advantages of the individual enterprise is the ease of getting started. Many people are attracted by the appeal of running their own show, whether in a small store, on the farm, or in painting houses, and without the individual enterprise their desires would go unfulfilled. Yet this very advantage may also be called a disadvantage. The individual enterprise can get started on the relatively small savings of one person but too often it cannot achieve the scale of operation which will yield a reasonable income. Hampered by low income and without access to additional funds, the small firm cannot be expanded to reach the volume of business essential to success. Further, there is seldom any reserve for the inevitable rainy day and when trade slackens the small weak firms are the first to go.

The difficulty of raising capital is the most serious but not the only disadvantage of unincorporated business. Another arises from its small scale. Persons of ability are attracted to large organizations where there is greater scope for self-expression and advancement. The small business must be content with the less able and less ambitious people.

In the partnership we find other difficulties. One is the need for agreement among the partners on all major decisions. Another

is the problem of reorganizing the business whenever one partner dies or withdraws. Finally, there is the added risk arising from "unlimited liability". A wealthy partner with a small share in the business can find himself obliged to pay most of the firm's debts — and selling personal property to do so — if his partners cannot pay their share.

Summing Up

The unincorporated business organization works well enough in industries where the capital required is small, as in the medical profession or in law. But in most industries the disadvantages are likely to far outweigh the advantages. Even in agriculture, where small-scale units are more efficient than in most other industries, the typical firm is greatly handicapped by the difficulty of borrowing money.

In the past, unincorporated business has served as a stepping-stone to greater things. The T. Eaton Company and the Ford Motor Company are conspicuous examples of successful corporations which began as individual enterprises. But in the present day that road to business success is more closed than open. Many individual entrepreneurs fail and among those who manage to stay in business many earn less than they could earn working for someone else. Very often they work very long hours. Whereas many Canadian workers have the eight-hour day and the five-day week, the farmer and the proprietor of the corner store may be on the job for twelve hours a day and work on Sunday too.

In Canada, the importance of the unincorporated business sector is declining. Thirty years ago individual proprietors and partners earned approximately one-quarter of the national income; today their share is less than 15 per cent. Over the same period corporations have made large gains. Nevertheless, the individual enterprise persists in large numbers. In a few industries it can be an efficient form of organization. And even where it cannot it continues to attract many individuals who ignore the odds against them because they prefer to be independent.

2. THE CORPORATION

Origins

The corporation is a relative newcomer, a by-product of the "industrial revolution" which began less than 200 years ago. Before that time the typical unit engaged in production and trade was small. Individuals working alone or with partners could raise the capital necessary for the efficient conduct of the business. But when power-driven machinery was introduced the most efficient way to use it was in plants housing many expensive machines and employing large numbers of workers. Such undertakings required more capital than a single factory owner, or even several partners, could supply. The difficulty was particularly apparent in the application of steam power in transportation. A railroad from London to the cotton factories in Lancashire could not be built by a succession of small firms, each owning five or ten miles of the line! There had to be an organization big enough to do the whole job, a new kind of business that could raise large sums of money. The modern corporation was developed to meet this need.

The corporate form of organization made large-scale production units possible and, in many lines of production, large units are the most efficient. The large plant and the large firm (which may own many separate plants) may produce more cheaply for several reasons. The firm which expands in size can achieve the specialization and division of labour which we described in Chapter 3. For example, it can reorganize management, setting up separate departments to specialize in production, accounting, selling, purchasing, advertising, research and personnel. The large firm may also obtain discounts and rebates because it buys its supplies in large amounts. The unit cost of railway and truck transport, of advertising and promotion and other selling costs will be lower for a large volume of sales than for a small volume. The large firm also has an advantage in raising funds to finance its operations.

All of these economies of large-scale production add up to greater efficiency, hence lower costs. This means an advantage in competition. In many industries, therefore, the force of competition compelled individual firms to achieve the economies of large-scale production, or go out of business altogether. Thus the corporation became the dominant form of business organization.

The corporate form of business organization has flourished for reasons other than the efficiency of large-scale production. It opened the door to the human desires for bigness for its own sake, and for power and the profit and prestige that go with power. But before we can assess the social gains and losses that accompanied the growth of corporate business we need to know more precisely what a corporation is and how it works.

Legal Status

Legally, a corporation has the status of a person. This artificial person can own property, it can sue and be sued and do many other things that people do. In short, it has an existence of its own, quite apart from the people who own it. This separation of the firm from its owners limits the risk of the individual investor. Thanks to a simple legal device, the business firm has the power to owe money and its owners cannot be made to pay its bills out of their personal accounts. While the business itself may fail, the most the investor can lose is the money he put in. This fact of "limited liability" is one of the chief differences between the corporation and the older forms of business organization.

The legal status of the corporation reduces the risk of investment in another way. The business is not forced to close when any of its owners dies. Given this continuity of life, the corporation is able to undertake and complete long-term projects. The individual owner, meanwhile, is always free to transfer his share of the business other to individuals if he wishes.

Raising Capital Through Stocks and Bonds

To get started in the first place the corporation issues "shares". If it plans to raise $1 million, for example, the corporation may sell 100,000 shares at $10 apiece, or one million shares at $1 apiece. An established corporation may also issue more shares from time to time to secure additional capital.

The most important shares are called "common shares" or "common stock". The common stockholders share in the profits of the business, receiving payment in the form of dividends. (If there are no profits, of course, there will be no dividends.) The common stockholders are, in fact, the *owners* of the corporation. Thus one way the corporation raises vast sums of money is by having a multitude of owners to contribute capital, instead of one or a few individuals.

A corporation may raise some of its capital by selling "preferred stocks". Preferred stockholders have a limited share in profits — say 6 per cent of the face value of the share — but their share comes out of profits first. Thus they sacrifice the possibility of larger dividends for greater safety. Although the preferred stockholders are owners, as a general rule they do not exercise control of the business.

The corporation also raises money by selling another kind of security called "bonds". This is a way of *borrowing* money for long periods of time. Stocks and bonds are quite different. The bondholders are not owners; the stockholders are. When you buy a bond you are simply lending money to the corporation. The bond is a loan contract. It states that you, as holder of the bond, will be repaid the face value of the bond in a certain number of years, perhaps, ten, fifteen, or twenty years, and that you will be paid a *fixed* interest, say 5 per cent of the face value of the bond each year.

As a bondholder, you take less risk than stockholders but you lose the chance of earning as large a return. If profits are large, the common stockholders may receive 10 or 12 per cent on their investment but you will earn only the fixed rate, say 4 or 5 per cent. However, you do have the advantage when profits are low or nil. The bondholders are paid before profits can be calculated for the stockholders. Even if a firm is losing money it may continue to pay the interest on its bonds. Of course, if the losses continue and the firm goes into bankruptcy, then the bondholders may lose part or all of their investment.

Advantages of Stocks and Bonds

Stocks and bonds offer many advantages. First of all, the investor's money is not tied up indefinitely. There are organized markets for the purchase and sale of outstanding securities, and the investor who wishes to convert his stocks or bonds into cash simply sells them to someone else. He will gain or lose on the sale if the price has changed since he bought them. (Stock prices in particular are subject to change, depending as they do on profits. Indeed, for many investors, the possibility of a "capital gain" through a rise in price is the chief inducement to buy stocks.) But the main point is that all corporate securities *can* be bought and sold easily. This fact alone makes them much more attractive than lending to or financing unincorporated business firms.

A second advantage of buying common stock in a corporation is that the investor does not take the risk of "unlimited liability". Unlike the owner of an individual enterprise or partnership, he risks only the money that he paid for his stock. Corporate stocks, therefore, are a safer investment.

Finally, the corporation has the great advantage that it can tempt every taste. To people who want a *safe* investment, with low but steady earnings, the corporation offers bonds. It can sell preferred stocks to those who will take a somewhat greater risk than the bondholders in return for the chance of somewhat larger earnings. And to those who prefer a chance for the largest earnings and who are willing to take the risk of getting nothing at all, the corporation offers common stocks.

Management and Control

Most large corporations have a great many owners and, as the shares are freely bought and sold, the owners are constantly changing! How, then, can the owners direct and manage their own business? The answer is that the owners cannot and do not actually run the business themselves except in very small corporations. The jobs of management are performed by the executives of the corporation: the president, the production manager, the sales manager, and so on. These men and women are employees and they work for salaries, not for profits. They may also own stock and receive a share in the profits, but as managing executives they are hired by the company and paid salaries.

At the same time the owners of the corporation do have a measure of control. They do not manage the business but they do have the power to change the policies by which the business is run. This power is exercised through the board of directors which is elected by the common stockholders. These stockholders can approve the policies of the corporation by voting for the present board of directors — or they can voice dissatisfaction by voting against them. This means, at least in theory, that the owners direct their own business. The system works well when the number of owners is small, but the large corporation raises special problems, which are described in Section 3.

Growth of Corporations

We have seen why the corporation is much better able than other forms of business to secure funds. Through the sale of stocks and bonds a single corporation may assemble the savings of hundreds or thousands of individuals. There are some corporations with over a million owners! At the same time there has evolved a flexible formula for the operation of the business. Management is given a free hand within the limits of the policy laid down by the board of directors, while the last word remains with the people who buy the common stock.

In short, the corporation provides a form of organization that meets the needs of modern large-scale production.

Although it originated with large undertakings — such as the railroads — the corporate form spread gradually into other industries: manufacturing, mining, finance, utilities, construction, wholesale and retail trade. It has proved useful in small-scale business as well as in large. Indeed, small- or medium-sized corporations are far more numerous than business giants such as General Motors, International Nickel and the Canadian Pacific Railway. But the large corporation has a position of power in the economy not reflected by mere numbers. To understand our economy we must appreciate the "bigness" of big business.

The Concentration of Industry

In the United States in 1958 there were 70 companies whose individual assets exceeded one billion dollars. The largest 200 corporations held between 20 and 25 per cent of the nation's wealth and together they employed one out of every eight workers! Wealth, production and employment are similarly concentrated in Canada. For illustration we go to a recent study of Canadian manufacturing. In one-third of the industries covered, fewer than 5 corporations accounted for 80 per cent of the total employment. In half of the industries 80 per cent of the total employment was concentrated in 9 or fewer corporations. Comparing the degree of concentration in manufacturing industries between Canada and the United States, the

---

Fewer than 4 largest firms supplied *80% of total employment* (1948) in each of these industries:

aluminum, primary	steel ingots and castings
matches	glass
cement	bicycles
gypsum products	petroleum products
automobiles	nickel
cotton thread	aircraft
cigarettes	cordage, rope and twine
pig iron	railway rolling stock

Source: Gideon Rosenbluth, *Concentration in Canadian Manufacturing Industries* (New York, 1957).

study concluded that "with very few exceptions, comparable industries are more highly concentrated in Canada".

The extent to which Canadian corporations are owned abroad — particularly by Americans — is another important feature of Canadian business. In manufacturing, petroleum, mining and smelting, foreign ownership of Canadian corporations exceeds 40 per cent and the Canadian corporations that are owned in the United States are usually controlled there as well.

These are some of the highlights of our corporate economy. We live in the age of corporations, many of which are large and powerful, and many of which are controlled abroad. Unquestionably, these large-scale corporations bring us many advantages — but they are also the source of problems. We shall consider, first, the problem of minority control within the corporation and the concentration of wealth and power which results. Secondly, we shall discuss the problem of monopoly.

3. PROBLEMS WITH BIG BUSINESS

Control in the Large Corporation

As we have seen, the common stockholders of a corporation can exercise control through the annual election of the board of directors. Each share carries *one vote*. The individual with 10,000 shares has a thousand times as many votes as the individual with 10. The individual shareholder need not attend a meeting to cast his votes. He can vote "by proxy". To do so, he gives written consent to another individual, who is attending the meeting, to vote on his behalf.

In a small corporation, it is not impossible that all stockholders will attend meetings, voice their opinions, vote, and generally keep an eye on their interests. But in large corporations the great majority of stockholders usually do not bother to vote. Most of them own only a few shares. They live in many different parts of a vast country. The expense and trouble of attending the annual meeting — to cast a negligible vote! — would deter them, even if they understood and were concerned with the conduct of the business. And very few can be expected to have a thorough knowledge of the business. Under these conditions control of the corporation easily passes into the hands of a *small group* of larger stockholders who do take an active interest in the business.

There is no single pattern that would describe the actual situation in every large

corporation in Canada. To be absolutely certain of retaining control the minority group would have to own — or secure proxies to vote — 50 per cent of the voting stock. But as a general rule much less than 50 per cent will do. For the typical giant corporation in the United States 20 per cent of the voting stock is more than enough to maintain effective control.

Suppose five individuals, owning $40,000 in stock apiece, together control a million-dollar-share corporation. In addition to the capital supplied by all the stockholders the minority group controls the capital obtained from the issue of preferred stock and the sale of bonds. Suppose that in addition to the million dollars raised by sales of common stock, another million had been raised by sales of bonds and preferred stocks — then the same five individuals would control assets purchased with $2,000,-000. Nor does this mark the limit. The assets under their control may be multiplied again through a holding company. This device is commonly used in Canada.

The Holding Company

A holding company is a corporation set up to hold the securities of other corporations. To illustrate, suppose there are five companies actually producing and selling to the public. Together, the five companies are worth $20 million with "capital liabilities" of $6 million in common stock, plus $4 million in preferred stock, and $10 million raised through sale of bonds. Now suppose we set up a holding company to buy $3 million of the common stock. To raise the $3 million, we could sell $1 million of bonds, $1 million of preferred stock, $500,000 of common stock to the public, and buy $500,000 of common stock ourselves. With 50 per cent of the common stock we would control the holding company. But because it holds 50 per cent of the common stock in five operating companies, our $500,000 investment gives us not just control of a $3-million company but of five companies worth $20 million as well. For every dollar we put up, we can control $40 worth of assets in the operating companies!

We can go even further. We can now set up Holding Company Number 2 and let it buy the $500,000 of common stock we held in Holding Company Number 1. Again by selling bonds, non-voting stock and some common stock to the public — to the extent of, say, $400,000 — we can control Holding Company Number 2 by buying $100,000 of its common stock. Through Number 2 we now control Holding Company Number 1 and through it we control the five companies that actually produce something for the public. This is called "pyramiding". For a $100,000 investment we control $20 million of wealth in the form of actual physical plant and equipment.

The Dangers of Control

The facts of minority control within the corporation have far-reaching implications. Because the vast majority of stockholders play a passive role, control has been separated from ownership. As a result, the small group of larger stockholders control the destinies of big corporations — and even huge segments of industry. But is this really so bad? It can be argued that *all* stockholders have the same interest: having profits as large as possible. And what do corporation politics matter to the rest of us?

To take the second question first, the facts

of control within large corporations are a matter of concern to everybody, even those who never buy a penny's-worth of stock, because control over vast companies is bound to confer *power*. And the presence of such powerful groups in industry is not easy to reconcile with the kind of democracy we want to have.

At the same time the interests of the great majority of small shareholders are *not always* the same as those of the small group which controls the corporation. For example, the group in power may be too eager, at times, to plough profits back into the business. This is quite legitimate when expansion is justified, but they might also be influenced by considerations of personal prestige, by the desire to be associated with an even bigger company. If such personal ambitions are the reason for retaining profits and keeping dividends low, then the interests of the vast majority of shareholders are not being served. The small group also has the opportunity to award its own members and friends and relatives unnecessarily high salaries and bonuses, which lower profits and dividends. They may have the corporation make contracts with other companies they control, even when better offers are available. In short, the individuals who control the large corporation are not compelled to serve the interests of all the shareholders. And they would be more than human if they always did so.

Big Business and the Problem of Monopoly

The second problem arising with our large corporations is the decline of competition. This, too, is a matter of concern to everybody because the consumers' interest is served by having as much competition as possible. Where sellers are few consumers are usually obliged to pay higher prices. This is a monopoly situation, and the emergence of the large corporation is, in part, responsible because large sellers inevitably mean fewer sellers. You cannot have twenty or thirty companies the size of Ford or General Motors in the automobile industry

— the market could not absorb their output. The same is true in many industries. There simply is not room for more than a few large companies, and small companies — if they manage to survive — do not produce enough to provide effective competition.

This high degree of concentration is partly explained by the greater efficiency of large-scale production units. As we have seen, the economies of large-scale production contributed to the growth of corporations. But greater efficiency is not the whole explanation. Concentration also results from the pursuit of monopoly profits. The desire to reduce competition and administer prices to secure monopoly profits is a powerful motive in the business world, and large corporations are in a strong position to pursue this objective.

They may pursue it in many ways. For example, a holding company may be used to concentrate the control of many operating companies. Another common corporate practice is "interlocking directorates". The same directors sitting on many company boards are in a position to co-ordinate monopoly practices among the several companies. Then there is the merger. In a merger, separate companies unite to form a single company.

Another device that is often used by big business firms is the trade association. This is simply an association of the firms that make up an industry. In a concentrated industry the association will have as members the large firms who control the bulk of the industry's production. While such associations serve innocent and legitimate purposes, they also provide an excellent device for establishing a combine to set prices and otherwise exploit the public. A famous economist remarked long ago, "People of the same trade seldom meet together, even for merriment and diversion, but the conversation ends in a conspiracy against the public, or in some contrivance to raise prices."

This is not to say that the large corporation is undesirable. Without it, large-scale production could not have developed as it did and consumers have gained much from the greater efficiency of large-scale production. Nor are corporation practices always directed against consumers. The holding company may be set up quite legitimately to provide a united and stronger credit base for its companies, with the economies of finance being passed on to consumers. The merger may be justified by economies in production that benefit consumers. The trade association has many legitimate uses. Nevertheless, the unpleasant consequences of large corporations are real enough and must be balanced against the benefits they confer. Here the public faces a dilemma: how to enjoy the benefits of large-scale production without being hurt by the market power of giant business units.

Protecting the Consumer's Interest

It would be no solution to break up the large corporations, although this most drastic remedy has been applied occasionally. (In 1956, Canadian Industries Limited, a giant producer of chemicals and explosives, was required by the Canadian government to split into two separate companies.) But so many big corporations would lose the advantage of large-scale production if they were split into smaller units that no one seriously urges breaking them up as a general policy. Instead, as we saw in Chapter 3, Canadian governments *limit* the power of large corporations by regulating prices in the utility field and by forbidding certain monopoly practices.

A second line of attack is to use some other form of business organization. Neither the individual enterprise nor the partnership could fill the place of the private corporation, but there are two other alternatives: the public ownership of corporations and co-operatives. Both play a considerable role in the Canadian economy.

4. PUBLIC OWNERSHIP OF CORPORATIONS

Ownership and Management

The publicly-owned corporation, like any other corporation, is a business firm selling to the public. The chief difference is in the way it is owned. Instead of having individual shareholders such corporations are owned by a government, which may be a city or rural municipality, a provincial government or the federal government in Ottawa. Since governments represent the public, these corporations are actually owned by the community which elects the government. Well-known examples are the Canadian National Railways, the Canadian Broadcasting Corporation, the Bank of Canada, Ontario Hydro, the Saskatchewan Power Corporation, the Nova Scotia Electric Power Commission, and the Toronto Transit Commission.

The publicly-owned corporation is run in the same way as the private corporation with one major difference. The executive officers of a privately-owned corporation are responsible to the board of directors and, through the board, to the shareholders. The officers of a publicly-owned corporation are responsible to the government concerned and, through the government, to the people who elect that government.

Another difference between the two kinds of corporations may be seen in their aims. The private corporation is in business solely to make profits for its shareholders. The publicly-owned corporation is generally expected to show profits too but other considerations may come first. As we go on to look at the origins of public ownership we shall see why some other aim may take precedence over profits.

Origins

One reason for public ownership has been mentioned: it is a way to avoid the monopoly power of a private corporation. In the public utility field monopoly power is particularly strong because a local company will generally have the field to itself. Without government intervention, the only limit on rates would be "what the traffic will bear". To protect consumers, therefore, the government may buy out the private shareholders and take over the business. In this way urban transportation, gas, light and power companies in many municipalities across Canada became publicly-owned corporations. Such companies are not bound only by profit considerations. They can consider the interests of the whole community, which may be better served by low rates than high profits.

A good example of a combination of provincial and municipal action is the Ontario Hydro-Electric Commission. Hydro-electricity would have developed under private ownership in Ontario, as it did in Quebec, but Sir Adam Beck, leading founder of the Commission, insisted on public ownership to avoid the dangers and limitations of private companies in the production and distribution of electricity.

A second and very important reason for public ownership in Canada has been the weakness of private capital. Time after time, in different parts of the country, the development of resources has depended upon government assistance because the vast sums required were beyond the means of private capitalists. In some cases assistance has taken the form of financial aid to private corporations; in others, governments have made the developmental expenditures themselves through a publicly-owned corporation.

Both methods were used to build our railways. A most successful private corporation — the Canadian Pacific Railway — was actually started as a federal government enterprise. Seven years later, in 1880, a private company undertook to complete the line, but to do so it required generous government assistance. This included $25 million in cash, 25 million acres of land, the more than 700 miles of railroad already built by the government, and monopoly privileges for 20 years. Unquestionably, the building of our first transcontinental railroad was a spectacular achievement and the founders of the company deserve the credit our history books bestow. But the achievement was not solely due to private efforts. Without large-scale aid from the government the Canadian Pacific Railway could not have been built.

Government aid was also freely granted as two other transcontinental railways, the Canadian Northern and the Grand Trunk Pacific, were built after 1900. The National Transcontinental, the eastern section of the Grand Trunk Pacific, was built by the government. The Intercolonial also deserves mention. At the time it was built, immediately after Confederation, private capitalists would not undertake the job, so the first railway link between the Maritimes and central Canada was built by the Canadian government.

Provincial governments also entered the railway field. Because there was a strong demand for a railroad to open up the resources of the north and no private company willing to undertake the risk, the Ontario government built the Ontario Northland to James Bay. The Pacific Great Eastern in British Columbia is another example of public ownership to develop frontier areas. On the prairies, the three provincial governments went into the telephone business in the early days when no private company would undertake to meet the demand for telephones.

In these several illustrations we find public ownership introduced either to hasten development of resources or to meet the needs of pioneer settlements when private corporations were unwilling to do so. When there has been a strong demand from the public to have some particular service and no rush of private companies to supply it, Canadians have often turned to public ownership.

In the origins of the Canadian National Railway System we find a third reason for public ownership. The several lines which comprise the present system were built at different times and in different ways. Some were publicly-owned and some were private companies. The private companies included the Grand Trunk, the Grand Trunk Pacific

and the Canadian Northern as well as several smaller companies. By 1917 these railroads were all in financial difficulty. The federal government was obliged to meet their financial obligations and, then, to keep the lines in operation, assumed ownership. In 1922 these were united with the other government lines to form a single company.

One last example of public ownership of the corporation is the Bank of Canada. This is our central bank, which we study in Chapter 10. As we shall see, the business of a central bank is altogether unsuitable for a private company. Although the Bank of Canada does make profits the work it does to stabilize prices, income and employment is vastly more important. In a publicly-owned corporation, the public interest can be put above the pursuit of profit.

Conclusions

We have found four distinct reasons in Canada's experience for the public ownership of corporations. There are some kinds of business that private companies would not undertake because the risks are too great, others in which private companies could not earn a profit, and still others in which private companies would make too much profit! There are also special fields in which the larger public interest must come before the pursuit of profits. The Bank of Canada, the Canadian Broadcasting Corporation and Central Mortgage and Housing Corporation all fall into this category.

It is clear that the success of a publicly-owned corporation cannot be measured in terms of profit and loss alone. If its business is running a railroad through a thousand miles of non-revenue-producing northland it may well incur losses, but the public at large will be more than compensated if an expansion of trade and industry results. Similarly, when agriculture or house-building are held back by the unwillingness of private companies to make mortgage money available, the community gains by having a government company fill the gap.

In the utility field the success of public ownership must be judged by the prices consumers pay for the company's services. Although public ownership will eliminate the monopoly profits of a private corporation, it does not always mean lower prices to consumers. The city-owned electric power utility in Saskatoon, for example, follows a policy of monopoly prices. Its high profits go to the city. This means that the company's light bills are being used to raise city revenues that would normally be raised through taxes. Consumers would be better served by low prices and low profits; hence public ownership in this instance does not serve the interests of consumers. Public ownership is not always a successful remedy for monopoly: results depend upon the policies of the publicly-owned corporation.

5. THE CO-OPERATIVE

Many Canadians think the remedy for monopoly lies in *more* government regulation or *more* government ownership, but there are many who find an answer in an altogether different form of business organization — the co-operative. This fifth kind of business firm differs greatly from the other four.

A Co-operative Store

To see what a co-operative *is*, let us compare three stores in the grocery business: an individual enterprise, a private corporation, and a co-operative. The first two, although poles apart in size and number of owners, have this much in common: both are selling groceries, to all comers, for the purpose of making profits for their owners (the proprietor and the stockholders). Their *customers* have no personal relation to the business. Of course, some of the stockholders in a big chain store may shop at one of its branches but this is of no concern to the company. The co-op store is different. Its customers own the business. Its primary purpose is not to reap profits but to lower the cost of groceries to its owners. If it is successful its owners will "profit" by buying their groceries for less than they would pay at other stores.

The Patronage Dividend

How can the members of an efficient co-op get their groceries for less? The main reason is that the surplus earnings, which in a private corporation go to the shareholders, go to the members of the co-operative who shopped at their co-operative store. Surplus earnings are distributed among the members in amounts based upon their patronage. If Mrs. Jones spends $100 at the co-operative each month and Mrs. Brown spends only $50, Mrs. Jones will get a "patronage dividend" which is twice as large as Mrs. Brown's. But both will get their groceries for less than they would pay in other stores because part of what they spend comes back to them as patronage dividends.

The patronage dividend is the basic principle in every co-operative enterprise. You may wonder why. Must the co-op earn a surplus? Instead, why not pass the savings on to members by setting lower prices? There are several reasons. One is that if prices were lower *anyone* could take advantage of co-operative savings by shopping at the co-operative store: there would be no incentive to join the co-operative association. The co-op must have an interested, active membership to maintain the business and see that it is run efficiently. The patronage dividend encourages people to become members and very often supplies the means of paying for membership. People who are unable to buy a membership share in advance can still join and pay for their share with their patronage dividends.

Another disadvantage of setting lower prices is that this policy would invite a price war with the nearby chain store. In such a battle victory would almost surely go to the chain store with all the financial resources of a powerful corporation behind it.

Owners and Managers

The owners of a co-op are members of a co-operative association. To become a member you buy a share. By itself, this share does not entitle you to any of the surplus earnings of the business, as it would in a private corporation. In a co-op your share earns a fixed interest payment and your chief return is the patronage dividend. To earn it you must *use* your co-op.

The day-to-day business of a co-operative is run in much the same way as it is in any other corporation. There are the executives employed by the co-op, and a board of directors, elected by the members, which is responsible for policy. In voting for the board of directors, however, we find an important distinction. In a private corporation you have as many votes as you have shares; in a co-op the rule is one vote for each member. No matter how many shares he owns each member has only one vote; each has an equal voice in the control of the business.

Even with this democratic principle co-ops encounter some of the same problems that large private corporations do. For one reason or another many co-op members do not use their vote, and a large co-op is usually run by a small group of active members. Nevertheless, a major difference remains. If you wished to force a change in policy in a co-op you would need to round up the support of a majority of members but you would not have to purchase shares. In an ordinary corporation only the wealthiest shareholders are able to buy up or get proxies for a majority of the shares.

Raising Capital

The sale of shares to members provides the initial capital for a co-op to get started. Thereafter, the co-ops must rely on retained earnings, loans from other co-ops, and on the sale of shares to new members. To raise more money through the sale of shares the co-ops *must* attract new members because there is no incentive for members to buy more than the one or two shares needed to join.

Another major limitation is that the co-ops cannot appeal to the investing public. Private corporations have the advantage of a wide range of securities and also of special institutions, such as the stock exchange, which grew up with the corporation to attract private savings into common shares. Co-operatives have to rely very largely on the co-operative movement itself to provide capital.

It is true that many co-ops do find the capital they need for expansion; some have entered the realms of big business. Nevertheless, the difficulties of raising funds must be counted as a major limitation of the co-operative form of enterprise.

Principles of Co-operation

To sum up we may list the five basic principles of the co-operative corporation:

(i) open membership to all, regardless of class, colour or creed

(ii) equal voting privileges; one member — one vote

(iii) fixed interest on share capital

(iv) selling at prevailing prices

(v) distribution of surplus earnings by patronage dividends

To this list of principles many co-ops add a sixth — cash trading. A majority also devote some part of their earnings to educational programmes to promote the growth of co-operation.

Kinds of Co-operatives

A co-operative business does not need to be a grocery — or even a store. A co-op can be set up to supply any service to its owners. This may mean selling something (such as groceries or hardware or health insurance) that its owners want to *buy*, or it may mean marketing products (such as fish or fruit or wheat) that its owners want to *sell*. Those organized to sell *to* their members are called consumers co-ops, and the ones which sell *for* their members are called marketing co-ops. The co-op grocery store described above is an example of consumer co-operation. Marketing co-operatives are organized on the same basic principles, but the members are producers, usually farmers or fishermen, who set up a co-operative business to market their own products. Here lower costs mean a higher return for producers — again distributed in the form of the patronage dividend.

Consumer co-ops have been very successful in Great Britain and in other countries of north-western Europe. They have had less success in North America. In Great Britain co-op stores handle eleven per cent of the total retail trade. Some of the stores are small, catering to the needs of rural districts; others are as large as the private corporations they compete with. A single local association in London has over 2 million members. The local co-ops own their own wholesale organization and the large wholesale co-ops have branched out into production, acquiring flour mills, cargo fleets, and plantations in many parts of the world. Thus the co-ops as a group are big business and they offer a wide variety of services, from clothing and groceries to insurance and medical services.

In Canada, as we shall see, the greatest co-operative development has been in marketing. Ranging from the giant wheat pools to tiny livestock shipping clubs, the farmers' co-operatives play an important role in our economy.

Origins

Why have co-operatives? Why do consumers go into the grocery business? Why do farmers and fishermen set up their own marketing organization? The answer is that they are dissatisfied with other forms of business. Consumers may think that prices are too high, and blame the storekeeper for taking too much profit. Farmers may feel the prices they are getting are too low, and blame the middleman for taking too much profit. Both may be right. The stores may have enough monopoly power to keep their prices a little higher; the companies who

buy farm products may also be able to pay farmers less than they should. Thus, in either event co-ops are really an attack on monopoly.

It was a monopoly situation that produced the first successful co-operative. This happened in Rochdale, England, in the 1840's, a period of deep depression that earned the name "the hungry forties". In Rochdale, as elsewhere, unemployment was widespread, wages were low, and the misery of workers was increased by the high prices and shoddy goods in small retail stores. But in Rochdale a group of unemployed weavers found a solution: they set up their own store. And they ran it on co-operative principles, the principles described on page 41. In time their experiment succeeded and the principles of the Rochdale pioneers became the basis of co-operation throughout the world.

Marketing Co-operatives in Canada

In the coal-mining communities in Nova Scotia co-op stores have a long history (the British-Canadian Co-operative Society was founded in 1906) but in most parts of Canada, until very recently, co-operative business made its appeal mainly to producers. A famous illustration comes from the prairies. In the early 1900's pioneer farmers were dissatisfied with the prices they got for their wheat. They distrusted the large elevator companies to which they delivered their grain, and also the grain dealers who sold the grain on the Winnipeg grain exchange. And so, like the Rochdale weavers, the prairie farmers went into business for themselves.

They organized the first co-operative company to sell grain on the Winnipeg market. The original Grain Growers Grain Company (later United Grain Growers) was followed by co-operative elevator companies in each of the prairie provinces. Later, in the nineteen-twenties, prairie farmers pooled their wheat and sold it co-operatively through a central selling agency. Nowadays all western grain is sold through a federal government agency, the Canadian Wheat Board, but the farmers are still in the elevator business. These giants of the co-operative movement provide elevator service for approximately half the crop, which makes them very big business indeed.

In dollar volume of business the prairie elevator companies greatly outdistance all other Canadian co-operatives, but in the co-operative movement success cannot be judged by size alone. The small co-op can be just as effective in securing better prices for the farmer as a large one, and co-operative business can be particularly helpful to small farmers. The typical small farmer cannot afford to move his livestock to market. On his own he would be obliged to take whatever price was offered at the farm. But if several small farmers form a co-op to ship and sell their stock in the market, their chances of getting better prices are greatly improved. In the case of prod-

ucts such as eggs and milk many dealers prefer to buy in carload lots and, as a result, the small farmer has difficulty securing reasonable prices for his small quantities. But a farmer's co-op can collect the products of many small farmers, grade and package them, and deliver them to the city in the large quantities that are more easily sold.

These facts are well known in Nova Scotia, a province famous for its co-operatives. This fame rests not on the age or size of co-operatives but rather on their success in raising incomes both of producers and consumers. Thirty years ago, when the modern movement began, low incomes were a problem everywhere, but the great depression had struck Nova Scotia with particular force. Agriculture had long been depressed and the further loss of income — in agricul-

Nova Scotia Information Service

Packaging of fish at a plant of the United Maritime Fishermen Co-operative, at Cheticamp on Cape Breton Island, Nova Scotia.

ture, in the fisheries, in all industries — produced a crisis which demanded a solution.

Could co-operation help to raise the cash incomes of farmers and fishermen? A small group of men at St. Francis Xavier University and in the provincial Department of Agriculture thought that it could. As a first step they encouraged the formation of study groups in which farmers and fishermen could be trained in the principles and methods of co-operation. Next came buying-clubs to purchase farm or household supplies, and very often a full-fledged co-operative store would follow. The same co-ops could turn to marketing the things produced by its members: eggs, milk and other farm products; lobsters and fresh fish in the case of fishermen's co-operatives. Over the past 20 years this co-operative movement has expanded greatly and today Nova Scotia has a higher percentage of its population belonging to co-operatives than has any other province. Although Quebec has the largest number of co-operatives and the prairie provinces (particularly Saskatchewan) the largest memberships, nowhere is the participation ratio so high as in Nova Scotia.

Co-operative marketing associations are found in all parts of Canada and have well over a million farmer members. Almost one-third of all farm products sold commercially are sold through the co-ops. In some cases, notably wool, hay and seeds, maple products, honey, and the storage of wheat and other grains, the proportion is much higher. Co-ops are extensively used in the dairy business and in the marketing of fruits and vegetables. In British Columbia the local co-operatives handle most of the fruit crop while government marketing boards, which actually sell the crop, administer a pooled price.

Consumer Co-operation

The last two decades have witnessed a spectacular growth in consumer co-ops in Canada. Earlier, most of our purchasing co-operatives grew out of farmers' organizations, such as the United Grain Growers Company. Originally established to sell grain for farmers, the U.G.G. branched out into buying farm supplies for its members and has had both retail and wholesale stores for many years. Today there are a great many purchasing associations and co-operative stores, selling farm supplies (feed, fertilizers, gas and oil, machinery and building materials), and also groceries, auto accessories, clothing, home furnishings and many other consumer goods. There are ten co-operative wholesales. In the east the co-op wholesales also act as central marketing agencies for local marketing co-ops. In the west they have followed the lead of the British co-operative wholesales and branched into production. Thus Federated Co-operatives Ltd. owns coal mines, timber berths, sawmills, oil wells and refineries. The Saskatchewan Wheat Pool owns a large flour and seed mill.

In spite of the expansion, the co-operative's share of the total business, both in retail and wholesale trade, is still very small. But co-operative stores are firmly established and have shown that Canadian consumers as well as farmers can help themselves by going into business. Moreover, their competition compels other firms to reduce prices and maintain efficiency. As a result the total benefit is far greater than their size alone would indicate.

We do not have space to describe the many other services that Canadian co-operatives provide: insurance (fire, life, and hail), medical expenses, restaurants, boarding-houses, funeral homes, freezer lockers, light and power, community services (such as snow-ploughs, community halls, and so on), and credit. This last, however, deserves special mention.

Credit Unions

The credit union is a co-operative of a special type. Its purpose is to encourage thrift among its members and to make loans at reasonably low interest rates. Credit unions are formed by people with a common bond of association, such as a lodge or parish, employment in the same company, or residence in a certain community. Like any co-op, a credit union is owned and controlled by its members on the Rochdale principle of one vote per member. To join you pay a small entrance fee and buy a share. (Saskatchewan law, for example, sets the fee at 25 cents and shares at $5 each.) You then use the credit union, just as you would a bank, as a place to deposit your savings and a place to borrow money.

As a member, you can borrow at a limited interest rate. In Saskatchewan the highest credit union lending rate is 12 per cent; the most typical is 6 per cent. These rates are much lower than the 16 to 24 per cent charged by many consumer finance companies and by stores providing instalment credit. The great advantage of the credit union to anyone with a low or moderate income is obvious. Members rely on their credit unions to finance their cars, refrigerators, record players, farm implements, and all manner of costly, durable goods.

The credit union pays a fixed interest, usually 3 or 4 per cent, on share capital; it also pays a lower interest, say 1½ per cent, on deposits. Some even pay patronage dividends to borrowers in the form of "interest refunds". But generally credit unions prefer to charge lower interest rates and to give members more services instead of interest refunds. Services include chequing privileges, life insurance equal to each member's savings deposits, and loan insurance to cancel the debt to the credit union if a borrower dies.

In addition to the local credit unions there are also central credit unions in each province to which the locals belong. The purpose of the centrals is to lend to and hold deposits of the locals. Thus a "central" acts as the *credit union* of the local credit unions in a province or region. The provincial centrals, in turn, look to a "national central" — the Canadian Co-operative Credit Society — to which they may belong.

Like other kinds of co-ops, the credit unions developed in response to a need. In 1900, when Alphonse Desjardins established North America's first credit union in Lévis, Quebec, low-income families in Montreal were paying interest rates of 100 per cent and more! That first credit union was followed by many more as the movement spread throughout Quebec (where today there are over a million members), into Ontario, to the other provinces of Canada and into the United States as well. That there is *still* a need for the service of credit unions is evident in the doubling of their membership over the past ten years. Today over 2 million Canadians belong to credit unions.

Advantages and Disadvantages of Co-operatives

Like any form of business organization the co-op has both strong points and weaknesses. On the plus side is the financial gain for members. Wherever there are private companies making monopoly profits the co-op can obtain more favourable prices for its members, whether they are farmers or consumers. A second advantage is its success in reconciling big business with democracy. The co-operative form of enterprise provides for a large-scale organization while preserving democratic control. Although minority control does occur in large co-ops, the ordinary member need not accept the passive role of the small shareholder in a private corporation. He does have an equal vote with the other members and if he takes an active interest in the business he can expect to have some influence on policy.

The chief weakness of the co-operative business is the difficulty it faces in raising capital. It cannot attract the investor's money as a private corporation can. As a result, co-operatives have to rely on their members: withholding profits from old members or finding new ones. Sometimes these sources prove adequate, as witness the Rochdale weavers who opened their business on $140, or the Lévis credit union with its initial capital of $26! Many co-ops got started in a small way and grew into successful enterprises. But the fact remains that many co-ops have been handicapped by lack of funds. The difficulty of raising capital has prevented the co-op from making further inroads upon private enterprise.

Another limitation of co-operatives is that their present success is confined to a few fields. For the most part consumer co-ops are active in the very lines where profit margins are lowest. The big chain grocery stores in Canadian cities operate on a low margin per dollar of sales. Therefore it is difficult for the co-operatives in competition with them to pay large patronage dividends. (The situation in rural districts is different. The country general store is often in a near monopoly position, and a local co-op can secure larger gains for rural consumers.)

To make *greater* savings in cost the co-operatives would have to move more into manufacturing where, because of concentration, monopoly elements are more common. But the higher profit margins in manufacturing may be due to the greater *risk* as well as monopoly. While people go on buying groceries, year in, year out, the sales of refrigerators, automobiles and other consumer durables drop sharply whenever there is any slackening in trade. In addition to the greater risk, the manufacture of consumer durables requires a very large investment. Moreover, these fields are already occupied by powerful private companies who would not stand idly by while co-ops took over a large share of their business.

The co-operatives have moved into manufacturing of oil and gasoline, flour, light implements, bags and other items for which they have assured markets through the co-op stores. But unless there is a revolution in their approach, it seems unlikely that co-operatives will ever compete with private corporations in the major manufacturing industries. Nevertheless, in trade and particularly in the marketing of farmers' products, the co-ops play a useful part in our mixed economy.

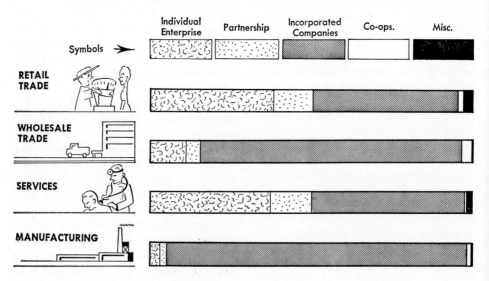

PERCENTAGE OF TOTAL SALES OF THE DIFFERENT KINDS OF BUSINESS FIRMS

QUESTIONS FOR DISCUSSION

1. Let us say that you have $2000 and the opportunity to buy a small café. Naturally you would investigate the business and its prospects very carefully, but what could you say off-hand about your capital position in this venture? List some of the factors the prospective proprietor should take into account.

2. Make a list of twenty business firms in your community from different fields of industry. What percentage do you find are individual enterprises or partnerships, what percentage are corporations?

3. Mr. Johnston and Mr. Jones are partners in a grocery store. Their business is a good one but they think it would be better if the store could be renovated and service expanded. What problems would be solved if they incorporated and could sell shares to two wealthy relatives?

4. What is the difference between stocks and bonds? When a company is making large profits, would you prefer to have its stocks — or bonds? Why? What if the company is not making a profit? Give three reasons why stocks and bonds are effective devices for raising money.

5. Explain how an individual enterprise is owned and managed. What changes would result if the business were incorporated but the former owner held all the stock? Who are the owners and who are the managers in a corporation where the stock is widely held? Explain how the owners have a voice in the management of their business.

6. Explain why a large corporation can be controlled by a small number of shareholders. How could this affect your interests, supposing you owned a few shares in a big company? Can the large corporation affect you as a consumer?

7. In any edition of the *Canada Year Book* you will find a section called "The Growth of Manufacturing in Canada". Statistics for manufacturing in Canada from 1870 to the present day are given in Table 1. Notice first the *number* of establishments (column 1), say in 1870, 1890, 1917, 1929, 1939, and 1957. There are now fewer establishments than there were 70 years ago! This shows that business firms have been increasing in size rather than in numbers. Proof of this can be had by looking at the increases in column 2 — amount of capital employed — and columns 6 and 7 — the value of output. For the years mentioned above, divide the number of establishments into the total capital to show the *average* value of capital employed for each establishment. Divide the number of establishments into the value of output to show the average production for each establishment. See how your figures, spanning more than 80 years, support what was said in this chapter about the growth of large-scale production.

8. In the United States privately-owned power companies pay for full-page magazine ads to carry the message that competition from *publicly*-owned power companies is unfair. Do you agree? Can you give reasons for having publicly-owned power companies? Supposing a similar charge was levelled against the Canadian National Railways, how would you defend public ownership of the C.N.R.?

9. A distinguishing feature of the co-operative is the owner's special purpose for being in business. Compare this purpose with the aim of the proprietor in an individual enterprise or of the stockholders in a private corporation. Is there anything in common between a co-operative corporation and a publicly-owned corporation?

10. Describe the main feature of any co-operative business. How many co-operatives are there in your community? What services are performed by these local co-operatives?

Chapter 5

Labour Organization

Most of you have heard of the U.A.W., the C.L.C. and other combinations of letters which stand for labour organizations. What they are and what they do are described later in this chapter. But to understand the labour union and its place in our mixed economy we shall have to begin at the beginning and survey the labour scene at the time when the union made its first appearance.

1. BACKGROUND OF THE LABOUR MOVEMENT

This takes us back to early nineteenth-century England. The "industrial revolution" was well under way and long-established methods in production were giving way to the new. Machine industry had begun to replace traditional handicrafts, mills and factories were multiplying and the railway builders were revolutionizing transportation. It was a time of rapid change and the basic changes in production methods called forth new institutions. As we have seen, business men responded by devising a new form of organization. Now we must see what the new methods in production meant to labour, and why labour too had to take action.

The Factory Worker

There were no factories in pre-industrial England. As a general rule cotton was spun, cloth was woven and metal work was done in the home, with the aid of simple tools which were owned by the worker. The position of the factory worker, therefore, was altogether new. The new machines were too expensive for him to own. They were simple to operate and so efficient that his old skills were as obsolete as his tools. The worker was left with nothing to offer to earn his living except his labour.

The same is true, of course, of most workers today. But we have had time to grow used to the idea and, more important, the modern factory worker can earn a very good living. In the early nineteenth century many workers could not earn enough to support their families, however long and hard they worked. And when a man's wages would not feed and clothe and house his family, his wife and often his children worked too. In the 1830's some 55 per cent of all factory workers in England were women. Almost half the factory workers were under 18 years of age, and in the cotton mills one quarter were under 14. Many employers preferred to hire children because they could do the job and cost less than adults. The widespread use of child labour inspired many protests, including these lines:

> "The golf links are so near the mill
> That almost every day
> The little children at their work
> Can see the men at play."

Most of the early factories were poorly ventilated, dark and noisy. If the operations required heat or dampness or created dust the surroundings were even more unhealthy. Safety precautions were few and accidents were frequent. The danger of accidents was increased by the monotony of the work. Under these conditions men, women and children tended tireless machines for 12 to 14 hours a day, 6 days a week. In the rush season in the mills even the children worked an 18-hour day! Official reports describe sleeping children being carried to the factory in the morning, still clutching the bread they were too tired to eat the night before. A Royal Commission investigating child labour in the mines quoted a boy of seven and a half who claimed to have been down three years. Said he: "When I first went down I couldn't keep my eyes open; I don't fall asleep now; I smokes my pipe."

Labour in a Price System

Today it is hard to believe that people actually lived and worked under these conditions. How did it happen? To answer this question we need to know something about the position of labour in a price system.

In a free price system wages are decided by the actions of the buyers and sellers of labour. To illustrate, let us say that mine owners offer wages of 40 cents a day. If, at that wage, they can hire all the men they want then 40 cents a day will be the miner's wage. The wage will rise if 40 cents a day does not bring enough men to the pits, and it will fall if enough men will work for less. The low wages of early industrial England, therefore, must be viewed from two sides: buyers (employers) and sellers (workers).

First of all, the offers of employers cannot be judged by modern standards. The productive efficiency of workers was so much lower than it is today that no employer could afford to pay 40 cents *an hour*, much less a modern wage scale. Second, when we turn to the sellers' side, we find a great many men and women seeking jobs. This large supply of workers also contributed to low wages. From many parts of England they streamed to the new industrial towns, driven from farms and villages by the new methods in agriculture and from traditional craft industries by the new machines. Although his wages were low, the factory worker was better paid than farm labourers and handicraft workers, and certainly he earned more than the unemployed! In an economy where no better opportunities existed, factory employment had to be accepted by working men and women.

Traditionally, in England, the welfare of the working class had been a responsibility of the community as a whole. Wages were often fixed by public authorities and a comprehensive system of poor relief took care of those who could not earn enough. But in the early nineteenth century these regulations were swept away because they interfered with the movement of labour. The people who elected governments (not until the 1880's did the workers have the vote) believed in the absolute reign of the price system. This, they said, would assure the most efficient use of resources, hence the largest output of goods and services, the greatest wealth for the nation. Government regulations could only hinder the working of the price system and reduce wealth. The government, therefore, should cease to concern itself with wages. Like any other price, wages must be left to the actions of buyers and sellers alone; employers and workers must be free to conclude their own bargains.

Supporters of the price system overlooked the fact that in the "bargaining" between employers and workers the strength was on the employers' side. In mine or mill or factory the individual worker could be easily replaced. His work required little or no training and many others were able and eager to take his place. In consequence, the individual worker could not *demand* higher wages or better working conditions. Even if he quit his job, his protest would not win a penny more for his fellow workers. In a free price system, therefore, and especially when there was unemployment, the average worker could not expect to improve his lot so long as he bargained alone. And so, in the earliest days of modern industry, workers turned to group organization to protect themselves.

Labour Organizes

One of the earliest protests against the conditions of life and work in an industrial economy came from a wealthy mill owner, Robert Owen. With a small group of supporters Owen spent many years on schemes designed to change the economic order, and although most of the early Owenite experiments ended in failure, out of Owenism came three separate movements which have helped to shape our modern world. One of these was the co-operative movement described in Chapter 4. The second, Chartism, was designed to improve conditions through political action. Eventually working men and women did get the vote but in the late 1840's the Chartists appeared to have failed and their movement broke up. The third movement was the labour union movement which, after early failures, eventually achieved success.

The whole idea of the union was to give the workers some power in order to force concessions from individual employers. The individual worker has little bargaining power. But what if *all* the workers in a factory should band together and speak with a single voice? What if *all* refused to work until wages were raised and working conditions improved? Then labour would have power on its side too. In the words of a union song:

> "The boss won't listen when one
> guy squawks
> But he's got to listen when the
> union talks."

Working men and women wanted better wages and working conditions than the price system would provide; the *union* was their means of seeking them.

Opposition and Growth

The story of the union movement from its beginning almost to the present day is a stormy one. The early unions in England were faced with laws which forbade associations of working men, and even after the legal barriers had been cleared away many employers continued to fight the unions,

often successfully. In North America the struggle was even more prolonged. For decades after the unions had been generally accepted in England, Canadian and American employers in large numbers continued to resist.

Resistance took many forms. The employer might simply refuse to meet with union officials. Or he might get rid of a troublesome union by firing all its members. The Ford Motor Company in the United States used this method more than once. Strikes were broken by importing new factory workers by the hundreds from remote country places where unions were unknown. Sometimes employers got help from the courts. Thus the company might break a strike by having it ruled illegal. A great many employers resisted less openly but just as effectively by means of the "company union". To understand this tactic we must see the difference between two kinds of unions.

The Company Union

Labour's unions are organized on a national or a regional basis. The reason is that labour wants *one* strong independent union to confront all employers in an industry. The company union is made up of employees of a single company and has no connections with any other group of organized workers. By encouraging employees to form a company union the employer not only avoids the much bigger and stronger unions which are organized to suit labour's needs, but he may be able to control the company union. So labour rejected the company union and fought for unions of their own choice organized in their own way.

Union Recognition

Opposition from employers, together with labour's determination to organize, resulted in episodes of violence and occasional bloodshed. The opposition was not strong enough to stop the unions but it did prevent them from growing rapidly. As recently as 1938, for example, there were scarcely any unions in the Canadian textile industry. Yet wages were incredibly low and the hours of work so long that the International Labour Office placed Canada (along with Japan, India and China) among the few countries which had not achieved the 48-hour week! A Royal Commission which investigated the industry found employers' opposition the main reason for the failure of unions. The president of one company testified:

"The men can belong to any union if they like. We do not ask a man if he belongs to a union or what religion he is, but the board of directors refuse to recognize the Union, any Union."

In other words, this company would not meet with the unions' representatives. It would not "recognize" the union as the official bargaining agent of its members.

This flat refusal to concede the union any place in labour-management relations was a common attitude among North American employers. Many unions, therefore, had to fight first of all for "recognition". Before they could hope to win higher wages — or anything else — they had to force employers to accept the principle of collective bargaining. And as long as the unions had to fight for recognition their members and strength could increase only slowly.

In recent years the growth of unions has been speeded up as a result of actions taken by the third party in all labour-management relations. This third party, government representing the public interest, had traditionally played a negative role, which meant its support was more often on the side of the employers than of the workers. Finally, in 1933, American unions got the public support they needed to win their biggest battle. A law passed by the government of the United States made it *compulsory* for employers to negotiate with the union chosen by the employees — provided that the union had majority support. This gave the unions legal status. No longer could a company fight a union by ignoring it, by imposing a company union, or by intimidating or otherwise preventing its workers from signing up. Companies *had* to negotiate with their workers through the workers' union.

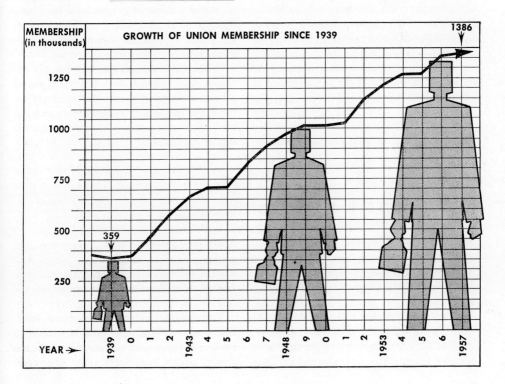

GROWTH OF UNION MEMBERSHIP SINCE 1939

Canadian unions had several years to wait but eventually similar legislation, passed by governments in Canada, strengthened the position of the unions in this country and enabled them to go ahead at a rapid pace as they had in the United States.

Kinds of Unions

The earliest unions were those of the skilled craftsmen. The members of these unions have in common a particular trade or craft — carpentry, printing, blacksmithing, machine operation — and their unions are therefore known as "craft" unions. A carpenter might work in the construction industry, or the wagon industry or any other, but he joins a union with other carpenters. Skilled workers have usually had an advantage over unskilled workers and through their unions they further strengthened their positions. For a long time progress in the labour movement was confined to the craft unions.

The industrial unions came later. These unions are called "industrial" because they are organized on the basis of particular industries. Each union includes workers of many different occupations and of varying degrees of skill. Assembly-line workers, welders, painters, machinists and every kind of labour employed in the manufacture of automobiles: all are eligible to join the U.A.W. This kind of union is much more useful to the unskilled and semi-skilled workers in modern mass production indus-tries than the old craft union. Today, both kinds of unions are found in all the western democracies. The craft union still has an advantage for many kinds of workers but the industrial union has become increasingly important.

Labour and the Government

From 40 cents a day to $4.00 an hour; from the 72-hour week to the 44: these show how far labour has travelled. Between the 1840's and the 1950's the conditions of earning a living were radically transformed. This is not the result of the unions alone. The union has been one means of getting the things that labour wanted, but many of labour's objectives have been won through action by the government. For example, governments have passed laws prohibiting child labour and protecting women and young people. Hours of work, safety and health of workers, indeed all the objectives of labour have attracted the attention of governments. So labour has had two strings to its bow. Some objectives have been won directly by the unions, some indirectly as the unions brought pressure on governments to pass the laws that labour wanted.

In the next two sections our topic is the union: the function and the structure of unions in Canada today. In Section 4 we return to the role of governments and describe their many points of contact with the labour movement.

2. COLLECTIVE BARGAINING

What a Union Is — and Does

First and foremost, the function of a union is to bargain for its members. Its objectives may be higher wages, or holidays with pay, or job security or some other condition of work, but it is something to be won *for* its members *from* the employer. Unions are not designed to fight the battle for all workers. The International Brother-hood of Carpenters and Joiners has one primary aim: to secure better wages and working conditions for carpenters. The United Auto Workers has the same aim for workers in the automobile industry.

This does not mean that unions are indifferent to what happens outside their own ranks. Every union has an interest in the whole labour movement. But the main interest and the main job for each union remains the more limited one of bargaining for its own members.

The union works on the principle of "collective bargaining", which means simply that the union speaks for all its members in the employ of the company. Workers without a union must bargain as individuals. When the individual worker seeks a raise it is for himself alone. No worker has the authority to speak for any other. And the company can refuse each worker in turn. This is "individual bargaining", or every man for himself. But if the union's demands are not met, at least in part, the company knows that all employees may go on strike. Collective bargaining, therefore, strengthens the employees' position.

Negotiations and Contract

Once a union has been "recognized" by a company the way is clear for collective bargaining. Negotiations take place at regular intervals — once a year or possibly once every two or three years — when officials of the union and the company meet at the conference table to settle on wages and other aspects of company policy affecting labour.

Before negotiations begin, both sides prepare their case with care. The union picks its best men for the job, and these may be assisted by skilled professional negotiators from union headquarters. They go to the conference table with specific demands. To illustrate, let us say the union asks for an increase in wages of 20 cents an hour. Company records have been studied, and the union men have brief cases bulging with figures to support their argument that the company can afford the higher wage schedule. The company, on its side, has an offer in mind — say 10 cents an hour — and its negotiators work hard to show that this is the most the company can afford to pay. Then the real bargaining begins. The air is filled with facts and figures, speech-making and haggling, as the one side tries to get as much as it can, the other to yield as little as possible. And in this atmosphere of give and take a new wage contract is hammered out between hard bargainers on both sides of the table.

National Film Board Photo

Union-management negotiations round the conference table.

Whether the final result is closer to the union's 20 cents or the company's 10 cents will depend upon the relative strength of the two sides. A strong union may be in a position to get most of what it asks; a weak union will often settle for a fraction of its original demands. Strength on both sides may vary from one year to another. The union's chances are generally best when the business is flourishing, and are almost always diminished by recession and unemployment. In recent years, with inflation a major problem, many unions have succeeded in getting wages linked to the consumer price index. Then any increase in prices which moves the index up a certain number of points means an automatic increase in wages without further negotiations.

Besides wages the unions will have other demands to negotiate. For example, there is the problem of "union security". Since the union's strength is based on its numbers, the union must protect itself against loss of membership whether through actions by the company or simply from inertia and indifference among the workers. Whenever possible it tries to get the company to agree to include certain union safeguards in the contract. One of these safeguards is the "check-off", which means that union dues are deducted from wages by the company and forwarded to the union. Another is the "maintenance of union membership" clause. This requires that union members may not leave the union during the life of the contract. If the union is strong enough it will force the company to require all new employees to join the union. This is called the "union shop". The "closed shop" requires even greater strength to win. In a closed shop all employees must join the union.

Other topics of negotiation include seniority rights and hours of work. The union may want the work week shortened, or different pay rates for overtime. If it thinks the safety and health of its members are not sufficiently protected it will ask for company action. Then there are the so-called "fringe benefits", such as holidays and sick leave, pensions, and health schemes. Finally, union and company must settle on a method for handling complaints and grievances that may arise during the life of the contract.

Thus point by point the union representatives spell out their demands, and point by point the company representatives counter with what they are prepared to yield. It usually takes some time before agreement is reached on all the topics covered by a contract. Nevertheless, both sides are anxious to reach an agreement because both will suffer if they fail. Most negotiations end with agreement and the signing of the contract. This contract sets down, in detail, every point settled by negotiation. The union promises not to call a strike during the life of the contract and the company gives its word not to close down the plant. And so until negotiation time comes again, when the contract must be re-negotiated, labour-management relations are governed by the contract which *both* have had a hand in writing.

The importance of collective bargaining can be judged from the fact that in Canada today there are more than 6000 contracts in effect covering over a million and a half workers. Through collective bargaining, workers express their views on every aspect of employment. They feel better off and more secure because they have a voice in deciding the company's labour policy. But it is not only the workers who stand to gain from the use of collective bargaining. The company is assured peaceful relations with its employees, possibly greater efficiency. And where both sides can settle their differences around the conference table relations are likely to remain peaceful.

The Strike and the Lock-out

Collective bargaining does not always follow a peaceful course. Suppose the union will not go below 20 cents an hour in its demands and the company will not offer more than 10 cents. What happens when union and company cannot agree? One possibility is that the union will call a strike. By stopping the company's operations the union hopes to *force* the company to meet its terms. A strike committee is formed and union members are instructed to stay off their jobs until the dispute is settled. However, the strike itself does not settle the issue. The dispute may be settled on the union's terms, but a strike can also end in victory for the company. The outcome of any strike depends on the circumstances. If all employees belong to the union, and particularly if replacements for the strikers are hard to find, and if the union has ample funds, the union will likely win at least part of its demands. But unions are not always in this strong position and, when they are not, the company may be able to hold out longer than its employees.

The strike is very costly all round. The workers draw no pay and their strike benefits are less than wages. The strike benefits paid by the union out of its strike funds deplete the union's treasury. The company loses money if it cannot operate. The public is inconvenienced. When union and company are evenly matched a strike may last for weeks or months, causing hardship to all concerned. Yet in spite of all these costs we would be wrong to conclude that the strike has no merits. It is the strike — or, more precisely, the *threat* of a strike — that gives the union a bargaining position in dealing with management. In spite of its disadvantages the strike remains the most powerful weapon a union has.

Who is to blame when a strike occurs? Most people say the union and certainly it is the union that calls out the workers. But the basic trouble is the deadlock in negotiations. It makes as much sense to blame the company for not going over 10 cents as to blame the union for refusing to take less than 20 cents! When *both* sides refuse to budge, we must hold both sides responsible. Either side could prevent the strike by giving ground to the other. Precisely the same reasoning applies to the lock-out. In a dispute the employer may try to force the union to come to terms by closing down the plant. The workers are "locked out". Again, although the company takes the initiative, both sides are responsible for the failure to reach agreement.

Conciliation and Arbitration

Failure to reach agreement does not always lead to a strike or lock-out. Another possibility is conciliation. Here union and company agree to invite an impartial outsider to study the facts of the dispute and suggest a compromise. Either side is perfectly free to turn down the conciliator's solution, but very often it is one that both sides can accept. In Canada, the federal government and most of the provinces provide a conciliation service. They set up conciliation boards when called upon to help settle disputes. Most of the cases that go before a conciliation board are settled without a strike.

Conciliation is also widely used to settle disputes when a strike is already on. In a few industries of special importance — the railroads, mining, and the utilities — conciliation *must* be tried before either company or union can slow down or stop production. The law does not require them to accept the conciliation board's decision, but the conciliation procedure provides a "cooling-off period" which may make it easier to reach an agreement.

Arbitration is another method of settling disputes between management and labour. As with conciliation, the union and the company invite a third party to find a solution, but in arbitration both sides agree in advance *to accept* the recommendations of the arbitrator or arbitration board. In Canada certain kinds of employers and workers are required by law to submit their disputes to arbitration; this is known as compulsory arbitration. Usually it applies where the public insists that the strike and the lock-out be made illegal. The municipal fire-fighting services are a good illustration. Compulsory arbitration, however, although widely used in some countries, has not been popular in Canada because it deprives individuals of freedom of action: workers cannot strike; employers cannot use the lock-out.

Industry Agreements

Most negotiations take place between a union and a single company. For the union, however, the signing of a single contract is not the only goal. Wherever possible organized labour tries to get the same contract with *all* the companies in an industry. Auto workers, for example, would not be content to have a good contract only at General Motors, because if Ford and Chrysler pay lower wages auto workers at General Motors could not hope to improve their contract at their next negotiations. Even worse, if a high wage company loses business to low wage competitors, the union with the good contract may lose all it has won. So labour tries to get the same contract with all the companies in an industry. This is the chief reason why most unions are organized on a national basis. Instead of one union for auto workers in Oshawa and another one in Oakville and still another in Windsor, it is all one union: the U.A.W. The one union negotiates with Ford, General Motors, and Chrysler.

Occasionally the union negotiates with several companies in an industry at one time. The contract is then called a "trade agreement"; all matters affecting labour in the entire industry are covered in the one agreement.

Union Abuses

What about the debit side? A few sensational cases of corruption have been turned up in the United States and the unions concerned have usually been front-page stories in Canadian newspapers. But since it is generally admitted that such abuses are rare, even in the United States, the more serious charge against the unions is that they misuse their power. Both within its own ranks and in its relations with the general public the big union does raise problems.

Like the rank-and-file corporation shareholder the rank-and-file union member does not participate in policy-making decisions. He does have much more influence and greater powers of control because, in the election of local officers, each union member has a single vote. But union officials do not always represent the views of the majority, and they can sometimes remain in office with only an active minority's support.

When we turn to the community as a whole we find that the power of big unions may conflict with the public interest. As we have seen, the public bears part of the costs of a strike although usually most of the cost is borne by the workers and the company involved. But when a major strike occurs in a key industry such as steel the number of other industries affected could raise the steel strike to the status of a national crisis. In this event government may step in to force big business and big unions to come to terms. The post-war problem of inflation points to another danger. Again the policies of big business and big unions may have undesirable results. We shall consider this problem in Chapter 11.

3. ORGANIZED LABOUR IN CANADA

We have seen why labour has its unions and what these unions do. Now let us look at the union picture in Canada. How far have the unions progressed? How many Canadian workers belong to unions? What *kinds* of workers belong to unions? We should also like to understand the *structure* of labour unions. Every trade unionist has his local union, but a majority are also members of a big national union. Then there are the labour congresses, notably the Canadian Labour Congress. Where does the Congress fit into the union picture?

Union Membership

Most Canadian workers do not belong to

a union. Only about a third of our labour force — and not counting agriculture — are union members. The percentage is similar in the United States. In two provinces, British Columbia and Newfoundland, one out of two members of the labour force (including agriculture) is in a union, but in Quebec the proportion drops to one in four. Ontario with one out of three stands at the national average.

It is true that the influence of unions does extend beyond their actual membership. For example, when the union signs a contract with an employer the terms of the contract usually apply to *all* employees in the plant, not only to the union members. Thus in 1957 there were approximately 1.6 million workers covered by collective agreements while the total union membership was only 1.4 million. In addition, the gains made by the unions spill over into non-union shops when employers are forced to pay union wage rates to get enough labour. Nevertheless, the chief benefits of labour unions do go to union members, and only one out of three Canadian workers actually belongs to a union.

Unions are found throughout Canada and in most industries but they have made much more progress in some industries than in others. Heading the list is transportation where 70 per cent of all workers belong to unions. Manufacturing, public utilities, forestry, and construction all have slightly over 40 per cent; mining has slightly less. In trade and finance the proportion drops below one-third. Lagging far behind are the "service" industries, such as restaurants, laundries, and government. Here only one worker out of six is a union member.

The railways and the large manufacturing industries (steel, automobiles, agricultural implements and pulp and paper) account for a high proportion of total union membership. The railways alone have over 10 per cent of the national total and manufacturing as a whole takes in 40 per cent. The rapid growth of our manufacturing industry is one reason why the last twenty years have

witnessed a large increase in union membership. Unlike the United States, where union membership began to climb rapidly after 1933, rapid growth in Canadian unions came during and after World War II. In 1939 there were only 360,000 workers in unions. During the war union membership doubled and since 1945 it has almost doubled again. These increases reflect not only the new labour legislation which came during and shortly after the war but also economic growth and prosperity which have favoured expansion of the unions.

The Local Union

The structure of the trade union movement is like a pyramid. The broad base is formed by several thousand local unions; above them are a smaller number of national and international unions; at the top is the labour congress. The whole structure rests on the locals and their strength determines the character of the entire union movement.

The local union is formed by the workers in a single plant or in a local industry. For example, the employees of Massey-Ferguson Ltd. in Toronto have their own local and the employees of Massey-Ferguson Ltd. in Regina have theirs. Similarly, carpenters in the Edmonton area have their local union while carpenters in other places are in the local of their own city or district. The local union may be organized on the basis of a common craft — as with the carpenters — or it may be an industrial union whose membership is open to workers of every kind in a single plant or factory, as at Massey-Ferguson Ltd.

There are more than 6000 local unions in Canada today. All but a small fraction (some 400) are part of larger organizations which are called the "parent union". These larger organizations are formed by federations of the locals. The size of a local union depends upon the size of the plant or the areas from which it draws its members. If you worked in a big steel plant or automobile factory you might belong to a local which had more than 16,000 members. But most local unions in Canada have less than

200 members and the very smallest have less than 10.

The rank and file member participates in union activities at the local. Here he attends meetings, pays his dues, elects his officers and delegates. His complaints about the job or his demands for action on wages and working conditions are aired at the local meetings. In some cases the task of bargaining is undertaken by the local alone although more commonly the parent union lends assistance.

National and International Unions

As we have seen, labour prefers to organize on a national or, at least, a regional basis, wherever possible. And so most local unions have joined forces to form organizations which include all the workers in a craft or all the workers in an industry. In applying this principle unions often ignore the boundary between the United States and Canada. A great many unions cover the field in both countries. These are called international unions.

In Canada 71 per cent of union members belong to international unions. These unions have headquarters in the United States though the larger ones also have Canadian head offices. In either case the action taken by the Canadian section of the union is determined by Canadian officers in the light of wage and working conditions in Canada. Another 25 per cent of Canadian unionists are in unions which either span the nation or a single province. This leaves only 4 per cent of total union membership in 400 local unions with no outside connections.

Altogether there are 171 national and international unions in Canada, of which 111 are international and 60 are either national or regional in scope. The unions vary in size. Among the national unions the largest is the Canadian Brotherhood of Railway Employees and Other Transport Workers. It has 252 locals with 34,000 members. Some of the internationals are even larger. The United Steel Workers has 75,000 Canadian members, the United Brotherhood of Carpenters and Joiners 68,000 and the United

Auto Workers 60,000. Although most Canadian unions have less than 5000 members the big unions account for a greater proportion of the total membership. The largest twenty take in more than half of all union members in Canada.

The typical Canadian union member, then, belongs not only to a local but to a larger organization in which his local is one of many. And a majority belong to one of the *big* unions. The big unions, whether national or international, are generally more active and exercise more control over their locals than the smaller, less powerful organizations. Commonly, union headquarters set the objectives of collective bargaining for all the locals. For example, the executive of the U.A.W. decides whether auto workers negotiate for a 10 per cent wage increase or a 20 per cent increase, whether they ask for a shorter work week this year or next. Its representatives assist each local executive whenever a contract is negotiated with an employer. If negotiations break down, permission from headquarters may be required before the local can call a strike. But even where the local union has more independence, the support of the parent union is desirable because the parent union has the skilled personnel to analyse local conditions and advise locals on bargaining policy. Furthermore, it is the parent union that collects and administers strike funds. It is also the national office that has the power to call out other locals in sympathy strikes. Thus in a strong and powerful union the local shares in the strength of the parent organization.

The Labour Congress

Probably the best known organization in the labour movement, apart from a few of the largest unions, is the Canadian Labour Congress. The Congress is not a union at all but a central organization established and financed by the unions. Its powers come from the unions that support it. To the individual union member the Congress is not nearly as important as his local or his union whose job is to protect his immediate

Canadian Labour

Delegates cheer the re-election of Congress officers at the 1960 Convention of the Canadian Labour Congress in Montreal.

interests and win concessions from his employers. Nevertheless, all union members have much to gain from a central organization and unorganized labour may also share in these benefits.

The chief function of the labour congress is to bring pressure on governments to pass the laws that labour wants. When an organization that speaks for more than a million workers urges the 40-hour week the public and members of parliament are bound to pay more attention than they would to the same request from individual unions. Legislation of this kind clearly benefits the union member because the more he can win as a legal right the less he has to win through bargaining with his employer. Unorganized labour gains too because laws affecting labour usually apply to all workers. A central organization can work for the objectives that all working men and women have in common.

Canadian labour has two congresses: the giant C.L.C. and the much smaller Canadian and Catholic Federation of Labour. The C.C.C.L. represents the Catholic unions in

Quebec whose total membership is just under 100,000. Most of the other unions in Canada are represented in the C.L.C. Since they have over three-quarters of all union members in their ranks, their Congress speaks for more than a million unionists.

The C.L.C. dates back only to 1956 and is therefore a recent arrival on the national labour scene. However, Canadian labour has had some kind of central organization ever since the eighteen-eighties when the Trades and Labour Council was formed on the model of the newly established American Federation of Labour in the United States. For many years the A.F.L. and the T.L.C. were largely limited to the craft unions. When the big industrial unions appeared in the 1930's the well-established and powerful craft unions vigorously opposed the new principle of industrial organization. But the industrial unions were successful and established their own central organizations — the Congress of Industrial Organizations (C.I.O.) in the United States and its Canadian counterpart, the Canadian Congress of Labour (C.C.L.). There followed a period of competition between the rival congresses. Instead of working together and presenting a common front, each was more concerned with increasing its own power. The A.F.L. and the T.L.C. tried to preserve their lead by organizing new unions of their own on an industrial basis. On occasion both A.F.L. and C.I.O. had rival unions in the same industry! Needless to say, the rivalry between two congresses did little to advance the cause of organized labour and after twenty years both sides agreed to a truce. In 1955 the A.F.L. and the C.I.O. joined forces, establishing the pattern for the union of the T.L.C. and C.C.L. in Canada. The result of this marriage is the one big organization, the Canadian Labour Congress, and the end of the bitterness, effort and expense which went with the old rivalry.

At the present time the C.L.C. is pressing for an improved scheme of unemployment insurance, a national legal minimum wage of one dollar an hour, the 40-hour week in all provinces, and a national law requiring two weeks' holiday with pay for all workers. Its programme also includes more general objectives, such as improved social legislation, an improved national pensions plan and a national labour code.

Besides acting as labour's spokesman, the Congress devotes its energies to maintaining and increasing the strength of the whole union movement. Thus the C.L.C. has research and educational divisions to study labour's problems and to educate union members in union principles and citizenship. It also plans organizational activity. A major concern is the problem of organizing the great majority of Canadian workers who are still outside the union movement. Another objective is to bring the C.C.C.L. and all unaffiliated unions into the Congress so that the C.L.C. would represent all the unions in Canada.

4. LABOUR AND THE GOVERNMENT IN CANADA

In a price system governments are assigned a minor role and nowhere has this role been so slight as in nineteenth-century England. Yet even there the need for *some* government regulation made itself felt. When large sections of public opinion rebelled at the employment of children the government was forced to intervene with laws governing employment in factories. One of the earliest of the Factory Acts forbade the employment of children under nine! Eventually these acts put an end to child labour, reduced the hours worked by women and young people, and forced employers to make better provisions for their workers' safety. Today we take such regulations for granted. But we do not always recognize the need for further action by the government. Although the worst evils have been remedied, governments may still improve the position of labour in a price system. Let us look briefly at the role of government in Canada.

The Government and Wages

The aim of minimum wage laws is to assure that every worker gets a *living* wage. As we shall see, minimum wages in Canada fall short of achieving this objective, but before we turn to Canadian legislation we may ask why minimum wage laws are needed. After all, don't the unions look after wages? The answer is that unions do not protect all workers. They cannot always secure a reasonable wage for their own members and they cannot help workers who do not belong to any union.

Take the first case. A union may confront an inefficient company that cannot afford to pay the going wage rates. If higher wage rates would put the company out of business, what can a union do? Here is a job for governments who, in effect, say: "If a company cannot pay the minimum wage and stay in business, the country is better off without the company." Only governments, who represent all of us, can take this kind of responsibility. The union may have the power to close down the company but its members may not *want* to look for other jobs. If higher wages cannot be won within the framework of collective bargaining the union is powerless to act.

In the second case — that of unorganized labour — one solution would appear to be to extend the range of unions. But the difficulties of organizing a union vary greatly among different industries and occupations. Where workers are widely scattered (as with farm labourers, domestic help, and employees in small shops and offices) or when they frequently move from job to job (the seasonal workers) the difficulties are likely to be insurmountable. It is true that a great many workers who could organize effectively are still outside the union movement and, eventually, are likely to have their unions. But at the present time minimum wage laws are needed for a high percentage of our labour force and there will always be workers who cannot be protected in any other way.

The need for minimum wage laws is particularly clear in the so-called "sweating system". Indeed, the plight of "sweated workers" was one of the main reasons why governments began passing laws on wages. To find evidence of the system we do not have to return to nineteenth-century England. We find it in twentieth-century Canada. Sweating can occur in any industry, but it has been most common in the textile industry among workers who are employed in their own homes and who are paid "piece rates" — that is, so much for each piece of work completed. Most of these workers are women or children. Because they are widely scattered in separate homes they are not likely to have a union. Such workers can be paid very low wages, particularly when job opportunities are scarce. What is worse, when workers are

powerless to resist, low wages can be cut to even lower levels so that workers are forced to protect their incomes by working longer hours and turning out more finished pieces.

In the last depression "sweating" was a common practice in Canada. Because women and young people were desperate for work unscrupulous employers could reduce piece rates and other employers were obliged to follow suit to stay in business. In Canadian textile factories machine operators earned $9.00 for a fifty-five hour week. Textile workers in the home earned less than half as much as the factory worker and put in longer hours! The widespread use of the sweating system in the nineteen-thirties explains why minimum wages in some provinces apply only to women. These laws curbed the worst abuses but "sweating" has not entirely disappeared.

Today all provinces in Canada except Prince Edward Island have minimum wage laws. This means that employers are required *by law* to pay a certain minimum wage. In Saskatchewan, for example, employers cannot pay less than $32 a week for full-time workers, excepting farm help and domestic servants. The minimum wage for employees under 18 years of age is $30. But minimum wage laws do not always have such wide coverage. In two provinces, Nova Scotia and Ontario, the laws apply only to women workers or to industries where most of the workers are women. In five provinces (Newfoundland, New Brunswick, Manitoba, Alberta and British Columbia) there are separate regulations for men and women. Only Saskatchewan and Quebec provide the same minimum scale for men and women.

Hours and Working Conditions

In the business of earning a living a good wage is only half the battle. The hours you work and the kind of place you work in are equally important. Government intervention to limit hours of work and improve working conditions can be traced back to the English Factory Acts. In Canada, the federal government and the provinces have

Goodyear Tire & Rubber Company of Canada

Good working conditions may be seen in this picture of the Goodyear Rubber Company's new plant in Medicine Hat, Alberta — good lighting, modern, efficient equipment, adequate space, cleanness, and proper ventilation.

continued the British tradition but the rate of improvement has been slow. Only twenty years ago the 10-hour day and the 55-hour week were common for Canadian factory workers. These were the actual limits allowed for women and young people under provincial laws. There were no limits on the hours of work for men, but generally they worked the same 55-hour week. At that time normal hours of work in most other

Maximum Hours of Work, Selected Provinces

	Newfoundland	Nova Scotia	Quebec	Sask.	Alta.	B.C.
coal mines		8-hr. day		8-hr. day 44-hr. wk.	8-hr. day 48-hr. wk.	8-hr. day 44-hr. wk.
factories	none	regulations apply only to boys and girls under 16	10-hr. day, 55-hr. wk. for women and boys under 18	8-hr. day 44-hr. wk.	8-hr. day 48-hr. wk.	8-hr. day 44-hr. wk.
shops	8-hr. day, 54-hr. wk. in some areas	none	60-hr. wk. for women and boys under 18, in larger towns	8-hr. day 44-hr. wk.	8-hr. day 48-hr. wk.	8-hr. day 44-hr. wk.

Note: In Saskatchewan limits apply unless time and a half is paid. In addition, Factory Acts prohibit employment of women beyond 48 hours. In Alberta limits are 44 hours a week in four cities.

Source: Department of Labour, Provincial Labour Standards, November 1953.

advanced countries were 48 hours a week or less!

Even today the 8-hour day is not universal in Canada. Only Ontario and the four western provinces have limits on hours worked which apply to all workers except those on farms and in domestic service. In these five provinces workers do have the 8-hour day and a 44- or 48-hour limit to the work-week. (Ontario, Alberta, and British Columbia place absolute limits on hours. The law in Saskatchewan and Manitoba requires employers to pay time and a half for anything beyond the 8-hour day or in excess of 44 or 48 hours a week.) In the other five provinces there is no special legislation on hours of work. Some workers have limits on the hours they work because their jobs come under an Industrial Standards Act, a Factory Act or a Mines Act, but this protection may not apply to all workers. In Quebec and New Brunswick, for example, the limit on hours under the Factory Acts applies only to women and to boys under eighteen.

Backing the Unions

Although our list of labour laws is not complete, we have shown why governments have a role to play. Even in our age labour is sometimes "sweated", and some employers impose excessive hours. And only the government can remedy abuses when, as often happens, the unions are powerless to act.

For organized labour governments perform another vital service: they supply the legal basis for collective bargaining. In the days when the union had to fight for recognition from the company many unions never got to the conference table. Today, Canadian employers *are compelled* to bargain collectively with their employees, because governments have passed laws obliging them to do so.

To establish its legal rights, the union must show that it was freely chosen by a majority of the workers it claims to represent. On this condition it is "certified" by the government. Laws of this kind have been passed in all provinces and for workers in interprovincial industries, which come under federal jurisdiction, by the federal government in Ottawa. The same laws forbid the use of "unfair labour practices", such as firing union leaders, or interfering with the workers' choice of a union. Labour, on the other side, must comply with certain standards governing union practices. For example, a union cannot coerce prospective members. Thus Canadian governments lay down rules to govern the relations within unions and between employers and the unions. Within this framework the union principle of collective bargaining has grown in strength and extended its range in Canada as in all the western democracies.

Conclusion

Today the labour union is firmly established, and the big union is as much a part of our economic system as the big corporation. Both, as we have seen, made their first appearance at about the same time and in response to the same condition: the introduction of factory methods of production. The corporation supplied a form of business organization that spawned the giants of industry we have today. But the bigger and more powerful business firms grew the more unreal was the notion that wages were best left to the bargains made between individual workers and their employers. Thus the union principle finally won general acceptance and as unions grew in size and strength both sides of the wage bargain became more nearly equal.

The labour union is here to stay. There is as little likelihood of going back to the free market in labour as there is of scrapping the big corporation. Like the corporation, free trade unions are essential to our system. The only industrialized countries without them are totalitarian states like fascist Spain and communist Russia.

QUESTIONS FOR DISCUSSION

1. The "closed shop" has been won by certain unions of skilled workers in the building industry, in printing, and in the manufacture of clothing. Give reasons why the "closed shop" is seldom found in other industries. What are the advantages of the "closed shop" compared with the more common "union shop"?

2. In a booklet designed for Canadian immigrants ("Working and Living Conditions in Canada", April 1959), the Department of Labour states: "In most Canadian industries union membership is on a voluntary basis." Do you think that the union shop falls within this category? Do you think the individual should be free to choose whether or not he joins the union? Because there are strong arguments on both sides of this question it would make a good topic for debate.

3. When union and company fail to agree, the central issue need not be higher wages. The following examples are selected from the major work stoppages in 1957:

(i) The strike of aluminum workers at Arvida, Quebec. One of the main issues was the union's request for a master agreement to cover all the company's plants in Quebec.

(ii) The strike at Murdochville, Quebec. In this dispute the central issue was the recognition of the United Steelworkers of America as bargaining agent.

(iii) The C.P.R. firemen's strike was a result of the company's request to remove firemen from diesel engines in freight and yard service.

What do all three issues have in common? For the remainder of the school year let the class keep a list of all strikes reported in the local paper. Make notes on the issues involved, the course of negotiations before the strike, the role of conciliation, and the end result.

4. The time lost through strikes and lock-outs is often exaggerated. In 1957, for example, a total of 249 strikes occurred of which three-fourths lasted less than 15 days, with a majority of these ending in less than 5 days. Altogether, the total time lost is estimated to be 0.14 per cent of the total time worked by paid workers. On the other hand, 6000 aluminum workers were on strike 4 months; the Murdochville strike (1000 workers) lasted nearly 7 months. In the case of the C.P.R. firemen the repercussions were far-reaching. The union called out 2800 firemen, whereupon the company laid off 65,000 employees and suspended all railway operations; a large section of the transportation industry came to a halt for 10 days.

Write briefly on the pros and cons of the strike. It is clear which evidence would be emphasized by individuals who are opposed to the right to strike, but be sure to include both the general and the specific cases in your evaluation.

5. Average weekly earnings in Canadian industry as a whole (excluding agriculture) at Dec. 1, 1958, were $71.56 (D.B.S. Employment and Payrolls). Earnings were highest, on the average, in mining, in certain manufacturing industries (petroleum and coal products, paper, non-ferrous metals, chemical, iron and steel products and transportation equipment) and in the public utilities. Lowest average earnings were reported by the service group ($49.26) and people in the manufacture of clothing ($46.58). Manufacture of other textiles and of leather and the trade group were also well below the average. What relationship can you find between wage rates and the strength of unions in different industries? Can you think of other factors, in addition to the varying strength of unions, which would account for different wages? Could these other factors help to explain the industrial distribution of unions?

6. Under provincial law a union is certified when it can show that it was freely elected by a majority of the workers. As we have seen, labour prefers to organize on a national or regional basis, yet unions with no outside affiliations are sometimes certified. Are there any real advantages to labour in the independent union?

Chapter 6

Family Income and Expenditure

1. THE CONSUMER'S ROLE

A major function of our economic system is to satisfy the wants of consumers by producing the kinds of goods and services that they demand. Now that we have looked at the principal actors in the world of production — the different kinds of business firms (Chapter 4) and the men and women who make up the labour force (Chapter 5) — we go back to our starting-point. What part do consumers play in the complex organization which exists to serve them?

In our economic system the consumer's role is fundamental. Consumers do more than simply *buy* the goods and services that have been produced; they also *decide* what kinds and quantities of goods and services will be produced. In many countries consumers do not have this power. Their governments decide what kinds of beef, pork, shoes, houses, sewing machines, and cars will be produced, and how much. In a price system, however, these decisions are left to

Robert Simpson Company Limited

Consumers make their wishes known by what they buy.

The main floor of Simpson's department store in Toronto exemplifies the vast array of goods and services available to Canadian consumers.

the free choice of consumers. Hence consumers actually direct production.

The system was described briefly in Chapter 3. As we have seen, consumers make their wishes known by what they buy. Producers, in search of profits, must produce the things that people will buy and so are led to produce the things that people want.

This does not mean that the consumer's every wish will be fulfilled, nor that all wishes will influence the actions of producers. Wishes must be backed by purchasing power. If you have a dollar you can command the labour of others, but only to the extent of that dollar. The poor man's wish for an expensive convertible has no meaning for production, and many much more modest wishes go unexpressed through lack of means. Nevertheless, we all have *something* to say about production. When we buy one thing instead of another we are voting for the production of the first, and

against the production of the other — thus consumers are given a large measure of control over production. This is one of the greatest merits of a price system.

To study the consumer's place in the scheme of things we begin with consumer spending. Why do consumers buy what they do? The forces that influence consumer choice are, in the final analysis, the forces that determine the pattern of production. We shall investigate these forces in Section 2. In Section 3 we balance theories with facts. We examine the actual spending patterns of Canadian families and see how forces described in Section 2 have influenced decisions in buying. Of the several forces none is more important than the size of the family income. So a special section (Section 4) is devoted to the incomes of Canadian families. Finally, in Section 5, we come to the practical question of spending wisely: what are the secrets of the wise consumer?

2. THE BASIS OF CONSUMER CHOICE

Watch any girl buying a dress. As she picks and chooses, looking at this, that, and the other one, we know that she is trying to get the most for her money. In other words, she is trying to satisfy her desire for a dress as fully as possible with the means at her disposal. Or take three men each with an extra $200 to spend. One might buy a television set, another an outboard motor, while the third takes a trip with his family. These three decisions in spending reflect their different tastes or wants. And so it is with all consumer spending. Our individual tastes or wants govern our behaviour as consumers. But the wants themselves are shaped by several forces. The next step is to see why we want the things we buy.

Custom and Fashion

In many ways we are all slaves to custom. We buy turkey for Thanksgiving and toys at Christmas because it is the custom to do so. Indeed, the kinds of food that Canadians buy every day, the clothes we wear, the houses we live in: all reflect the customary patterns of eating, dressing and housing in Canada. Canadian families living in India or even in England soon change their shopping habits. In England, for example, they adopt the custom of afternoon tea. They buy more buns and pastries, fewer steaks and pork chops than they did at home. They find, too, that the automobile is not regarded as an essential. While the average family in Canada owns a car, an English family with the same income is much more likely to do without. Thus the things that consumers choose to buy are not everywhere the same, because consumers are influenced by customs and these differ greatly from place to place.

Fashion is not the same as custom, for fashions come and go while customs are slow to change. Yet fashion has a profound effect on consumers' choices. It is fashion which explains why Mrs. Brown buys a new party dress before her old one wears out, and only fashion could keep the ladies' hat

industry in business. The man of the house may think himself less influenced by fashion — since styles in men's clothes change more slowly — but the male consumer is seldom unmoved by the yearly style changes in automobiles.

Teen-agers are the most slavish group of all. Whether the current craze is rock-'n-roll records or leather jackets or the duck-tail bob, most young consumers feel bound to conform. And even younger Canadians are not immune. When the hoola-hoop fad swept the country a few years ago thousands of Canadian mothers were driven out to buy hoops for their children. Few consumers escape the influence of fashion.

Advertising

Advertising is another powerful force shaping consumers' choice. Familiar trade names attract us. Whether we are shopping for a new refrigerator or a can of beans we are likely to choose a brand that has been advertised. We buy the names advertised on our favourite television programmes, even those drummed into our minds with jarring jingles. It does not matter that the jingle is unpleasant; we cannot forget the name! Under the pressure of advertising we also buy things we would not otherwise have bought. This is demonstrated by tests of impulse buying. In these tests store sales of any product, say, for example, a certain hair tonic, are recorded for a few weeks. Then colourful displays of the tonic are set up in the same stores and sales are recorded for another week. The result is a spectacular increase in sales in the second period. Since it is unlikely that people should suddenly need more hair tonic, we conclude that they must have responded to the displays.

Many kinds of advertising and promotion are designed to create new wants. They make us feel unhappy with our present lot and so lead us into buying what we would not have wanted if we had been left alone. It is this kind of pressure which drives us to keep up with the Joneses next door and drives them to keep up with us. Not all advertising is of this kind. Indeed a great deal of advertising gives us useful information about products and their prices. This is the essential social function that advertising should perform: to educate consumers to the available alternatives so that they can spend their incomes wisely and satisfy their wants as fully as possible.

Income Limits the Satisfaction of Wants

The most powerful influence on family consumption is the size of the family budget. No matter how fashionable it is to own a TV set, or how beguiling the ads., or how much we enjoy television, to buy a set we must have the money. How consumers spend their money, therefore, depends very largely on how much money they have to spend. A man with an income of $20,000 a year will spend his money differently than a man with $3000. Not only will the $20,000 a year man buy *more* things but *different kinds* of things as well. He may buy a Cadillac and three suits a year while the other buys a Ford and one suit every three years. These differences in their purchases are explained by the difference in their incomes.

Consumers with very low incomes have the least choice; almost all their income must go for the essentials — food, clothing, shelter. Consumers with higher incomes can afford greater variety and better quality in food and clothes, live in better homes, and spend more on other things. In the next section we shall seek some concrete illustrations.

3. FAMILY SPENDING IN CANADA

To study consumers in action let us look at the shopping patterns of Canadians. What things do they buy? How much do they spend on "essentials"? How much on "luxuries"? How does the spending pattern of low-income families differ from that of middle and high-income families? To answer these questions we look at spending done by families, rather than individuals. The reason is that most consumers live in families where one or two persons earn the income and decide how most of it will be spent. The family is the spending unit.

The following table sums up the findings of a survey of family spending in the larger Canadian cities. Total family expenditure has been divided to show what proportion was spent on food, what proportion on clothes, and so on. Column 1 gives the pattern for all families. Columns 2 and 3 show the difference in the pattern for low-income families and high-income families. (The low-income families include only those who spent less than $2500 during the year. The high-income families are those who spent $6000 or more.) Of course, the percentages in each column do not apply to each and every family included in the col-

TABLE 3

Family Spending Patterns in Seven Cities, 1955

Percentage Spent On:	(1) By All Families	(2) By Low Income Families	(3) By High Income Families
	Per Cent	Per Cent	Per Cent
Food......................	25	37	19
Housing and Household Operation.......................	21	27	17
Furnishings and Equipment................	6	4	8
Clothing...................	9	7	9
Total Above......	61	75	53
Other Things......	39	25	47
Total Spending	100	100	100

Source: City Family Expenditure, 1955, D.B.S. (Reference Paper, No. 83)

umn. Some families spend more on some things, less on others. The percentages do show the average pattern which emerges from the spending by all families: the percentage of total expenditure by all families which was spent on each item.

We see at once (column 1) that a high proportion of spending goes to satisfy the basic wants: food, clothing, and the home. Food alone accounts for one-quarter of the total expenditure by all families! When we add rent (or mortgage payment), the costs of running a house, such as heating and lighting, and the outlay on furniture and clothing, we find that 61 per cent of the total is used up. This leaves only 39 per cent for other things and some of these are scarcely less essential than the first four items. Medical care, for example, which claims 4 per cent, cannot be called a luxury. The heading "other things" also covers the cost of running a car or buying bus tickets, insurance, movies and other entertainment — in short, everything else that Canadian families buy.

Low Incomes and High Incomes

Columns 2 and 3 show how the spending pattern of consumers is influenced by their incomes. The low-income families, we find, are more restricted to essentials. Food alone absorbs 37 per cent of their total spending and the four basic items take three-quarters. That leaves only 25 per cent to spend on all other things. If one takes out the other "musts" such as bus fares and medical care, there is very little left for education, entertainment, travel or luxuries of any kind.

Families who spend $6000 a year or more (column 3) spend a smaller than average percentage on food and other essentials. Almost half of the total is spent on other things. Among "other things" taxes take 6 per cent, as compared with one per cent for low-income families, but there is still a comfortable margin left over. And this margin provides for a much greater variety in spending.

The high-income families would also spend a great deal *more* on each item than the average, the low-income families a great deal less. Table 3 does not show actual dollar expenditure but a few illustrations may be taken from the survey. The average amounts spent on food, for example, were $817 a year by the low-income families and $1344 a year by the high-income families.

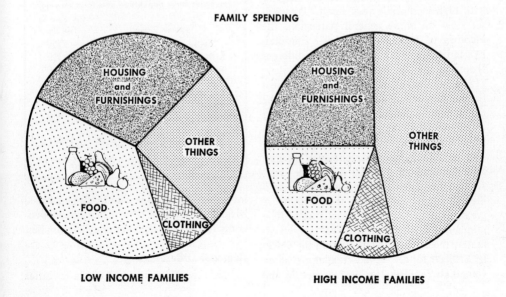

FAMILY SPENDING

LOW INCOME FAMILIES   HIGH INCOME FAMILIES

The extra $500 obviously allows a choice of more expensive foods and much greater variety. Going down the list we find that high-income families spent more than twice as much on housing, more than four times as much on clothes, and more than six times as much on furniture and other equipment for the home. The average expenditure on this last item by low-income families was less than $100 a year. The gleaming new appliances in our stores are seldom purchased by this section of Canadian consumers. Going on to "other things" the differences are even more striking. Expenditure on cars and their operation worked out to an average of $380 a year for all families, but low-income families spent an average of $20 while high-income families spent an average of almost $1300 or 65 times as much! Higher incomes permitted the one group to spend four times as much on enter-tainment and more than four times as much on tobacco and alcoholic beverages.

Family Size

While consumers' choices in buying depend, to a large degree, on the size of the family income, there are other important factors that influence family spending. The *age* of the family, for example, affects the shopping list of the average Canadian family, and so does the *occupation* of the head of the household. More important than either is the *size* of the family. Large families must spend a greater proportion of their total budget on food than smaller families. The family survey found that families with four children spent 32 per cent on food while couples with no children spent only 22 per cent. Large families also spent more on clothes but relatively less on housing and home furnishings.

4. FAMILY INCOME IN CANADA

In Chapter 2 we looked at the distribution of income in Canada and noted the high degree of inequality. Many individuals have medium or low incomes, and the number with high incomes is very small. We shall see now the same general pattern in the incomes of Canadian families. Families, like individuals, are awarded very different shares in the national product.

The percentage of *families* in the lowest income brackets (Table 4) is lower than the percentage of *individuals* (Table 2) because families, on the average, have higher incomes than individuals. However, as with individuals, only a very small percentage of families have incomes of $10,000 a year or over. Approximately two-thirds of Canadian families have incomes of less than $5000. A great many are actually below $3000. The number of families below $3000 is approximately the same as the number in the $5000 to $10,000 range. If we could look at *all* Canadian families the percentages in the

TABLE 4	
Distribution of Incomes of Canadian Families, 1957	
(excludes farm population and farm income)	
Income Group	Per Cent of Families
Under $1000..........................	3.0
$1000 to $1999........................	12.1
$2000 to $2999........................	14.3
$3000 to $3999........................	18.9
$4000 to $4999........................	16.9
$5000 to $9999........................	30.6
$10,000 and over......................	4.2
Total..................................	100.0

Source: *Distribution of Non-farm Incomes in Canada by Size, 1957, D.B.S.*

lower-income groups would be increased because the incomes of farm families are generally lower than incomes of urban families.

Regional Differences

The several regions of Canada differ

greatly in population, resources, and development. It is not surprising, therefore, that incomes also vary from one region to another. Among urban families average incomes are highest in Ontario and lowest in the four Atlantic provinces. In Ontario only 12 per cent of urban families fall in the lowest-income bracket (under $2000). The national average is 15 per cent and in the Atlantic provinces the proportion is a very high 30 per cent! Ontario also has a much higher proportion of families with incomes over $5000. Forty-two per cent of all families in Ontario are above that level as compared to 35 per cent in the country as a whole and only 19 per cent in the Atlantic provinces.

In Quebec, British Columbia, and the prairie provinces the pattern of urban family incomes conforms closely with the national average. Quebec and the prairie provinces, however, have a great many farm families and the picture would be greatly changed if farm families were included in the comparison.

Family Size

Still other differences in family incomes appear when size of income is related to the size of the family. Large families tend to have higher incomes than small families. The reason is that large families are more likely to have two or more persons bringing home a pay cheque. In some families both parents work and, more often, sons and daughters are employed.

The large family, however, needs a larger income. If we divide family income by the number of persons in the family — to get income *per person* — we find that the large family is generally worse off than the small family. On the average, families of two persons have the highest income per person, families of three people come next, and so on. The importance of family size can be judged by an English study (the Beveridge Report) which showed that extreme poverty was more often the result of a large family than of low wages! In Canada, a study of the effects of family size on the budget of

Canadian families helped to pave the way for the introduction of family allowances.

Farm Income

No official study of family incomes among the farm population of Canada has ever been undertaken. We do know that on the average families are larger and family incomes much lower on farms than in the city, and we can compare incomes per capita for the farm and non-farm populations. Over the thirty-two years from 1926 to 1958 the average income of the farm population in Canada was 40 per cent of the average income of other Canadians. That means that over the past generation people not on farms earned, on the average, $2.50 for each $1.00 earned by farm people. The years from 1942 to 1953 were years of unusual prosperity for agriculture, but even then farm income per capita rose to only 43 per cent of average non-farm income. Since there are farm families with incomes as high or higher than the average city family income, it is clear that very low incomes are much more the rule among farm families than among city families. This great difference in the economic well-being of farm and urban families explains why there is a continuous migration from farm to city.

Inequality of Income and Production

Since income is an important factor in consumer choice, the *distribution* of income greatly influences the pattern of consumer expenditures. The pattern of consumer expenditures, in turn, governs the actions of producers and, for that reason, the inequality of income affects the kinds and quantities of goods and services produced. The products that absorb most of the spending of the lower-income groups are turned out in quantity. But only a handful of families with very high incomes can command the production of yachts, mink coats, winter trips to Nassau and other luxuries. Thus the pattern of production in Canada is shaped by the pattern of family income described above.

At this point we do not ask *why* this particular distribution of income prevails. We simply state the facts and from these facts we conclude that Canadian consumers do not have an equal voice in planning production. An income of $3000 cannot command the labour of others to the same extent as an income of $10,000. On the other hand, actual purchases by all the low- and medium-income families have considerable influence because these families are so numerous. Among urban families, as we have seen, almost 30 per cent earn incomes of less than $3000 and only 4 per cent earn $10,000 or more. In a later chapter (Chapter 14) we shall return to this question and explain the distribution of income.

5. WISE CONSUMPTION

The heart of the consumer's problem is choosing what to buy. There are so many things to buy and, usually, so little to buy them with. With 25 cents to spend, will you buy a soda or a magazine or save the money towards buying a sweater at some later date? What the economist can say about this problem of choice is simple common sense: that we should spend our money so that a dollar spent on any one thing gives more or at least as much satisfaction than if it were spent on something else. If the soda will give more satisfaction than any other way of spending a quarter, that's the thing to buy. The economist does not ask whether or not Mrs. Brown's wants are foolish or if Mrs. Jones is a spendthrift. All that matters from the economic point of view is that consumers should be free to choose and should actually choose the things that give them the most satisfaction.

It is no easy task nowadays to spend wisely. There are so many things to choose from! And some are so highly technical it is difficult to know what is a good buy. Through lack of planning our expenditures and through ignorance of all the alternatives open to us, we do not consistently get the most for our money. Fortunately there are some rules to guide us.

Budgets

Many people find that it helps to keep a budget. When you write down the money you have to spend (your income) and the things you *must* buy, you know exactly what you can spend on non-essentials. A long-run goal, such as a winter coat or even a university education, can go into your budget too under an entry for "saving". If you have a job after school that pays $10 a week your budget might look something like this:

School supplies.........	$ 1.00
Bus fare...............	1.00
Clothing...............	2.00
Movies, Cokes, etc.......	2.00
Savings................	4.00
Total..............	$10.00

Each item, of course, is up to you. Your own wants or preferences determine whether you spend more for one thing and less for something else. With a larger income you could increase the expenditure on each item, add other items to the list, or save more. The important thing is to stick to your budget once it is made. It is, after all, your own planned programme on the best way to spend your income.

The family that keeps a budget makes sure the rent and light bill are paid before new slip covers are bought. Their budget will show whether the family income can stand a regular monthly payment on a car. Best of all, these families do not have to wonder where the money goes; they know! And they will know how to adjust their spending pattern from time to time to assure the greatest possible satisfaction out of the family income.

Using Credit

It is easy to spend more than your income. You can open a charge account or buy on the instalment plan; you can borrow from a bank or a finance company. Business firms are constantly urging us to do these very things. Is this a good way to buy, or should we limit spending to the money we have in our pockets?

The first thing to remember is that credit *costs* something. Interest and service charges may add as much as 20 per cent to the cost of a television set purchased on the instalment plan. The cheapest way to buy it is to pay cash. And paying cash has another advantage over credit: it is impossible to spend too much. Ten dollars a month on the instalment plan may sound easy, but can you be sure of having the ten dollars every month? If you cannot meet the payments back goes the television set to the store and you lose the money you have already put into it. A cut in pay or the loss of a job makes instalment payments even more difficult to meet. For such reasons it is wise to make allowances for possible changes in your income when you plan to buy on credit.

At the same time there are some good reasons for using credit. Few people would ever own a house if they had to save up the full purchase price, and it is quite sensible to pay for a house as you use it. The same is true of other large durable items such as automobiles and household equipment. Credit makes sense for the young couple who need a great many things to start housekeeping and who can expect a higher income as time goes by. Very often it is worth the extra cost to get things now instead of later. In other words, it increases our total want satisfaction to pay as we use the commodity. Hence credit, used wisely, can work for consumers. It is the misuse of credit that gives credit a bad name.

Shop Carefully

It is usually a good idea to shop around before you buy. If you take the first coat you see you may miss a better one down the street. Another mistake is to buy something just because it is on sale. Sale goods are not always cheaper. They may be lower in quality as well as in price, and only the careful shopper can tell when she is really getting a bargain. Nevertheless, you can make a dollar go farther if you plan your buying to take advantage of sales, buying a new winter coat at the January clearance sales and next summer's bathing suit in August.

Look for Quality

A cheap suit is no economy if a few extra dollars would bring a year or two of extra wear. Good quality goods are usually cheaper in the long run. A problem here, however, is how to recognize good quality. High school courses in Home Economics teach future consumers something about food and clothing; many boys are skilful in judging second-hand cars. Yet we cannot all be experts on all the things we buy. How, then, can we judge quality?

It helps to know something about your store or dealer. Is it a firm that usually sells high-quality goods? Will it refund your money if the goods are not satisfactory? On some things there are labels you can read. You can find out if a sweater is wool or nylon, whether it will wash, its origin. The manufacturer's name is sometimes a guide to quality. Companies that spend a lot of money on a brand name are usually interested in their reputations, not in passing off poor-quality goods. Then, too, you can read the ads. Underneath all the superlatives you may find a solid core of information about the product and this is what to look for in advertising.

More useful to consumers are the special magazines — such as Consumers' Report — which give the results of laboratory tests on nearly all the standard things we buy. Here we meet the products with the familiar brand names, stripped of their makers' claims and graded impartially as Best Buy, Acceptable, or Not Acceptable. Whether you are buying face powder or furniture, it is good sense — and good fun — to check Consumers' Report. An unknown detergent may turn out to be the Best Buy and a highly advertised and widely used appliance may be rated Not Acceptable. Without being an expert you can have expert advice on choosing among different brands — and become a wiser consumer.

Governments Help Consumers

Recognizing the difficulties of judging quality, the government has provided services to assist consumers. Pure food laws prohibit the use of harmful preservatives, and even harmless substitutes are forbidden unless their presence is clearly stated on the label. Similar laws assure that drugs are safe to use. There are also government grading services. For example, all beef that passes inspection is graded: red brand for top quality and blue brand for standard quality. The housewife need not be expert in distinguishing one piece of beef from another; she simply selects the grade she is willing to pay for. Similarly, with a can of peas she can choose between fancy quality, choice quality, and standard quality which are clearly marked on the labels. Besides beef and canned vegetables, government inspection and grading services cover poultry, milk, butter, cheese, eggs and canned fruit.

Quite recently the federal government introduced a system of inspection and grading which goes beyond food products. The idea is to establish certain standards of quality for many products, so that when Mrs. Housewife buys a fur coat with "national standard" on the label she knows the coat has met the required standards for its price range.

Another service to consumers is the supervision of advertising. While it is hard to believe there is any limit to the claims some producers make for their products, they are nevertheless forbidden by law to use false or obviously misleading statements. Labels also must be accurate. The label "pure wool", for example, means just that; a vest that is 90 per cent wool and 10 per cent cotton cannot be represented as pure wool.

Not all government programmes are being applied vigorously. They could be greatly extended and it would be very helpful to consumers if they were. The more information the government can give us about the things we buy the easier it is to make wise decisions in our buying.

QUESTIONS FOR DISCUSSION

1. Whether the economy is based upon direct production or a high degree of specialization the end of economic activity is the same. What is the end of economic activity? In the first case, when single family units consume their own production, consumers clearly direct production. Explain how production is made to conform with the wishes of consumers in a *specialized* economy. How is "consumer sovereignty" affected by inequality in the incomes of consumers?

2. Why do consumers buy the things they do? The question is asked not only by economists but also by merchants and manufacturers. Advertising agencies are spending millions of dollars on studies of consumer motivation. Increasingly, the makers' claims are made to fit our deepest longings; products and packages are designed to appeal to desires and needs we are hardly aware of ourselves. The growing field of "motivational research" is vividly described in *The Hidden Persuaders* by Vance Packard (Pocket Books Inc. c-288). Read the book and discuss whether "MR" works for consumers or against them.

3. It is often said that America and Canada have become nations of conformists. Much of the evidence points this way: the cars, the TV sets, the ranch-style bungalow with the picture window are much the same from B.C. to Maine and from Edmonton to Miami. At the same time, because North Americans have a great many *more* products to choose from than at any time in the past, there would seem to be more opportunity for expressing individual taste. Do you think Canadians spend their

incomes as independent individualists, or are they more influenced by what their friends and neighbours do?

4. What is a luxury and what is a necessity? Strictly speaking, cars and refrigerators are not necessities. But because a majority of Canadian families have them the average young person expects to own them in the future.

Let each student prepare a minimum list of the things he will need if he is to feel that he is getting a fair share of the world's goods. Compare this list with a list your parents might have compiled at the same age.

Because more and more things are within reach of the average person, our society is sometimes called "the affluent society". To Canadians of fifty years ago, if they could have foreseen it, our affluent society would have seemed a Utopia. Does it seem that way to you? Explain.

5. Table 3 is based on a survey of family spending in seven Canadian cities in 1955. Do you think a survey of *farm family* spending would differ appreciably? Why?

As a class project, make a budget for a student going to university next year. Find out what room and board would cost and include travelling expenses. How much would he need for fees, books, clothes, bus fare, entertainment? When all the items have been filled in, compare the percentage distribution of the total with the percentages given in Table 3.

6. Compare the distribution of *family* income (Table 4) with the distribution of *individual* income (Table 2 in Chapter 2). What are the major points of difference? — of similarity? In recent years we have heard a good deal about the "levelling" process — the elimination of poverty and the disappearance of class distinctions. To judge by the ads, the "good life" is available to all. Using the data on family income presented in this chapter, write briefly on the differences in living standards which still persist in Canada.

7. Of all the different economic groups with a common interest, consumers are among the least well organized. The Canadian Association of Consumers has only 17,000 members although there are millions of consumers. In view of the much higher participation ratios in labour unions, trade associations, and farm organizations, Canadians seem to be indifferent to their interests as consumers. Does this mean that consumers have no problems? Do you think that inertia is an important factor or that consumers' problems cannot be solved by group action?

As a class project, compile a list of difficulties that may be encountered in shopping and mistakes you have made. (Parents should be glad to help.) Identify the problems which can be solved by the individual and those which require collective action and government aids.

PART II

Chapter 7

A Bird's-Eye View

When an immigrant steps off the boat in Halifax, what sort of country lies before him? Very often our prospective citizen has only the haziest notion of what Canada has to offer, and many young Canadians are not much better informed. If you were asked to describe this country and its opportunities, what would you say?

Fifty to sixty years ago the immigrant's questions could be answered easily enough. When good land was cheap on the western prairie you would have advised him to seek his fortune there. But what of today's immigrants? And, coming closer to home, what of today's high school graduates? Will they look for jobs on farms? Or does their future lie in factories, in stores or offices? In short, we want to know what most Canadians do.

In Chapter 2 we saw that the level of living in Canada is second only to the American. How many could name the

Photographic Survey Corporation Limited

Chrysler Corporation's administrative offices and production plants at Windsor, Ontario – an important contributor to Canada's growing manufacturing industry.

industries that give rise to this wealth? Certainly agriculture is one. Canadian wheat is known the world over and many other farm products find markets abroad. Some 18 million Canadians are fed each day and Canadian farms supply a high proportion of their food. And yet we cannot say that Canada is an agricultural country. The steel mills in Hamilton, the gigantic new Ford plant at Oakville: these are evidence of a large and growing manufacturing industry. Alberta owes much to a spectacular development in oil and natural gas, and many kinds of mining contribute to the nation's wealth. Thousands of Canadian communities depend upon the forest industries and, for British Columbia and the Atlantic provinces, the coastal fisheries could be added to the list.

Even then our survey is not complete, nor can we see the pattern. What are the leading industries in Canada? Which industries are new and expanding, which are stable or contracting? To answer these questions we present a bird's-eye view of the Canadian economy.

1. THE STRUCTURE OF INDUSTRY

The Problem of Measurement

To determine the relative importance of different industries the first step is to see what each one contributes to the national income. How much income is the result of production on Canadian farms, how much from production in mills and factories?

At first glance it would seem more reasonable to compare the value of their *output*; X billion dollars' worth of agricultural products, Y billion dollars' worth of manufacturers and so on. In fact this comparison would not supply the information we want. The reason is this: when the values of output of different industries are added some things are counted twice. Wheat, for example, is counted as an agricultural product. But some of the wheat is used to make flour, and when we value the output of the flour-milling industry we are counting the same wheat again. Then the value of the bread produced includes the value of the flour and wheat once more. To get round this difficulty we look instead at the *incomes* each industry creates. The incomes earned by farmers measure agriculture's contribution to national income; the incomes earned in manufacturing tell us how much that industry added to the total income, and so with all the industries in the country.

National Income by Industries

How much each industry contributed to Canada's total income in 1956 is shown in Table 5 below. You will notice that the industries have been grouped into three classes. The "primary" industries are those

TABLE 5		
National Income, by Industries, 1956		
	Millions of Dollars	Percentage Distribution
Agriculture..................	1,960	7.3
Mining, forestry, fishing, trapping....	1,799	6.7
Total primary..........	3,759	14.0
Manufacturing............	7,534	28.0
Construction................	1,624	6.0
Total secondary......	9,158	34.0
Transportation, communication and other utilities............	3,191	11.8
Trade..........................	3,624	13.5
Finance, insurance and real estate......	2,608	9.7
Services......................	2,863	10.6
Government................	1,733	6.4
Total tertiary..........	14,019	52.0
Total National Income................	26,936	100.0

Source: National Accounts, Income and Expenditure, 1926–56, D.B.S.

most directly connected with natural resources, that is, the land — as in agriculture — or the forests, the mines, the lakes and coastal fisheries. They do not cover the second stage in production when wheat is milled into flour and logs turned into wood-pulp. Processing of products comes under the heading manufacturing, which also includes fabricating, assembly, and many other operations in production. Construction is classified along with manufacturing to make the total for "secondary" industry. The third group, called "tertiary" industry, covers a wide variety of productive activity: railroads, banks, radio stations, stores and a great many other services to be described later.

Agriculture

We can say at once that Canada is not primarily an agricultural country. Agriculture accounts for only 7 per cent of all incomes. In countries where agriculture predominates its contribution is over 50 per cent. Canadians, and particularly western Canadians, are accustomed to think that agriculture is one of our leading industries. Its relatively small contribution to total income will surprise many readers. However, agriculture is more important than Table 5 would lead one to believe. We shall see why in a later section.

Other Primary Industries and Manufacturing

Mining, lumbering, fishing, hunting and trapping (the other primary industries), account for only 6 per cent of Canada's national income. If we add all the primary industries together we find their total contribution is only half that of manufacturing. Manufacturing, you will notice, gives rise to more income than any other industry. It is our biggest single industry.

This is another surprising feature of the Canadian economy. We do not usually consider Canada an industrial nation like the industrial giant to the south, yet the proportion of income which arises in manufacturing in the United States is not signifi-

cantly higher than that in Canada! However, the structure of the manufacturing industry differs greatly between the two countries. Heavy industry, for example, is not highly developed in Canada. And a very high proportion of our manufacturing is the processing of primary products. This means that our primary industries are very much more important than would appear in Table 5.

Tertiary Industry

Perhaps the most striking feature of Canadian industry is the importance of the third category. Here a single group — transportation, communications and other utilities — gives rise to much more income for Canadians than agriculture, and the whole battery of tertiary industry supplies over half of Canada's national income! This fact is less surprising when we reflect on how many and how important are the industries included. Transportation alone is an immense industry, taking in railroads, airlines and steamship companies, road transport and taxis. Another giant is trade. Here we find all our retailers — from the big department stores and supermarkets to the smallest corner store — and the complete network of wholesalers as well. The next group covers the banks, loan companies, investment houses, insurance companies, real estate and many other firms in the world of finance. The service industries are too numerous to list. Laundries, restaurants, theatres, doctors and lawyers, cooks and maids are a few examples. Finally, there are governments whose activities result in incomes for policemen and postmen, forest rangers, clerks and stenographers, and a host of other workers in the civil service. When we consider all these varied activities we can begin to understand the importance of tertiary industry.

Employment by Industries

By comparing the incomes in different industries we can point to the industries which are most important from the standpoint of *production*. From the standpoint of *employment*, however, the pattern may be rather different. The reason is that some industries use more labour, relative to output, than do others. Mining, for example, uses large amounts of capital and the labour ingredient is relatively small. Agriculture uses a great deal of labour. To answer the question — where do most Canadians find jobs — we must look at the different industries once more.

This table shows that manufacturing is our leading industry in terms of employment as well as output. In 1951 it supplied more jobs for Canadians than any other single industry. Almost as many Canadians were employed in manufacturing as in trade and agriculture combined. Manufacturing and construction together employed about one-third of the labour force. They also accounted for a third of the national income.

TABLE 6

Canadian Labour Force and National Income by Industries, 1951

	Per Cent Distribution	
	Labour Force	National Income
Agriculture................	15.6	12.5
Other primary..........	5.3	7.0
Manufacturing..........	25.7	28.6
Construction..............	6.6	4.8
Transportation, communications, utilities	8.8	11.3
Trade........................	13.4	12.5
Finance, insurance, real estate..............	2.7	7.8
Services and government............	20.4	15.5
Total (including industry not specified)	100.0	100.0

(Labour force figures are from the decennial census, 1951. This table also gives the income data for 1951. The pattern of income described in Table 5 was for 1956.)

CANADIAN LABOUR FORCE BY INDUSTRIES, 1951

(each symbol represents 100,000 workers)

Again we see the importance of tertiary industry. In 1951, 45 per cent of the Canadian labour force was at work in transportation, communications, trade, finance, service industries and government. And since the proportion of income arising in tertiary industry was smaller then (47 per cent as compared with 52 per cent in 1956), we might find a higher proportion of employment in these industries today.

When we turn to agriculture we find that the impression of size based upon income data must be revised. At the last census, although agriculture produced only one-eighth of the national income it employed about a sixth of the labour force. There were more Canadians working in agriculture than in stores. And if we take the male labour force alone we find approximately *one-fifth* of the total on farms.

Is All Industry Productive?

Some people think that the farmer is somehow more "productive" than other workers and many find a special merit in all the primary and secondary industries because these industries turn out tangible goods. However, the view that some industries are productive and others are not is mistaken. It is the result of thinking of production only in terms of growing wheat or making tractors. At first glance there does seem to be a difference between a product you can see and touch and the more intangible output of tertiary industries, but the difference is not really important. Production is *not* simply the process of growing something or changing a product from one form to another. Production takes in all kinds of jobs that contribute to the want satisfaction of consumers. *All add value to the final product.*

A good illustration is the transportation industry. The farmer's products are worth very little to the rest of us if they stay on the farm. The wheat must go to the mill, the pigs to the meat packer. The railroads and trucking firms that move these products to the places they are wanted add to the value of the product. The same argument

applies to trade. Imagine the inconvenience and expense of touring Canadian factories every time we wanted to buy something! Everything we buy is worth more to us because wholesalers and retailers have done the job of getting things to the right place at the right time.

If you run down the list of tertiary industries you can see that each provides some kind of service *that people want* — and that fact makes them productive. Transportation and trade put things *where* we want them; the banks and other loan companies help us to have things *when* we want them. These and the many other services supplied by governments, by the professions, indeed by all tertiary industries, are as much wanted by consumers in a modern economy as the tangible products of the farm and the factory.

And so the extent and growth of tertiary industry in Canada is not cause for concern. As final proof, try to imagine our economy if the whole lot were swept away. The farmer, it is true, might go on producing — but with very different results! With no transport to take his crop to market or bring him goods from factories, no banks or credit unions to lend him money, no one to sell gasoline for trucks and tractors, the farmer would cease to be very productive. In a modern, specialized economy all industries are interdependent; each one produces more as a result of the production of others. All contribute to the standard of living of the community.

The Development of Industry

You might still think we would be better off if more of us worked in primary and secondary industry. The facts, however, are just the reverse. Countries like Canada which have a high proportion of *tertiary* industry are the ones with the highest national income! The poorest countries rely heavily on primary industry. The bulk of their population *has* to be farmers or fishermen to produce enough food.

In almost every underdeveloped country today a major aim is to establish manufacturing. People look to industrialization to raise their incomes because countries which have secondary industry generally have higher incomes than those which do not. Nevertheless, manufacturing is not essential to a high level of income! In some countries — England, the United States and Germany among others — manufacturing makes a large contribution but in other countries, no less advanced, it is unimportant. New Zealand, for example, has very little secondary industry, yet its national income is one of the highest in the world.

What all the high-income countries do have in common is a high proportion of production in tertiary industries. This is the mark of an advanced economy. A well developed transportation system, banking facilities, and other aids to production increase the output of primary and secondary industries many times over. And this greater productivity — whether of butter and wool in New Zealand or of textiles and machinery in England — is the secret of wealth and high incomes. High productivity frees labour from the soil and the production of "things", and more and more workers are then available to provide medical care, education, recreation and the many other services that add to the variety and enjoyment of life.

Our Changing Economy

Given all these facts and figures our new Canadian would have some knowledge of the Canadian economy. He would know that agriculture, while important, is not the leading industry, that manufacturing employs 50 per cent more workers and creates almost four times as much income! He would recognize that Canada is highly industrialized, although she still looks to primary industries to determine her particular specialties. The importance of tertiary industry in Canada he would take as evidence of a high level of development. And our new citizen would know that wherever he finds work he will be eligible for a share in a high national income.

The new Canadian may also want to know how the Canadian economy is changing. The structure of industry in the nineteen-thirties and forties differed greatly from the structure in the nineteen-fifties, and further alterations may be expected in the nineteen-sixties and seventies.

In recent years the major change has been the decline in the importance of primary industry. Just twenty years ago the primary industries contributed one-quarter of our national income; today they produce only one-sixth. Twenty years ago manufacturing and construction were roughly equal to the primary industries. Now they contribute *twice* as much income.

CANADIANS WORKING IN AGRICULTURE, MANUFACTURING AND TRADE

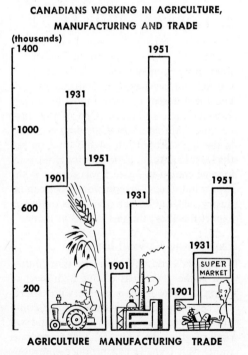

(thousands)

AGRICULTURE MANUFACTURING TRADE

Changes in Employment

The same trends appear in employment figures. A generation ago just under 30 per cent of the labour force was in agriculture (compared with 15 per cent today). Almost a third of the labour force was in the primary industries. Over the same period the proportion in manufacturing has increased from one-sixth to one-quarter. The position of tertiary industry has not altered as much. While some tertiary industries have gained ground, domestic service, like agriculture, has lost. On balance, tertiary industry employs a higher percentage of the Canadian labour force today but its share has not increased as much as manufacturing's.

In the short space of twenty years, then, the employment picture has altered greatly. The principal change for men has been the exodus from farming. The number in agriculture has declined from one in three to one in five. Today manufacturing and construction together employ almost twice as many men as agriculture.

The place of women workers in the economy has changed even more. A generation ago fewer women had jobs outside the home, and of those who did one in four was in domestic service. Today the proportion is one in fourteen. Today most women work in shops or offices or factories. In manufacturing, the ratio of men to women has declined from five to one to four to one. In trade, the proportion of women has increased from one-quarter of the male labour force to almost half.

2. INTERNATIONAL TRADE

Section 1 — the Structure of Industry — does not complete our bird's-eye view. Goods and services are produced *for sale* and the different industries must have *markets* for their products. One of the most striking features of the Canadian economy is the high proportion of the total output that is sold abroad. One-quarter of the total income shown in Table 5 was earned in the *export* industries. In contrast, American industry sells only 5 per cent of its output in export markets; the rest is sold at home.

Exports and National Income

Canada's concentration on export industries is the very basis of our high level of living. A few million people with the resources of a harsh northern climate could not possibly turn out the volume and variety of goods and services that Canadians want. But Canada can produce enormous quantities of wheat, newsprint, and base metals. By selling surpluses of these and of other specialties Canadians can buy from abroad the oranges, coffee, complex machinery and other things they want.

Canadians live well because they trade, and *how well* they live depends, very largely, on their exports. To have a high level of income Canada must have a high level of exports. This much could be inferred from the fact that one-quarter of our national income is earned in export industries, such as wheat farming, pulp and paper, base metal mining and smelting. But, in addition, exports create a great many incomes *indirectly*. When wheat farmers buy tractors and combines there are sales — hence employment and incomes — in the agricultural implements industry. And as all the export incomes *are spent*, all create employment and incomes in domestic industries. Thus, a high domestic income (such as the $27 billion in Table 5) reflects a high level of exports. Had exports not been large in 1956 Table 5 would show less income earned in almost *all* Canadian industries, because *all* would have sold fewer goods and services. The jobs and incomes of Canadians, wherever they happen to work, are closely tied to exports.

Exports in Canadian History

Canadians have always been export-minded. At different times and different places we have had the self-sufficient farmer (described in Chapter 3), but the economy as a whole has never been self-sufficient. From the very beginning of our history production has been concentrated on a few lines for export. And these specialty products, which we produced in enormous quantity, were exchanged for the many things that Canadians did not grow or make for themselves.

Until quite recently our specialties were always primary products. They depended on an abundance of natural resources and required relatively little expenditure on labour and capital, which are the scarce factors in new countries. Such products are called "staples". Much of Canada's economic history lies in the story of her staples.

First, on the Atlantic coast, there was cod. Later came the colourful era of the fur trade. Most of you know stories of the *coureurs de bois*, the Indians, and the great explorers of the fur-trading companies, but public school histories often neglect the economic side. Over a period of two hundred years the fur trade was the mainspring of the Canadian economy. While some land was cleared for farming and settlement spread, it was the sale of furs to Europe that provided goods and services for Canadian consumers, jobs and incomes for Canadian workers. It was the sale of furs that provided capital and made possible the establishment of local industry and the growth of towns. Over the same period the explorations of the fur-traders in search of new supplies of fur traced out the geographic boundaries of present-day Canada. Thus the trade in furs laid the basis of the economic and political development of the nation.

Early in the nineteenth century other staples appeared, first timber and later wheat and other products from the farms of Upper Canada. But none ruled as long or successfully as fur. Indeed, the whole nineteenth century was a series of ups and downs for the scattered colonies and — after 1867 — the young Dominion. The development of each region was closely tied to its success or failure in export trade. A region prospered and grew when it had a good staple and suffered hard times when its staple export failed. For example, the Ottawa valley

boomed in the days of the square timber trade but its fortunes waned after 1850 when supplies of timber ran short and markets disappeared. In the St. Lawrence valley region, where prosperity and growth were based on the expansion of agriculture and wheat exports, good times came to an end at the same time. Thereafter, economic development in Canada proceeded slowly and sporadically until, at the end of the nineteenth century, a new major staple appeared on the western prairies.

In this new specialty — western wheat — Canadians found the staple which could provide for rapid economic growth on a nation-wide scale. In the space of a dozen years, as Canada's vast empty prairies became one of the leading granaries of the world, exports of wheat expanded from a bare $12 million a year to well over the $100 million mark. The value of all exports increased threefold, and this boom in exports affected the whole of Canada. The sale of wheat created jobs and incomes in the transportation industry that moved the flood of wheat to market, in the forest industries that produced the lumber to build the West. It created jobs and incomes in the new prairie towns and cities that serviced the wheat industry and in the eastern factories that sold in the prairie market. As the boom continued industries throughout Canada were drawn into the expansion. It was an era of unprecedented prosperity and rapid economic growth — most of it based on exports! At no time in our history had staple production paid off so handsomely.

This particular chapter in Canadian economic history came to an end as the limits of settlement were reached on the prairie. Although wheat exports continued large they were no longer *growing*, so further expansion in the economy awaited the emergence of new staples. In the early nineteen-twenties the Canadian newsprint industry experienced a greatly increased demand for its product. To the south, American pulp and paper mills were running short of raw materials at a time when the daily newspaper was approaching mass circulation. Newsprint became a major export. The nineteen-twenties also witnessed a notable increase in exports of base metals (nickel, copper, lead and zinc). By the end of the decade base metals as a group ranked third and newsprint had topped wheat as Canada's leading export.

3. THE GROWTH OF MANUFACTURING

Before World War I

Manufacturing in Canada is essentially a twentieth century development. While the census of 1900 recorded a great many firms, most were small and many catered solely to a local market. Planks and boards, flour, butter and cheese, bread, textiles and leather goods were the leading manufactures. By 1914 the picture had changed considerably. The rapid economic growth, described above, created a favourable climate for Canadian manufacturers. Some industries, notably textiles, shoes and tobacco, were stimulated by the increasing size of the Canadian market; others, such as flour, responded to a growing world demand. The capital goods industries expanded as a result of the investment boom. Primary iron and steel, for example, was barely established in 1900. By 1913 Canada was producing well over a million tons of steel ingots and castings, half a million tons of steel rails, and an almost equal amount of other rolled iron and steel products. More than 80 per cent of pig iron requirements were being met from domestic production. Railway rolling stock had also become an important industry.

World War I and After

Industrialization in Canada is sometimes attributed to World War I. This view is mistaken, but it is true that very large gains were made during the war period. Canadian factories turned out more than a billion dollars of munitions (mainly shells and explosives). A large expansion occurred in the metal smelting and refining industries. The war also stimulated food processing to feed the allied armies and, by cutting off foreign suppliers, encouraged manufacturing for the home market. By the end of the war the value of the output of manufacturing had surpassed that of agriculture.

A major development in the nineteen-twenties was the rise of the automobile industry. By 1929 it ranked fourth on the list of all manufacturing industries. The other outstanding advance was in three resource-using industries: newsprint, base metals, and the production of hydro-electric power. Production in each more than doubled between 1921 and 1929.

World War II and After

Between 1929 and 1939 little progress occurred but the process of industrialization, halted by the great depression, was greatly accelerated after 1939 and Canada's manufacturing industry began to take on its modern form. Profound changes occurred during the war. The output of munitions and war equipment, less than $2 billion during the first war, totalled almost $10 billion during World War II and covered a much wider range of products. Aircraft and shipbuilding became major industries. Steel output doubled. In the chemical and electrical apparatus industries, output increased even more. New industries were born, including optical glass, synthetic rubber, high-octane gasoline and nylon yarn. Among the most important developments was the expansion of productive capacity in the aluminum industry. Canadian output increased by 400 per cent.

Although the switch to peacetime production involved large cut-backs in some industries, such as aircraft and shipbuilding, Canadian manufacturing as a whole went

Aluminum Company of Canada

Kitimat in 1950 — a remote wilderness in northern British Columbia.

Aluminum Company of Canada

**Ten years later — a vast industrial complex which has greatly increased
Canadian production of aluminum.**

on to new gains. Foreign competition did not reappear immediately. Not until 1949 did imports begin to invade the preserves of Canadian manufacturers on any large scale. In the meantime Canadians were buying cars, furniture, clothing, appliances and electrical goods in record quantities. Their purchases not only stimulated consumer goods industries but also, indirectly, increased the demand for capital goods and the output of basic industries such as steel. In the 1950's the Korean war and high levels of defence-spending provided a new stimulus and expansion continued at an impressive rate. To cite one example, the number of cars from Canadian factories in 1953 was almost double the number in 1949.

Another element in the post-war expansion has been the growing world demand for Canada's specialties. Take the aluminum industry. Canadian production totalled 430 million pounds in 1945; 1000 million pounds in 1952. At that date the vast new plant at Kitimat was still under construction and, when Kitimat began producing (1954), the same company launched a programme to expand its capacity by two thirds!

Manufacturing Today

Today Canada is ranked sixth among the manufacturing nations of the world. Her mills and factories turn out most of the products that are manufactured anywhere—from pork to pig iron and from steel to stockings. The ten leading manufacturing industries are shown in the accompanying table. These ten accounted for 38 per cent of the total sales by manufacturing industries in 1957.

Only three are major exporters (pulp and paper, smelting and refining and sawmills). The other seven produce mainly for the domestic market: petroleum products, cars and trucks, meat and dairy products for Canadian consumers; iron and steel for Canadian factories, transportation equipment for Canadian industry.

	Millions of Dollars
Pulp and paper	1412
Petroleum products	1377
Non ferrous smelting and refining	1280
Motor vehicles	949
Slaughtering and meat packing	907
Primary iron and steel	705
Sawmills	556
Butter and cheese	470
Aircraft	424
Railway rolling stock	387

Summing Up

At mid-twentieth century we find an economy greatly changed from the economy of 1900 — and even from the economy of 1939. In a period of less than two decades (1939 to 1955) the real output of manufacturing industries is estimated to have increased threefold. Secondary and tertiary industry, selling in the domestic market, account for a growing portion of output, employment and income. The range of productive activity has broadened and the relative importance of older industries has declined.

At the same time, however, the modern economy retains many links with the past. The new industrialism should not obscure the continuing importance of staple exports. Pulp and paper, base metals and lumber, although manufacturing industries, supply staple exports which accounted for 40 per cent of Canada's total export sales in 1957. By adding five other major staples — wheat, petroleum, iron ore, uranium and asbestos — we take in 60 per cent of total exports. Accordingly, because prosperity in Canada depends upon a *high* level of exports, our fortunes remain closely tied to the fate of a few staples.

4. THE CHANGING LEVELS OF INCOME, EMPLOYMENT AND PRICES

In Section (1) our bird's-eye view was centred on the Canadian economy of the late nineteen-fifties. After all, it is the economy we live in that concerns us most. And yet this economy cannot be understood if our view is limited to the current scene. We may describe the economy in terms of different industries but we must not forget that the *result* of production in these industries varies from year to year. Their output may be large — or not so large. They may run at full capacity, or very much below. Also, over the years, their capacity will grow, and the growth in output must be checked against the growth in population. As the numbers of people increase our output of goods and services must keep pace.

To round out our bird's-eye view, then, we need an estimate of performance. How does the Canadian economy today compare with the economy of ten, twenty or thirty years ago? We look back in time because only the perspective of the past can tell us where we stand now.

Changes in National Income

The national income is higher now than at any time in the past. But how much higher? Can we say, for example, that Canadians are twice as rich as they were twenty years ago? Let us look at the record. Table 7 shows the national income in

Canada for five selected years, and because these years represent either high points or low points, they show us the entire range of income over the last thirty years.

In column 1, the income payments in each year have been totalled, just as income payments in 1956 were totalled in Table 5.[1] Now if we compare these different years we run into difficulty. In any year the total value of goods and services depends not only on the quantity produced but also on the *prices* which express their value. If prices doubled, the total value of output would be doubled although physical production had not increased at all. National income, which is the same as national output, is also doubled. But this kind of increase does not reflect any *real* increase in our incomes. Higher incomes are spent on goods and services with correspondingly higher prices. To measure the *real* change in income, whether up or down, we must take out the effect of price changes. This has been done in column 2. National income in each year is given in constant prices (the prices of 1949). As a result the income figures in the column are expressed in dollars which have the same purchasing power.

In column 3 we allow for the growth of

---

[1] The figures are not strictly comparable with figures shown in Table 5. For example, the latter includes income arising in Canadian industry which is paid out to foreigners.

---

	(1) National Income (unadjusted)	(2) National Income (adjusted for price changes)	(3) Adjusted National Income per Person
	(billions of dollars)		(dollars)
1928 High point for the twenties..............	4.7	6.7	684
1933 Low point in depression..................	2.4	4.2	394
1939 Recovery before the war................	4.2	6.9	614
1945 Wartime peak.................................	9.7	12.9	1065
1957 Latest year available......................	23.9	19.0	1152

TABLE 7

National Income—1926-1957

Source: National Accounts, Income and Expenditure, 1926–56, and 1957, D.B.S.

population. National income, adjusted for price changes, has been divided by the total population in each year to show income per capita.

When we look at column 1, Canadians appear to be very many times richer than at any point in the past. And the range of income over 30 years — from $2 billion to $24 billion!—appears very great. Of course, we know that the actual changes have not been so extreme, but even in column 2 the differences are impressive. Thirty years ago our national income was only one-third of national income today. And that $6 billion of income in 1928 represented the peak of a boom. Then came the great depression. When we look back from 1957 the loss of income does not seem very great, yet it amounted to more than one-third of the pre-depression level. Try to imagine the loss of one-third of all our incomes today! The two years, 1928 and 1933, clearly demonstrate why our bird's-eye view must include performance. The national income in 1928 reflects the real capacities of the Canadian economy at that time. In the depression Canadian industry was operating well below capacity and so national income was well below what it could have been.

After 1933 national income began moving up and, by the outbreak of war, it was back to the 1928 level (column 2). However, if we allow for the growth in population (column 3), we see that our incomes had not fully recovered. Since population had increased by more than a million persons, the 1928 level of income could not provide the same income per capita.

Over the last twenty years Canada has experienced a spectacular increase in national income. The increase during the war years almost equalled the total national income of 1928 and a similar amount has been added since. Canada's national income today stands close to 3 times higher than the best pre-war years. Of course, there are also

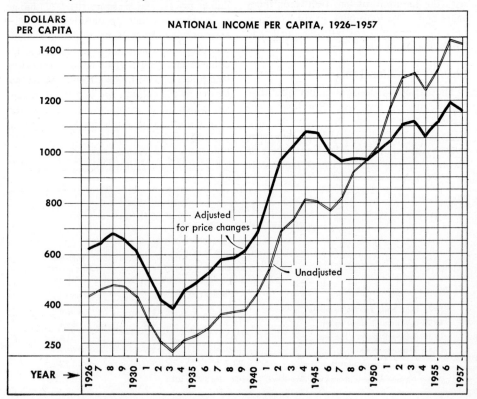

DOLLARS PER CAPITA

NATIONAL INCOME PER CAPITA, 1926–1957

Adjusted for price changes

Unadjusted

YEAR →

more people now and we find a somewhat altered picture in column 3. Per capita income took a great leap forward during the war and although it has continued to rise over the past 12 years the increase has been much less rapid. In other words, the postwar boom has not raised our incomes to the same degree as did the wartime expansion.

To see why, remember that Canada entered the war with a large reservoir of unemployed resources. As idle men found jobs and idle resources were put to work, the output of Canadian industry could increase very rapidly indeed. It could increase much less rapidly once all available resources had been drawn into production, and this point was reached in 1943. Since that time expansion has had to depend, very largely, on such factors as discoveries of new resources, growth of the labour force, new capital and improved methods in production. Column 3 shows that our national income has continued to grow, and Canadians *are* wealthier than they were twelve years ago. But the most striking contrast remains that with the pre-war economy. Canadians now produce almost twice as much per capita. They also enjoy more leisure as a result of the decline in the average hours worked per week.

Changes in Employment

Changes in national income go hand in hand with changes in employment. At high levels of national income there are jobs for all, and at low levels of national income there is much unemployment. Of course, there is some unemployment at all times. Even at the best of times there are people moving from one job to another and others who are temporarily out of work. In good years, however, these people can find other jobs, and so the number unemployed at any one time will not exceed 2 to 3 per cent of the labour force. This percentage provides a definition of "full employment". When unemployment is as low as 2 to 3 per cent of the labour force there are likely to be as many job vacancies as there are people looking for jobs.

Full employment is obviously desirable, yet over the past thirty years Canada has had full employment little more than half the time. The following graph shows how the Canadian labour force has fared as national income has moved up or down.

In the worst year of the depression, 1933, 20 per cent of the labour force was unemployed and another large fraction had only temporary jobs. For nine years, from 1931 to 1939, unemployment did not fall below 9 per cent of the labour force. In the best

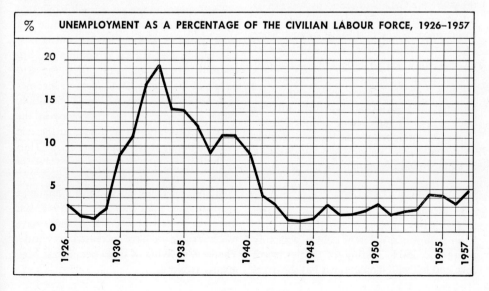

% UNEMPLOYMENT AS A PERCENTAGE OF THE CIVILIAN LABOUR FORCE, 1926–1957

year (1937) there were more than 400,000 Canadians without jobs. The persistence of mass unemployment meant that national income was far below what it might have been. Had the hundreds of thousands of unemployed been used in production, Canadian industry could have turned out many more goods and services — and created much more income.

When we look at employment figures we see why 1939 cannot be taken as the end of the depression. Although national income was back to the 1928 level, the labour force had grown (by 800,000 persons) and production techniques had improved, so that it was possible to create the *same* amount of income even with 11 per cent of the labour force unemployed. Income per capita, therefore, was still well below the level of 1928 (see Table 7).

The problem of unemployment was finally solved by World War II, and mass unemployment has not returned to plague us in the post-war period. Yet unemployment is still a problem from time to time. In 1954, for example, and again in late 1957 and in 1958, unemployment rose sharply, particularly during the winter months. Thus the figure — 4.3 per cent — in the graph is somewhat misleading. This percentage of unemployment represents the average for the year; the Canadian economy was not at full employment throughout 1957. In December unemployment stood at almost 7 per cent of the labour force and it continued to increase until March 1958 when it reached 10 per cent. This meant that more than 600,000 Canadians were out of work and looking for jobs. Unemployment on this scale, although temporary, cannot be dismissed as unimportant. In the next chapter we come back to the problem and ask *why* unemployment occurs.

Changes in the Price Level

In recent years Canadians have had less to fear from changes in employment than from change of a different kind — a rapidly rising price level. During the thirties prices rose and fell with employment but the over-riding concern was with the level of employment. During the war years the rise in prices was limited by government controls. But in the post-war years prices have been rising very rapidly indeed. Prices of most things have increased so much that a Canadian family needs more than $200 of income to buy what could be purchased with $100 twenty years ago. A shopping basket of groceries which cost $20 in 1940 would cost $40 or more today.

The increase in the price level is reflected in our latest figure for national income. In 1957 Canada's national income was almost $24 billion (see Table 7, column 1), apparently $14 billion more than the $10 billion of income in 1945. Yet our incomes had not really increased by $14 billion. When we allow for the difference in the price level (column 2) we find that the real increase was approximately $6 billion. Thus $8 billion — more than half the total increase — represents the rise in prices.

In spite of rising prices most Canadians are better off than they were in 1945, but there are some whose dollar incomes have not increased or have increased very little. The level of living of these people has been greatly reduced.

The Chapters Ahead

This account of major changes which have influenced our economic life completes our bird's-eye view. We are left with some very big questions. Why is it that Canadian industry does not perform at full capacity all the time? Why should there be times when many Canadians cannot find jobs? And why has our price level risen so rapidly over the past 15 years? In the fol-lowing chapter we investigate the changes in income and employment and later, in Chapter 11, the changing price level. To understand the forces at work we must also study money and the banking system. In Chapters 9 and 10 we see why these institutions are key components in a modern economy and how they are related to the problems of income and employment and the changing price level.

QUESTIONS FOR DISCUSSION

1. In an earlier generation, the number of immigrant arrivals in Canada reached a peak of 400,000 in a single year (1913). Immigration today is on a smaller scale, but to the immigrant of the 1950's, as to the immigrant of 1913, Canada represents a land of opportunity. Show how the *nature* of the opportunities has changed as the Canadian economy has developed. (For occupational trends in Canada, see *Canada Year Book,* 1943-44, p. 1066.)

2. According to Tables 5 and 6, manufacturing is the biggest single industry in Canada, and primary industry, including farming, appears relatively unimportant. In fact, our primary industries are of very great importance and will continue to be for many years to come. Explain this apparent contradiction. What is it that these tables leave out of the account?

3. In Farmer Brown's opinion, the trouble with this country is too many people doing useless jobs. Storekeepers, civil servants, lawyers, bankers: all could be better employed growing wheat or making tractors. Suppose our government were to follow Farmer Brown's prescription and put everybody to work making *things*. Would Canada be a richer country? Explain the error in Farmer Brown's analysis

4. What kind of industries predominate in poor countries and why? Most of these countries aim to develop manufacturing, but if we look at the high-income countries, listed in Chapter 2, we conclude that there must be different recipes for increasing wealth. By no stretch of the imagination can New Zealand be called an industrial nation. Yet New Zealanders have a higher level of living than the Belgians or Germans, both of whom are highly industrialized. Explain why, in spite of differences in the structure of industry, all three are high-income countries.

5. This chapter has supplied a bird's-eye view of the economy in which every high school student must eventually find a place. Some understanding of the structure of industry in modern Canada is clearly useful knowledge. But why should we look back? In the light of Henry Ford's famous pronouncement that history is bunk, why should we study exports in Canadian history or the growth of manufacturing? Write a brief note to show how these sections, together with Section 4, have added to your understanding of the Canadian economy.

Chapter 8

Changes in Income and Employment

1. PROSPERITY AND DEPRESSION

Why Do We Have Unemployment?

Every winter when activity in construction and other industries slows down, 250,000 to 300,000 Canadians are unemployed for varying periods of time. Seasonal unemployment is a serious Canadian problem. But seasonal unemployment cannot explain the dismal record of the 1930's nor can it account for 600,000 Canadians seeking jobs in March, 1958. Why should there be so much unemployment?

We cannot say that 600,000 Canadians chose to live on unemployment insurance benefits instead of wages because they valued leisure so much. Nor did they lose their jobs because the flow of goods from farm and factory had finally outrun our wants. As always, there was a host of unsatisfied consumers here in Canada and a hungry world beyond! Why, then, should more than half a million workers be idle? These men and women wanted jobs; the rest of us wanted the goods and services they could produce. We are forced to look for some flaw or defect in the economic system itself.

Unemployment, we learned in Chapter 7, is a recurrent problem. Our purpose now is to explain the different levels of employment. What is the secret of high incomes and full employment? And why, when we reach full capacity, can't we stay there? What *starts* the cut-backs in production, the loss of jobs and incomes? In short, why do we have unemployment?

This question is not an easy one. Even the economists are not fully agreed on the answer! Cycles of prosperity and depression have been studied over the past fifty years and different explanations have been offered. Like so many explanations in economics, however, it is impossible to test and reject or prove them in the laboratory. We must rely on actual experience. The problem is complicated by the fact that no recession or depression is precisely like the one that preceded it. Some are mild, some are severe. Some are long and some are short. But even the shortest and mildest of depressions is a social evil and today our government stands committed to do what it can to maintain full employment at all times.

In its approach to the problem of prosperity and depression the Canadian government, like many others, has been strongly influenced by the work of a British economist, Lord Keynes, and its version of the Keynesian theory will serve as our guide throughout this chapter. In the government's White Paper on Income and Employment (1945) we find the official view of the problem of keeping incomes and employment high along with a statement of policies designed to curtail depressions.

2. CHANGES IN INCOME AND SPENDING

Total Spending

The White Paper begins by stating that employment and incomes are provided by spending. In other words, the level of national income and employment depends on the amount of spending which takes place. To illustrate, suppose that in a given year all the spending in Canada adds up to $20 billion; obviously, then, $20 billion worth of goods and services can be *sold*. Now suppose that in the next year only $15 billion is spent. Then only $15 billion worth of goods and services can be sold. With smaller sales many business firms will decide to *produce* less, which means fewer jobs and less income. Thus a drop in spending causes a drop in incomes and employment.

An increase in spending works the other way. When the economy is not already at full employment, increased spending brings increased sales, hence more jobs and incomes. Thus employment and incomes depend upon *spending*. If we can explain changes in the level of spending we can explain changes in the level of national income and employment.

Why Spending Changes

If Canadians manage to spend $20 billion in one year, why should they spend only $15 billion the next year? To answer this we must look at the different *kinds* of spending. In the White Paper, spending is divided into four parts: spending by consumers, foreign spending on exports, business investment in plant and equipment, and spending by governments. Thus decisions to spend — or to not spend — are made by different people in very different circumstances. Their decisions depend upon different factors. To answer our question — why should total spending fall? — let us look first at consumers.

Spending by Consumers

Consumer spending is the largest component in total national expenditure. And so,

if spending falls, it would appear that consumers must bear much of the responsibility. Yet this is not the case. When total spending is high, consumers' incomes are high, and as long as incomes are high consumers are not likely to cut down their spending.

The behaviour of consumer spending can be inferred from what we learned in Chapter 6. How much a consumer spends depends upon his income. Consumers spend more when their incomes increase, less when their incomes fall. Consumers, therefore, do not *initiate* a decline in spending.

Of course, once total spending does decline, consumers' incomes will fall. Then consumer spending will decline. There will be further cut-backs in production, more workers dismissed, and still further losses of income. Once a recession or depression sets in the behaviour of consumer spending contributes to the difficulties. But we are looking for a change in spending which will *explain* a change in income. In other words, the change in spending must come *first*. This would appear to rule out consumers. To explain the initial drop in income we must go on to the other kinds of spending.

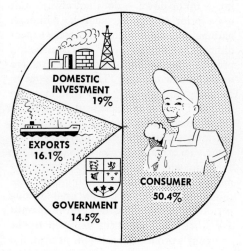

DISTRIBUTION OF SPENDING ON FINISHED GOODS AND SERVICES

DOMESTIC INVESTMENT 19%

EXPORTS 16.1%

GOVERNMENT 14.5%

CONSUMER 50.4%

Spending on Exports

The second kind of spending — foreign spending on Canadian exports — is quite different. Here we can more easily imagine a decline which comes at a time when our national income is high. The amount of spending on Canadian exports is decided by people and business firms in other countries, and they are influenced by their own national income, not by the size of ours. Exports may account for, say, $6 billion out of total national income of $20 billion in one year, but there is no reason why they must be $6 billion the next year. They may rise or fall. However high our national income, the exports which support that income may decline at any time because they are not, like consumer spending at home, closely tied to income at home.

Because a high domestic income in one year does not sell exports the next, a recession may start with a drop in exports. Of course, exports may also increase (making incomes increase) but in either event the change in exports — up or down — does not wait on a prior change in domestic income. Exports, therefore, play a strategic role in the determination of income and employment in the Canadian economy.

Spending on Investment

The same is true of private investment. A change in the volume of investment spending — up or down — does not always wait on a prior change in income. Although national income is high, investment expenditures may fall off as major construction projects are completed and no starts are made on new projects. Thus the decline in spending which marks the first stage in recession may be in investment spending.

Unlike consumer spending, investment is not always closely tied to the level of income. To explain why, let us imagine a big company which contemplates spending $50 million on new plant and equipment. Because plant and equipment are used for long periods of time the board of directors must ask what this investment will add to the company's profits, not this year or next, but in five, ten, or perhaps twenty years. Will it pay for itself through lower costs or greater output and sales? The decision to invest depends not only on current profits but on what profits *are expected to be* in the future. While it is true that large profits now make the future look bright, this by itself is not sufficient reason for spending millions of dollars on new plant and durable equipment. If the board expects that business will take a turn for the worse, new investment expenditures will not be made.

Similarly, in the economy as a whole, prosperity and a high national income do not automatically assure high investment. If business firms in general expect a turn for the worse, the volume of investment spending will decline. Like exports, then, investment spending can change without a change in income coming first.

A high national income does not guarantee our export markets nor a continuing large volume of investment. That is why, when the economy is prosperous, the first break in spending is likely to be in exports or private investment. It is a change in foreign spending on our exports and in home spending on investment goods that most often starts our economy on the downward path. And the process works in reverse. When the national income is low, exports or investment spending may rise, starting the economy on the upward path towards full employment. We say, therefore, that changes in exports and investment are responsible for most of the fluctuations in national income.

Multiplier Effects

To see how much a change in exports or investment can influence our fortunes — for good or ill — we must note that any change in spending operates with a *leverage* effect. In other words, when spending changes, the total change in national income will be some multiple of the initial change. And so, when exports rise, national income will increase by *more* than the addition to exports; when exports fall national income will fall even more. The same is true of a change in investment. Thus a loss of $100 million in exports or investment could mean a loss of $200 or even $300 million in income.

To see why, suppose wheat exports fall by $100 million. Immediately there is $100 million less income for prairie farmers. But this is not the only loss of income. Most of the lost $100 million was being spent. Country storekeepers, small town implement dealers, and many others who sell to farmers will find their incomes lower. Then there are the manufacturers who produce the things farmers buy. Their sales will be smaller too and workers in eastern factories will have less employment and earn less income. Others, farther removed, will be affected in turn and so the *total* loss of income will greatly exceed the initial drop in exports.[1]

This effect on incomes is called the "multiplier". And the multiplier works both ways. When exports increase, national income will increase by more than additional spending on exports. The student can trace through the same process described above. Start with the incomes of prairie farmers. This time there are *larger* incomes to be spent, hence more sales, more jobs and more income.

A similar train of events can be described for investment. Money spent on construction, for example, creates incomes for carpenters, electricians and workers in other building trades; also for the men in the woods and the lumber mills, in brick and glass factories and in all the industries that supply building materials. And as all these incomes are spent the construction dollar travels even farther afield. When construction is rising, therefore, incomes rise more than the increase in construction spending. And when construction declines not only the construction workers lose their jobs and incomes. The total loss of employment and income is much greater than the decline in investment.

The multiplier principle is based on a very simple proposition: incomes that *are spent* create other incomes. Any change in spending has this leverage effect. But the sequence of changes described by the multiplier usually begins with certain kinds of spending. Exports are of this kind and so are many types of investment. So it is that when they increase the whole economy benefits and when they decline the whole economy suffers.

Fluctuations in Exports and Investment

The Canadian economy is more sensitive than most to changes in its exports. In Chapter 7 we saw that approximately 25 per cent of the national income arises directly from the export industries. When you add the multiplier effects you can see that the level of exports is crucial. Canada cannot have a high level of income unless exports are high, and any considerable drop in exports has always meant falling income and rising unemployment.

In Canada, the role of investment spending is probably less critical than exports because much investment depends upon exports. However, the economy can no more stand the loss of a half billion dollars in investment than a half billion dollars in exports. Moreover, changes in the level of investment have often been extreme. In some years very large expenditures are made; in others, the flow of investment spending may come close to stopping altogether.

Why exports and investment should change as they do is a question we have yet to tackle. Given these fluctuations we can explain a rising national income on the one hand and recession and unemployment on the other. But why do the fluctuations occur? What makes spending on exports and investment rise and fall?

[1] How much will income fall? If we *assume* that people spend an average of 90 per cent of their income, then a loss of $100 million in export income will mean *additional* loss of income amounting to $90 million. Now think of a second round of spending. Assuming that 90 per cent of the $90 million would have been spent, its loss will reduce incomes further by $81 million. A third, a fourth and a fifth round of spending will find incomes lower still. You can see that the total loss of income will be much greater than the $100 million decline in exports. To the $100 million of export incomes we must add the $90 million of incomes it failed to create, the $81 million for the second round of spending, and we must *keep on adding* to account for all the incomes which still other rounds of spending would have made. In this hypothetical example the total change in income is ten times the initial change of $100 million.

B-A Oil Photo

Gas well at Lookout Butte, Alberta. Development of gas and oil resources has been an important element in post-war investment.

The Basis of Investment

Whether or not business investment takes place depends upon *expectations* concerning the future (see page 96). Investment expenditures are made when they appear profitable on the basis of *expected future sales*. Of course, business men cannot know the future, but each will have his own impression, and the factors which influence the expectations of one will usually influence others. Thus expectations at any one time are likely to be similar throughout the business community.

Among the factors which influence expectations the most important are signs of *growth* in the economy. A rapidly growing population is a particularly favourable influence. Increasing numbers of people mean that everything — from houses to hairpins — will be bought in larger quantities. To make the larger profits which go with larger sales, business firms have to expand capacity. Consider, for example, the outlook in the Canadian garment industry today compared with the prospects in the nineteen-thirties. Today higher birth rates and greater immigration add twice as many people to the clothing market each year.

Another element of growth that paves the way for investment is the opening up of new resources. Think of all the spending — on railroads, docks, loading facilities, whole new towns in the wilderness — required to develop the iron ore deposits in Quebec and Labrador! Spectacular resource developments have become almost commonplace in Canada since the war. And numerous small-scale developments that do not make the headlines have contributed even more to the stimulation of investment.

Aluminum Company of Canada

The development of Kitimat by the Aluminum Company of Canada necessitated the building of homes, shops, schools, library, hospital, churches, recreational facilities, restaurants – all the essentials of a living community.

A third stimulus to investment is innovation: the introduction of new techniques in production and new products for consumers. Immediately you will think of the vast expenditures on plant and equipment which television required. An even better illustration — to take an older example — is the automobile. The introduction of this single product called for huge outlays on new factories, new machinery and tools in the automobile industry itself and also in older industries, such as steel, glass, rubber and petroleum, to meet a greatly increased demand for their products. It created a whole new industry in garages and filling stations and opened up a huge field of investment for government spending on new roads. All told, the automobile called forth many hundreds of millions of dollars of investment spending.

In recent years there have been many innovations. Television is only one product in the rapidly expanding field of electronics. Radar, transistor radios, electronic computors and automation in many industries are all based upon developments in electronics. Atomic power, of course, is the most dramatic innovation. The jet engine, which revolutionized air flight, is another. These are but a few of the numerous innovations of our era that have stimulated investment in new plant and equipment.

Clearly, there have been many sources of growth in the post-war period. But the elements of rapid growth are not always present in the economy. Population may grow rapidly or slowly. Important discoveries of new resources and the introduction of new techniques and new products may or may not be numerous. As a result, the pace of investment is rapid at some times, sluggish at others. In Section 3 we shall see how greatly investment spending has varied in the past.

The Basis of Export Fluctuations

Why do exports rise and fall? To answer this question we shift our attention to the international economy of which Canada is a small part. Within that larger economy we find world-wide cycles of prosperity and depression generated by fluctuations in investment spending. Incomes in all countries rise and fall. And since our sales abroad depend upon incomes in other countries a change in their incomes causes a change in our exports.

Depression in other countries, and especially in our major export market, the United States, is transmitted to us through our export trade. Canada is particularly vulnerable to fluctuations in exports because so much of the national output is sold in export markets. Even when our own prospects for investment and growth are favourable the outlook can change rapidly as falling exports bring declining income and employment. Investment plans are then delayed and postponed till better times and the decline in investment spending is added to the decline in exports to strengthen the forces of recession.

3. SIXTY YEARS OF EXPORTS AND INVESTMENT

According to the federal government's White Paper, exports have been the chief determinant of the level of national income in Canada. Investment is ranked second in importance. When we look at the record — the behaviour of exports and investment over the past sixty years and the related changes in the level of national income — the facts bear out this theory. When both exports and investment have been increasing our national income has also increased and when both were large we enjoyed a high level of national income. When exports and investment have declined national income has fallen even further.

1900-1913

Consider first the great wheat boom in the early years of the century. In addition to the stimulus supplied by exports (see page 85) the Canadian economy experienced a great upsurge in investment. As settlers poured in to grow wheat thousands upon thousands of homes were built, whole new villages, towns and cities appeared on the prairies. Two new transcontinental railroads and a vast network of branch lines were constructed. The demand for goods of all kinds increased and business firms throughout the country expanded their capacity.

The importance of the basic factors of growth is clearly demonstrated. In this period there were two such factors: a new land resource in the vast agricultural frontier and a rapidly growing population. Both supplied a powerful stimulus to investment. As a result of the upsurge in exports and investment the Canadian economy reached very high levels of income and employment. For the first time Canadians experienced the prosperity and the rate of economic growth which they had hoped and planned for since Confederation.

1913-1929

Once the prairie provinces were settled and the rate of population growth slowed down, exports and investment were bound to level off. In 1913 and again in 1914 investment did decline and, if it had not been for the outbreak of war, Canada would have had a major depression at this time. Prosperity was maintained by wartime spending and for a brief period thereafter. But the post-war boom was followed by a severe depression. As exports plunged by more than 50 per cent, Canadians were forced to admit that expansion could not be continuous.

After the mid-nineteen-twenties wheat exports recovered and the new staples, newsprint and base metals, raised total exports to record levels. Investment also revived. In this boom, however, the growth elements in the economy were not so strong. The rate of population growth was lower than in the decade of the wheat boom. The automobile demanded large investment outlays but not as much as new railroads had done earlier. In short, there were few reasons why investment should go on increasing and, after 1929, investment collapsed completely. At the same time exports fell sharply. Thus the boom of the late nineteen-twenties came to an abrupt end.

The Great Depression

We come next to the ten lean years from 1929 to 1939. The story is told in the accompanying graph. Between 1928 and 1933 exports dropped by a billion dollars. Thus markets for a billion dollars of Canadian products disappeared into thin air! At the same time investment spending fell from the billion dollar level to a bare $140 million, a loss of almost 90 per cent of the spending in 1928! Confirming the theory of the multiplier, the decline in national income was *greater* than the combined loss of exports and investment.

These figures tell the bare story but they cannot convey the real meaning of depression. Behind them are prairie farmers who sold wheat for 30 cents a bushel (compared with $1.40 in 1928) and other farmers, stricken by drought, who had no crops to sell. Behind the statistics were several hundred thousands workers turned out of jobs and unable to find new jobs anywhere. Other incomes disappeared as small business firms went under. In a great many Canadian families no income was earned. Some lived, for a time, on savings, but most were forced to turn to private charity or government relief. In Saskatchewan, which was hardest hit, half the families in the province were on relief at one time. It was the worst depression Canadians had ever known. The fact that the depression was world-wide, that incomes fell in every country, was small comfort. And after the worst year, 1933, recovery was so slow that many Canadians seriously wondered whether the economy would ever run again at full capacity.

Current Prosperity

Prophecies of doom, so common in the thirties, have been disproved by our experience in World War II and after. After 1939 exports and investment began to increase rapidly and national income soon moved to new heights. Again there were markets and good prices for most of Canada's exports, and again conditions were favourable for investment. After the war important new elements of growth appeared. The baby boom and large-scale immigration provided a rapid rate of population growth. Towns like Leduc, Kitimat, and Blind River reflected the development of important new resources. New techniques in production and new products made their contribution to a host of investment opportunities. Investment spending in the postwar years increased more rapidly than exports (see graph). With only three interruptions, national income rose steadily. Unemployment, which reached large proportions in 1957 and 1958, was evidence of

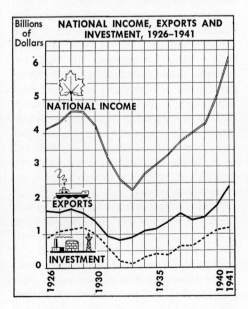

NATIONAL INCOME, EXPORTS AND INVESTMENT, 1926–1941

EXPORTS AND INVESTMENT, 1946–1957

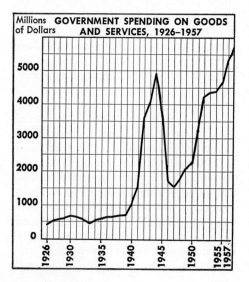

serious recession but not of full-scale depression.

Can Depression be Avoided?

Fifteen years of prosperity, however, do not erase the memories of the great depression. Few Canadians over the age of thirty believe that prosperity can last indefinitely. Will jobs and incomes vanish once again, as mysteriously as they have in the past? Fortunately, the experience of the nineteen-thirties is no longer so mysterious. We know now the importance of maintaining exports and investment spending. Can we, therefore, put this knowledge to work? Can we somehow prevent a downward spiral of income in the future *by keeping spending high?* To answer this question we must consider the role of governments.

4. CONTROL OF THE BUSINESS CYCLE

Spending by Governments

We need to recall that spending of *all* kinds provides employment and incomes. Through most of this chapter our interest has centred on two kinds only: spending on exports and spending on investment.

GOVERNMENT SPENDING ON GOODS AND SERVICES, 1926–1957

But when we come to the problem of *keeping* spending high we must take account of all four components. We begin with one that we have not yet examined: government spending on goods and services.

There are two reasons why government spending was not included in Section 2. One is that government spending has not always been a major component. In 1928, for example, total expenditure of all levels of government — federal, provincial and local — was only a third of exports and a much smaller fraction of consumer spending. Another and more important reason is that a drop in total spending is rarely initiated by a decline in government spending. In the past, governments, like consumers, increased their spending in good times and cut their budgets as incomes began to fall. Therefore, as a general rule, the behaviour of government spending could not be blamed for starting a depression.

This is not to say that governments acted wisely once a depression got under way. Because they cut expenditures at a time when *more* spending was required, governments could be charged with making a bad situation worse. However, although their traditional policy seems now to have been mistaken, we must remember that only within the last twenty years has the relationship between spending and incomes been fully appreciated. To cut expenditures when revenues are falling is sound business practice and, in the early nineteen-thirties, few people expected governments to do otherwise. Indeed, some people would still cry "unsound" if the government proposed to increase its spending to avert a major depression. We must remember too that a generation ago people believed government should stay out of economic affairs.

Today the situation is very different. For one thing, government spending is now very large. Owing to costs of defence and a greatly expanded social security programme, federal spending has increased to the point where it must be ranked with exports and investment as one of the major props of the post-war boom. A second change is less obvious but not less important. Governments have been assigned a new role. Instead of viewing the periodic bouts of hard times as inevitable, we now insist that governments take actions to keep our incomes high. Policies of the Canadian government are on record in the White Paper on Income and Employment and, although stated briefly and in a very general way, they indicate what governments might do to prevent a major depression.

A Public Works Programme

One way to meet a threat of depression is to require the government to spend *more*. A public works programme has two things in its favour. First, spending on highways, dams, public buildings and other public projects is investment spending. It hits the same industries and has the same multiplier effects on incomes as investment by private business: jobs and incomes are created not only on the spot but throughout the economy. A second advantage of a public works programme is that it can be appro-

priately timed. In other words, some government investment projects can be held in reserve until the need for more spending appears. While the government cannot put off paying the salaries of its postmen it *can* delay the construction of new post offices. Moreover, plans for new post offices can be drawn up in advance so that construction may begin on very short notice. Accordingly, the White Paper proposed a "reserve shelf" of public works of all kinds. Such a reserve shelf would put the government in a position to meet a decline in spending *immediately* with a large investment programme of its own.

At first glance a public works programme appears to be the solution. When spending falls the government will fill the gap by spending on roads and dams and public buildings. Unfortunately, the solution is not that simple. Certainly a public works programme can be helpful and, in a very mild recession, it might arrest the decline in income. But in a major recession or depression a public works programme could not itself stem the tide. In a private enterprise economy public works cannot absorb the huge sums required. A public works programme can be only part of a full employment policy. In the White Paper, therefore, the government proposed to influence spending of *all* kinds.

Encouraging Exports and Investment

The ideal solution would be to prevent a fall in exports and investment. The chief difficulty here is that spending on exports cannot be controlled. We cannot *force* other countries to buy in Canada! Our sales of wheat and newsprint — and of all other exports — depend upon how much foreign customers are willing to buy. If they decide to buy less, Canadian exports will fall and it would seem there is very little we can do about it.

Nevertheless, we need not accept an altogether passive role. As the White Paper suggested, our government can work with governments of other countries toward removing restrictions on world trade. This would help Canadian exports to grow in periods of prosperity. The acceptance of freer trade would also help to prevent the increase in restrictions which throttle trade in periods of depression.

When exports do fall there is still another remedy. If we wish, our government could finance exports. It could lend (or give) Canadian dollars to other countries so that they could buy more Canadian products. If a serious depression threatened, a strong case could be made for this policy. Although Canadian taxpayers would pay for some part of our major exports, more Canadians would have jobs and incomes, and *much less* tax money would be needed for relief.

Turning to investment, the White Paper proposed to encourage its flow by lowering taxes, by reducing interest rates and by making credit more readily available. Some specific proposals to encourage investment have been implemented, among them the Industrial Development Bank, the Farm Improvement Loans Act and large scale aid to housing.

Increasing Consumer Spending

A very important part in full employment policy was assigned to spending by consumers. In past depressions consumer spending fell because the decline in exports and investment reduced incomes. Suppose, therefore, when more spending is needed, the government stepped in and added to incomes. Consumers would oblige by spending more! Thus government can make spending increase by raising the *incomes* of consumers.

The government can raise incomes by increasing social security payments or by lowering taxes. Some social security payments — for example, unemployment insurance — rise automatically with a decline in employment. Others may be raised as part of the government's full employment policy. Lowering taxes furthers the same objective. For people who pay taxes a cut in taxes is the same thing as an increase in income.

There is a second way in which the government can call forth more spending from consumers. Consumers do not spend all of their income. They also *save*. (We define savings as the part of income not spent on consumption.) The act of saving in itself creates neither jobs nor incomes. It follows that when the need for more spending appears consumers should be encouraged to save less so that they will spend more. Again the government may intervene. The government can force the community as a whole to save less. Let us see how.

As a general rule, low-income families spend a greater proportion of their incomes than do high-income families. To make the community spend more the government may transfer income from consumers who save to consumers who do not save — or save very little. The transfer can be made through welfare payments financed by progressive income taxes. These payments raise the incomes of low-income families while the middle and high incomes bear most of the cost. This method is not a flexible one but where too little spending is a chronic problem it is a means of maintaining full employment.

Financing Full Employment Policy

To fight depression the federal government is committed to influence spending in the various ways described above. Now what about the cost? Should the government foot the bill from taxes, or should the government borrow the money as it did to finance a large part of the war? The method of financing employment policy makes a great difference to the result.

To see why, let us suppose that the government pays for its spending programme by raising taxes. Higher taxes mean that consumers will have less to spend. The increase in government spending, therefore, will be partly offset by a decline in consumer spending. Clearly this is not desirable when the situation calls for as much spending as possible. Suppose, then, that the government *borrows* the money. People who buy bonds are *saving*, so by selling bonds the government taps money that would *not* have been spent. In this way government spending can be increased without loss of consumer spending. A full employment programme should therefore be financed by borrowing rather than by taxing.

Indeed, the government should lower taxes. As we have seen, lowering taxes is another way to increase spending. The important thing is that the government should run deficits (that is, take in less than it pays out). And the Canadian government, according to the White Paper, is prepared to run deficits when depression threatens: to increase expenditures, reduce taxation, and borrow to finance the difference.

Not everybody accepts the view that governments should use deficits to fight depressions. Some argue that the government, like any business, must not spend more than it can pay for. An unbalanced budget, they say, is a dangerous thing. What this argument overlooks is that government is *not* an ordinary business firm. Its aim is not to make profits but to promote the general welfare of the whole community. If it can eliminate unemployment by going into debt the community will be better off if it does so.

Governments nowadays recognize that there is no need to balance the books at the end of each year. In a period of depression the government may spend more than it takes in for several years running. Then, when the economy recovers, it can let receipts exceed payments (a surplus) for a time and pay off the debts it has accumulated. As we shall see, although a *deficit* is the right policy when unemployment is the problem, a *surplus* is the right policy in years of high employment.

Will the New Policies Work?

As this book is written, full employment policies have not been tested against the onslaught of a major depression. What are the chances that they would meet the test successfully, that we can avoid a repetition of the nineteen-thirties?

It seems safe to say, first of all, that our chances of preventing a serious depression are better now than in the past because we know more about the causes. Our government is committed to do what it can to keep spending high — and this is a big step forward. It is true that public works programmes have been tried before without much success, but to argue that the White Paper's programme must therefore fail is to overlook two important developments. The government now has more than one weapon in its armoury. In addition to public works it also proposes to stimulate private investment and spending by consumers. If it were necessary, the government could also finance some of our major exports as it did in the period following the war.

Another reason for guarded optimism is that public works were not undertaken on a sufficiently large scale in past depressions and they were not introduced soon enough. In the nineteen-thirties Canadian governments used special works projects to relieve unemployment, but at the same time they curtailed many ordinary expenditures. The net result was that total expenditures on public works — by all levels of government — actually declined. The federal and provincial governments spent less on public works in 1933 than they did in 1928 and local governments failed completely to keep up their normal building programmes. The make-work policies in the last depression, therefore, are not a test of a public works programme. It is now recognized that governments must co-ordinate their public works programmes, spend *more* than they normally spend to offset the decline in private construction, and must act early in the recession.

On the other hand we cannot say that we have the cure-all for depression. No government can design policies that will keep private investment high at all times. If the underlying factors are unfavourable, the flow of investment spending cannot be maintained. The possibility of controlling exports is even more remote. Governments can offset moderate declines in exports and investment by increasing their own spending and by raising incomes and spending by consumers. But should exports and investment collapse, as they did in the nineteen-thirties, the amount of additional spending required to restore full employment would certainly be too large without the authoritarian controls allowed to government in wartime.

We conclude that no government, in a private enterprise economy, can fulfil a promise to keep income high at all times. But if full employment policies are wisely used, and if they are used in time, we may manage to avoid major depressions in the future. Even if we do not, depressions should be less serious than in the past. Welfare programmes have raised the "floor of depression". Old age pensions, family allowances, unemployment insurance, support prices for farm products and other welfare measures will maintain consumer spending at higher levels even though declines in investment and exports get out of hand. Moreover, we live in an era of cold war. High level expenditures on defence and preparation for war by governments at home and abroad — regrettable as they are in every other respect — do generate employment on a large scale, and help to maintain the general level of national income.

These same expenditures are also a chief cause of another major economic problem. Since the war it has not been unemployment but inflation that has imposed hardships on many sections of the population and threatened national economic disaster. To understand this problem — and to round out our understanding of the subject of the present chapter — we must examine money and the banking system, and their roles in the economy.

QUESTIONS FOR DISCUSSION

1. The White Paper on Income and Employment was published in 1945. At that time most people expected a few years of prosperity, followed by a deep and dark depression, and the White Paper reads as if its full employment policies will soon be used. However, apart from minor recessions, the boom has lasted for some fifteen years. Can you think of some of the growth factors in the economy, not evident in 1945, which explain why good times have lasted so long?

2. According to the Keynesian theory, changes in income and employment result from changes in the amount of *spending* that takes place. But although the largest part of total spending is done by consumers, the theory holds that *other* kinds of spending are the ones which matter most. Explain. How may consumer spending be used as part of a government programme aimed at keeping incomes high?

3. How did *your* community fare through the depression of the nineteen-thirties? See what you can discover about wage rates or farm income, unemployment, numbers on relief, standards of consumption, opportunities for young people, and so on. (Statistics may be found in public libraries but you may find additional useful information by talking to men and women of an older generation.) What grounds do we have for hoping that future depressions will not be as bad as the last one?

4. Ask at your local employment office to find out the scale of unemployment insurance benefits for insured workers, and the length of time for which benefits may be collected. How may the unemployment insurance programme cushion the impact of another depression?

Notice that if mass unemployment persisted for some time insurance benefits would run out; governments might once again be called upon to make large expenditures on unemployment relief. Using the lowest unemployment insurance benefits as a guide, make a rough estimate of the cost of supporting one million unemployed Canadian workers. Can you suggest *better* ways of spending the same amount of public money?

Chapter 9

Money and Credit

1. PRELIMINARY

The central topic of this chapter is both familiar and mysterious. Money is something we use every day yet, if we think about it at all, it raises some very puzzling questions. Why is it that a particular kind of paper, of no earthly use in itself, can nevertheless be exchanged for all manner of useful things? In other words, what makes it money? We may also wonder about the worth of a dollar. If, as so many people say nowadays, the dollar is worth 50 cents, what is a dollar? Can the value of our money change? Still another question is prompted by the knowledge that money does not grow on trees: where *does* money come from? And could we not have more of it?

The deepest mystery of all surrounds money's connection with the rest of the economy. If we could believe all the popular theories about the role of money we would have to think that money was respon-

sible for almost all our economic ills. Why has money been singled out from hundreds of components in the modern economy? Is it our monetary system that's at fault when things go wrong?

Money, then, raises a great many questions and not all of them can be answered in the present chapter. To begin with the first, Section 2 explains what money is and why we use it. In Section 3 we go on to the value of money and consider the effects of changes in its value. Section 4 brings us to the supply of money. We want to know how and why the supply of money changes and what happens when "too much" or "too little" is available. On this topic, however, we can only begin to trace the answers because we need an understanding of the banks (Chapter 11) to complete the picture. As a prelude to a study of the banking system, the last section in this chapter deals with the role of credit.

2. MONEY AND ITS USES

What Money Is

Money, to Canadians, is a dollar bill, a dime or a quarter; to the Englishman it is a pound note or a two-shilling piece. But there is no magic in these bills or coins that makes them money. At different times and places many different things have been used as money. Some North American Indians, for example, used wampum; the early fur-traders in Canada used beaver skins and, at one time, playing cards. In parts of Africa

the cow still serves as money. Money *can be anything*. What makes it money is that people consent to *use* it as money. In other words, if people take the Jack of Hearts or King of Diamonds as payment for a loaf of bread, then playing cards *are* money! Money, therefore, is anything which is generally and readily accepted as a payment. Our dollar bills and coins are money because all Canadians accept them.

Certain kinds of money do have advan-

DIFFERENT THINGS THAT HAVE BEEN USED AS MONEY

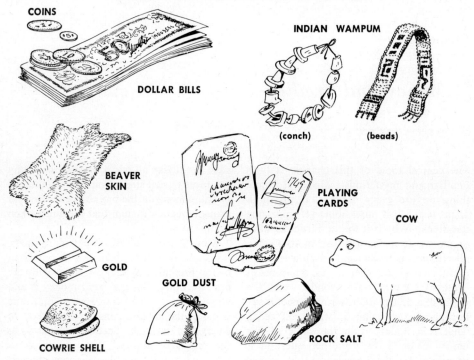

COINS

DOLLAR BILLS

INDIAN WAMPUM

(conch)   (beads)

BEAVER SKIN

PLAYING CARDS

COW

GOLD

GOLD DUST

COWRIE SHELL

ROCK SALT

tages over other kinds. Paper money is easy to carry around and, combined with coins, is convenient for making change. On both counts the cow and other livestock are quite unsatisfactory. All advanced countries use paper bills and, as we shall see later, a second kind of money, namely, bank deposits. Indeed, bank deposits are our chief kind of money because more payments are settled by the transfer of bank deposits than of anything else.

What Money Does

Since money *is* what money *does*, we have to know what money does — and it does several things. A modern country uses money in four ways.

A Medium of Exchange

Money, first of all, does away with the problems of exchange by barter. Without money, a baker who wanted apples would have to find someone with apples to trade who also wanted bread. But when bread and apples and goods and services of every kind can be freely exchanged for money the process of exchange becomes easy. Here money serves as a medium of exchange.

A Measure of Value

A second difficulty with barter is to compare the values of different things. Should a loaf of bread exchange for a pound of apples, or two pounds, or what? How cumbersome business and household accounting would be if we had to remember that a loaf of bread was worth a half-pound of apples, a tenth of a pair of shoes, and so on. We need a measure which can reduce all goods and services to a common denominator, and money supplies this measure. In much the same way the acre is a standard unit for measuring a field, degrees of fahrenheit or of centigrade are standard units for measuring temperature. Thus the Canadian dollar serves as the standard unit for measuring value. Price tags in dollars — or fractions of dollars — express in a simple and intelligible way the value of bread, houses, a day's work and everything else we buy and sell.

A Standard of Deferred Payment

Not all purchases are made with money. When you buy a toaster or a television set on the instalment plan you give a promise to pay later. This is not a direct use of money yet money is an essential part of the transaction. It is money that provides a means of deferring the debt and the future payments that will liquidate it. No dealer wants to sell cars to farmers on the basis of so many bushels of wheat delivered at intervals over the next five years. And few of us could offer anything as tangible as wheat. But since the payments can be arranged in *money*, future payment is as satisfactory to the seller as cash on the line.

"Budget terms" are widely used in modern business transactions.

In a modern economy deferred payment is far more than a convenience for con-sumers. Business firms also arrange to postpone payment, sometimes for 30 to 90 days, and sometimes for as long as 20 to 30 years. We shall see in Section 5 that a modern economy runs on credit, which is another name for deferred payment. This third use of money, therefore, is no less essential than the first two.

A Store of Value

In spite of the temptations of the instalment plan some people prefer to go without a car or television set until they can pay for it. Can you see that money makes *saving* much easier? Imagine a South Sea islander who takes a job in the hope of saving to buy a boat. If he is paid in coconuts (or, worse, in fish) he would find it difficult to save the rewards of each day's labour but with money his earnings could be stored easily and indefinitely. Thus money serves as a store of value. Instead of hurrying off on pay day to buy the week's supply of groceries we can, if we like, spread our spending over the week. We can also put part of our income away for future spending — to use in the event of sickness, retirement, or to buy a car or a TV set next year.

To sum up what we have learned so far, there is a little rhyme which goes like this:

> If you want to know what money is
> Ask what money's for:
> A medium, a measure,
> A standard and a store.

Money, in all four ways, is essential to the modern economy. Yet this very useful invention, for all its blessings, has created problems. The chief ones, which we consider now, have to do with changes in the value of money.

3. CHANGES IN THE VALUE OF MONEY

What Is a Dollar Worth?

It does not take us very far to say a dollar is worth a dollar, and this would not explain the common remark that the dollar now is worth 50 cents. But before we can tackle this problem we must first see what gives money its value in the first place. Look at a dollar bill and you see a piece of paper that, as paper, has no value at all. Its value is determined by what it will buy — a pound of coffee, ten chocolate bars, a teapot. A quarter is not 25 cents' worth of silver, but it will buy a quarter of one dollar's worth of other things (including silver), and *that* is what gives it value. The value of a piece of money depends on *how much* that money will buy. Because it can be so easily exchanged for goods that do actually have value, money acquires the value of those goods.

Why the Value of the Dollar Changes

How much you can buy with a dollar is called its purchasing power. This month it may be a little more — or a little less — than last month, and over a period of years the purchasing power of money may change considerably. The reason is that *prices* change. When prices of goods and services are falling each dollar will buy more and therefore each dollar is more valuable. The opposite is true when prices are rising. The dollar loses purchasing power; each dollar buys less. And so, although there is no price tag on the dollar to say what it is worth, we can tell what is happening to its value by looking at the prices of things the dollar buys.

When prices change slowly, changes in the value of money are small and need not greatly worry us. But over the past twenty years in Canada the general level of prices has more than doubled. Each dollar today, therefore, buys only half as much as it did in 1940: that is why we talk about a 50-cent dollar. Anyone who shopped fifteen and twenty years ago remembers that the dollar used to buy much more than it will today. To appreciate this shrinking dollar you can visualize your own position if tomorrow the price of everything you normally buy were to double. A milkshake would cost 60 cents, a $20 jacket would be $40 and a low-priced car would cost $5000. The purchasing power of your money would be cut in half! Clearly, changes in the value of money

are more than a mere nuisance. They make us richer or poorer. When the value of the dollar goes up or down the dollars in your pocket and your bank account stretch or shrink. It is well worth knowing how these changes may affect you.

Effects on Savings

Suppose that in 1939 Mr. Brown put aside a thousand dollars so that his infant son could have a college education. Eighteen years later, as young Brown left high school, those savings were worth only $500. Although the bank-book still showed a thousand dollars, each dollar would buy only half as much as before. Thus, Mr. Brown has lost half his savings. This is surely a frightening thought. Few people nowadays save money in a sock or under the mattress, yet savings can be lost even when they are in the hands of the bank!

One of the reasons we use money is to save for future spending. But since we risk losing part — or even all — of our savings through changes in the value of money, money's usefulness as a store of value is greatly reduced.

In the light of Mr. Brown's experience let us consider the different ways of saving. A bank account is often thought to be the safest way, but a bank cannot protect your dollars against rising prices. A wiser choice, when prices are rising, is to buy stocks or real estate because their prices go up too. By 1958 Mr. Brown might well have had two thousand dollars for his original one if he had invested his savings in shares or real estate. Buying shares, of course, brings other risks. If a business is not profitable the value of its shares will fall and again Mr. Brown would lose part, or all, of his savings. In this respect bonds are safer than shares. On the other hand, because the face value of a bond is fixed, bonds will be no safer than money in the bank if the value of the dollar falls!

In our example, Mr. Brown would certainly have been better off if he had bought shares or real estate in 1939. However, while it is easy to give the right answer now, in 1939 no one could foresee what would happen to the price level. For the same reason no one can prescribe the best way to save today. To make the wisest choice we must study the alternatives in the light of past experience.

Effects on Deferred Payments

Now let us see how changes in the value of money affect its use in the world of credit. This time suppose Mr. Brown bought a house in 1939, and made mortgage payments of $50 a month for twenty years. As those years of rising prices went by the Brown family would have to pay more for groceries and clothes, but the mortgage payment would stay the same. Moreover, the mortgage would be paid in dollars that bought less of other things, so the $50 a month would become easier to pay. In real terms, Mr. Brown would pay *less* for his house than he had bargained on. In a period of falling prices, however, the opposite would be true. Mr. Brown would pay *more* for his house because dollars become more valuable as prices fall. This is a major difficulty with deferred payments. Whatever the contract — a mortgage on a house, an agreement with an auto finance company, or a loan contract of any kind — the contract is made in dollars, and, if the *value of the dollar* changes, the *real* cost of the house or car will be more — or less — than the contracting parties expected.

Effects on Money as a Medium of Exchange

The effects of a changing dollar on savings and on contracts have been experienced by most Canadians. But changes in the value of money may be much greater than they have been in Canada. In extreme cases, money becomes valueless and no longer serves as a medium of exchange. This is what happened in the terrible inflation in Germany after World War I. Here prices rose not twenty times, not a thousand nor even a million times, but one million million times over the pre-war level! At the end, in 1923, it took 200 billion marks to buy a newspaper and the government was printing notes which bore the stamp 100,000,000,000,000 marks!

As the mark bought less and less many people refused to accept it. Farmers with butter and eggs would ask for dishes or furniture in exchange — anything rather than a basketful of marks which would be worth even less the next day. Thus money failed to serve as a medium of exchange; people went back to barter! The same kind of inflation — called hyper-inflation — occurred in several countries during and after World War II. When the value of money fell too far people reverted to barter or found a new money in commodities such as cigarettes which had the merits of acceptability and a stable value.

Hyper-inflation is rare. But it can happen. When it does happen money fails to do any of the tasks it is designed to perform. And much smaller changes in the value of money have the power to upset our calculations and do much harm, whether we are saving money, going into debt on the instalment plan, or simply spending money incomes. Certainly money would serve us better if its value stayed the same, but we do not have such an ideal money. Later, in Chapter 11, we shall see why.

4. THE SUPPLY OF MONEY

So far we have been talking about money as if we knew what it was, and, for most of us, a mental picture of money is probably limited to the dollar bill. But dollar bills are only one kind of money. They are bank-notes. These bank-notes, together with silver and copper coins, are called "currency". There is a second, more important kind of money called bank money. To understand our money system we must examine these two kinds of money separately.

Currency

We are all familiar with bank-notes and coins. Comparing their own with other currencies Canadians abroad will usually prefer their own. Of course it is more familiar, but it is also true that Canada's currency passes all the tests of a good currency. We have, first, a variety of sizes for convenience in making payments: five coins and eight denominations in bills (the one dollar, two, five, ten, twenty, fifty, one hundred and one thousand). Second, our currency is easy to carry and handle. This saves the wear and tear on pockets which goes with an excessive use of coins. But too much paper is also undesirable. A trip to France, where odds and ends of tattered, crumpled bills are counted out to pay for cigarettes, would show how well Canadian currency meets the third test — durability. Fourth, a good currency should be difficult to counterfeit. Finally, its supply should be easily adjustable to meet changes in the demand, as, for example, at Christmas when people *need* more currency. Canadian currency meets all these requirements.

The dollar bill is properly called a Bank of Canada note. Occasionally you may see a bill with Bank of Nova Scotia or some other bank's name on it. The private banks used to issue notes and these may still be seen in private collections of old currency. But today all notes are issued by the Bank of Canada which is an agency of the federal government.

Bank-notes do not last indefinitely. With frequent handling they get torn and thin, but we can always exchange a worn-out dollar (even if it is patched and held together with tape) for a crisp new one at any bank. The banks ship the worn-out notes to the Bank of Canada (where they are destroyed) and receive new ones in exchange. A one-dollar bill lasts on the average about nine

months. The larger bills are handled less and last longer.

Coins are not really different from paper money. The quarter, as we have seen, is not 25 cents' worth of silver. The metal in all coins, whether silver, nickel or bronze, is worth far less than the face value of the coin. Coins are used because they are more convenient for small transactions than paper. The one difference between notes and coins is that dollar bills are *unlimited* "legal tender": they have to be accepted as payment regardless of the size of the transaction. For example, a doctor cannot refuse to take dollars when I pay my bill, but he could refuse to accept eight bushels of wheat, or a parcel of two hundred nickels. Coins are only *limited* legal tender. They need not be accepted beyond certain specified amounts: silver up to ten dollars, nickel to five dollars, and bronze to 25 cents. If someone tries to settle a debt with you by paying one hundred quarters you can refuse and insist upon bank-notes for fifteen of the twenty-five dollars.

Bank Deposits

The second kind of money is not something you can touch and feel like currency. Nor is it a drawerful of bills and coins in the vaults of a bank. A bank deposit is simply an entry in a ledger which gives its owner the right to demand a certain amount of currency. To illustrate the difference between a bank deposit and currency, suppose you hand the bank's cashier two ten-dollar bills to deposit in your account. The addition to your account is *not* 20 dollars in currency. Ownership of the two ten-dollar bills passes to the bank and you now own twenty dollars in bank deposits. The bank *owes* you twenty dollars. The bank records its debt to you by crediting your deposit account by that amount. In other words, you *exchange* twenty dollars in currency for twenty dollars in the form of a bank deposit which is a debt of the bank to you.

If you now wish to buy something with your bank deposit you simply write a cheque which directs the bank to transfer a certain sum of money from your account to another. The cheque itself is not money. It is simply a device for transferring bank deposits from one person to another.

Bank deposits can be used to pay for things, to settle debts, and to save. Because they do the work of money, bank deposits *are* money. They are not legal tender and so you cannot force a person to accept your cheque. But your bank deposit can always be converted into currency at the bank and, on most occasions, bank deposits will be accepted as a means of payment. Because bank deposits are generally as acceptable as currency, are more convenient and are also safe, people have little need for currency. Many persons are paid by cheque and use chequing accounts to pay the rent, the gas company and the grocery bill. Business firms use bank money even more extensively. Indeed, in a modern economy, most transactions are settled with bank deposits. Currency is the small change of the system, used because of its convenience in small purchases.

Bank deposits, then, are the most important form of money. If we look at the total supply of money in Canada — on a particular day in 1960 — here is what we find:

	Millions of Dollars	Percentage
Coins	125	
Notes	1,596	
Total currency	1,721	13
Bank deposits	11,278	87
Total money supply	12,999	100

Source: Bank of Canada, Weekly Financial Statistics, March 24, 1960.

Currency was only 13 per cent of the total. Canadians had more than six times that amount in the form of bank deposits.

Where Money Comes From

To answer this question we had to know that there are two kinds of money. The supply of each is decided differently. Currency is supplied by the government: coins

are minted at the Royal Mint and the Bank of Canada issues all bank-notes or dollar bills. The supply of bank money cannot be described so easily. As we have just seen, bank deposits increase when people make deposits of currency. And so you might think that people and business firms with bank accounts decide the supply of bank money when they decide how much they will put in their accounts. But only a fraction of bank deposits originates in this way. Most bank deposits are created by the banks themselves. In the next chapter we shall see how and why.

Too Much Money

Earlier, in discussing the supply of money, we asked why cannot *more* of it be made. Would it not be easy for the government to print a crisp new ten-dollar bill for everyone in the country? This sounds attractive, but let us think about it. What would 17 million Canadians do with this extra $170 million? They would, of course, go out and spend it — or, at least, a large part of it. And sellers, their eyes on dwindling stocks, would raise prices (see Chapter 3, page 25). The extra money, therefore, would mean higher prices. If the economy were already producing at full capacity it could *only* mean higher prices because the quantity of goods and services produced could not be increased. Our ten-dollar bills would not buy more goods and services; we would simply pay higher prices. And so the extra money would not make us any richer.

With the supply of money it is not always a case of "the more the merrier". While your aim and mine is to have as much money as possible, the country as a whole can have too much! Actually there is no conflict of aims. The real goal, for the individual as well as the nation, is to have as many *goods and services* as possible. We must always remember that money is not a real commodity and what a dollar will buy depends on prices.

We should also keep in mind that governments cannot make us richer simply by printing money. The supply of money *can* increase too rapidly so that the community does have "too much money". At other times it may have too little. In either event the community will suffer, and for this rea- son we can blame the monetary system for some of our economic difficulties. We shall return to this question when we have exam- ined the banking system and how it creates money.

5. CREDIT

Many people use *credit*. They charge their groceries at the corner store and buy their TV set on the instalment plan. Sooner or later, when the bills come in, money does enter the picture and it is money, as we have seen, that makes the use of credit (deferred payment) easy. The widespread use of credit is an important feature of the modern econ- omy, and the use of credit has a special relation to the supply of money.

Personal Credit

Several kinds of credit are available to the individual. There are charge accounts and instalment plans. In addition, you can bor- row from firms that specialize in lending money — such as banks, finance companies and credit unions. But whatever its source, credit is never free. You must pay for it. You must repay not only the sum borrowed but also the costs and some of the profit of the business firm that provides the credit. The car dealer cannot tell the Ford Motor Company that Mr. Jones will pay the price of a car at $60 a month over the next three years! The dealer has to pay the company now. He wants the full price for the car to meet this obligation. So he arranges credit terms for Mr. Jones with another company that specializes in provision of credit. Mr. Jones pays for this service: the costs in- curred, the interest on the money and a payment to cover the risk of default.

All the costs incurred in providing credit are included in the "carrying charges" which are added to the monthly payments. These charges are likely to be high when credit is supplied by the seller (instalment plan) or a finance company. Banks offer cheaper credit — for those who can get a bank loan — and credit unions supply cheap credit to their members. The charge account is dif- ferent. Usually there are no extra carrying charges, but then the extra expense of offer- ing credit is added to the prices of the things we buy. Customers who pay cash share a part of the costs of providing credit to other customers.

Credit for Business

Personal credit, although widely used, is far from being the most important kind. You and I could get along, if we had to, without credit, but organized credit is essen- tial to modern business enterprise. If you consider the large expenditures in plant and machinery by modern industry the reason is easy to see. The cost of plant and equip- ment is so great that it must be spread over many years. Business firms often borrow money for as long as twenty or thirty years. Bonds, which were described in Chapter 4, are one of the chief instruments for securing long-term credit. People and business firms who buy these bonds are lending money to pay for new plant and new machinery.

The need for short-term credit — bor- rowing for one to three months — is not so obvious, but it too is essential in the modern business world. In its day-by-day transac- tions the typical business firm does not pay cash for goods received; instead, it arranges to pay in 30, 60, or 90 days' time. The retailer uses credit to pay the wholesaler, the wholesaler to pay the manufacturer, and the manufacturing company may borrow money to pay for its materials. Why is it worth postponing payment for such a short time?

The answer is that a firm can do *more* business when it uses credit. To illustrate, suppose the XY Shoe Store pays cash — say $5000 — for a thousand pairs of shoes which it expects to sell over the next two to three months. The store now has $5000 tied up in stock until the shoes are sold. But if it can *postpone payment* for the 90 days it takes to sell the shoes, the wholesaler can be paid with the proceeds from the sales. The transaction would require no extra cash, and so the XY Shoe Store can stock more shoes, do more business, and earn more profits. The extra volume of business will usually pay enough to more than offset the cost of the credit.

Now let us see where the short-term credit comes from. The individual, you will remember, has several alternatives — the store, the finance company, the bank, and so on. Similarly, our XY Shoe Store can obtain the credit it wants from a variety of sources. If the wholesaler will agree to wait 90 days for payment, the wholesaler supplies the credit. When this happens we say that the credit comes from a "trade" creditor because the two firms are in the ame line of business. Then there are the finance companies. Automobile dealers borrow extensively from the finance companies to pay for the cars they stock. Third, our XY Shoe Store may go to the bank. Indeed, the bank is usually the first choice. Banks specialize in this kind of commercial lending to a high degree, so much so that we give them the name "commercial banks".

Short-Term Credit and the Banks

In the world of short-term credit the banks occupy the most important position. Not only do they supply credit directly — as with a loan to the XY Shoe Store — but they supply a great deal of credit indirectly. Suppose, in our illustration, that the wholesaler supplied the credit by agreeing to wait 90 days. Although willing to provide a service to the customer, the wholesaler is no more eager than the retailer to tie up several thousand dollars and so will look to someone else to provide the credit. The obvious choice is his bank; the means of borrowing is known as "discounting". The wholesaler sells the bank its contract with the XY Shoe Store and receives the $5000 — less a discount. The discount is the payment to the bank for the service and it is the cost to the wholesaler of getting an immediate cash payment. Now the wholesaler has been paid for his shoes and the bank does the waiting for repayment. This means that the credit to the XY Shoe Store was actually supplied by the bank.

The contract between the XY Shoe Store and the wholesaler could be a promissory note (in which the store *promises* to pay $5000 in 90 days) or a 90-day draft (in which the store is *ordered* to pay). Both promissory notes and 60- and 90-day drafts are widely used for payments between business firms and both are commonly taken to the banks for discounting. Thus the banks, by discounting notes and drafts, supply much of the credit that business firms offer each other. Banks are also indirectly responsible for much of the credit offered by finance companies because the finance companies borrow extensively from the banks. Directly or indirectly, by far the largest part of all short-term credit comes from the commercial banks.

The credit functions of the commercial banks give them a key position in the economy. If the banks make credit hard to get, the XY Shoe Store and other business firms may have to pay for things with cash, which means fewer orders and fewer shoes to sell. When credit is easy more shoes can be ordered and more sales can be made. Easier credit, therefore, can speed up the pace of business. This does not mean that the banks *alone* decide whether the economy will stifle or prosper, but their influence is very great. To examine this aspect of a modern economy we must devote a special chapter to the banks and the banking system.

QUESTIONS FOR DISCUSSION

1. Long ago, tradition tells us, a great reformer in Sparta planned an ideal society in which all men would be equal. As part of this new order he intended to eliminate acquisitiveness and the desire for luxuries. To this end Sparta's gold and silver coins were replaced with iron money, and a very small value assigned to a great quantity and weight. We are told that a modest sum required a whole room to store it and a yoke of oxen to transport it (Plutarch's *Lives: Lycurgus*). Describe the effects this unique currency would have on trade (both domestic and foreign). Consider also its effects on saving, on spending, and on crime.

2. Consult an encyclopaedia to make a list of the different things that have been used as money. In the light of the four uses of money, consider the merits — and defects — of each. When did the Canadian colonies begin using dollars instead of English pounds? What reasons can you give for the change?

3. Suppose you have $500 and want to save it for a rainy day. If, by 1975, the price level had tripled, what would your savings be worth? Now imagine that a severe depression intervenes and the general level of prices in 1975 is 40 per cent below what it is today. What would be the effect on your savings? Taking account of the difficulty of predicting the future, discuss the best ways of saving.

4. Explain what a bank deposit is and why it is money.

5. In time of war governments always need more money: to buy munitions and supplies, to pay the armed services, and so on. In the past, many governments have resorted to the "printing press" method. That is, in addition to borrowing and/or raising taxes, the government simply *prints* more money. Explain the danger in this solution to the costs of war.

6. We have said that credit is never free. Can you think of some of the costs incurred by the merchant who provides credit? Perhaps a delegation from the class could query some of the local merchants in your town. Do you think that credit is worth paying for? Why do banks and credit unions offer cheaper credit than stores and finance companies? Why do business firms seek (a) long-term credit? (b) short-term credit?

Chapter 10

The Banking System

1. PRELIMINARY

In the last chapter we imagined what would happen if our government presented every person in Canada with a ten-dollar bill and we saw why, in an economy at full employment, no wise government would do such a thing. There would be *too much* spending. Because resources were already fully employed, output could not be increased. The increase in spending could only result in higher prices. At times this problem of too much spending *does* arise and it may be aggravated by a rapid increase in the supply of money. To investigate this problem we need to understand the banking system, because the largest part of the supply of money is created by the banks.

In one sense a bank is an ordinary business firm. Instead of shoes or eggs or farm machinery, its stock-in-trade is money. Its main business is receiving deposits and making loans to individuals and business firms. But this ordinary, everyday business of banks, which is described in Section 2, is not the whole story. Other business firms — insurance companies, saving societies, trust companies, credit unions, mortgage companies and finance companies — perform these same functions. Like the banks, many of these financial institutions will look after our savings and, like the banks, many will make loans to us. What makes the banks different — and worthy of special attention — is the fact that when banks lend they *create* money. Section 3 explains how the banks create money. In Section 4 we come back to the problem of controlling the supply of money. Here we examine the relation shown between the banking system and the government.

2. THE BANKING BUSINESS

We all know what a bank looks like. Almost every Canadian town, however small or remote, has a bank and our cities have very many. There are, however, only a handful of companies in the banking business. In contrast to the United States, where there are more than 14,000 separate banks, we have only nine banking businesses in Canada. The banks where you and I deposit our savings are all *branches* of one or another of these nine banks. The Canadian system of banking is called "branch banking". Although banks do much the same job, whether in Toronto, Chicago or Rangoon, the system used does make for differences in the way the banking is carried on. As Canadians, we can limit our study to branch banking. And since few Canadians have any occasion to deal with the head office, we begin our study with the ordinary, familiar branch bank.

The Branch Bank Receives Deposits

The branch bank is the place where you

and I have our accounts. Most of us have what is called a "savings account". The savings account is designed to serve persons who want to save and who write only an occasional cheque on these savings. For others, who want to deposit their pay cheque for safety's sake and pay their bills by writing cheques, a personal chequing account is more appropriate. A third kind of account is called a current account. These are the chequing accounts used by business firms.

The advantage of a savings account is that it earns interest. The interest is calculated on the minimum quarterly balance. The interest rate, which is changed from time to time by the bank, is low — lower than interest paid on many other forms of saving. But the low rate is compensated by the convenience of a savings account. Although banks can require seven days' notice of withdrawal, they never do. You can count on withdrawing your savings quickly and easily. And anyone can open an account with a deposit as small as one dollar. In 1957, of more than nine million personal savings accounts, well over half were less than one hundred dollars!

The Branch Bank Makes Loans

Receiving and paying out deposits is one side of the banking business. If this were all banks could do, banking would not be the very profitable business that it is! But there is another side to banking: *using* the money left on deposit. The most profitable use of funds is making loans to the public. This business is also carried on by the branch bank.

Personal loans were mentioned in Chapter 9. If you have a bank account and a steady job, one of the cheapest ways to borrow is through a personal loan from your bank. You may be asked to leave some "security", such as a life insurance policy or a government bond, but if you have good references for your character and can show that the amount of the loan is within your ability to repay, your chances of getting a loan will be very good. Most personal loans are for relatively small amounts. Added

together, however, the personal loans made by Canadian banks run into many millions of dollars.

Many more millions of dollars go into loans to business firms. Except for the very largest — which require approval by head office — loans to business firms are also made by branch banks. In the section on credit we saw that loans can be made directly to a business firm (for example, to the XY Shoe Store) or through the process of discounting. Banks find this kind of lending attractive because the actual sale of the shoes by the XY Shoe Store will provide the money to liquidate the loan. A large part of bank loans are of this "self-liquidating" kind.

Until recently most bank loans were short-term loans (30 to 90 days) and they went very largely to business firms in commerce and manufacturing. Under Canadian law banks are free to lend money to all industries, but banks, following their own safety rules, have ruled out certain types of borrowers. Farmers, for example, were generally ruled out because they needed longer-term loans. Since 1944 the government has guaranteed bank loans to farmers and fishermen. As a result, some of the intermediate-term credit needs of these producers are now met by bank loans. These guaranteed loans have been particularly helpful in the finance of purchases of farm machinery and equipment. A still more recent change occurred in the housing field. Since 1954 the government has allowed the banks to make mortgage loans on new housing. Many Canadians have borrowed from their banks to build new homes.

Canadian Bank Loans, December 1958	
	($ millions)
Personal (including home improvement loans)....................	898
Farmers...	368
Industry..	1166
Merchandisers...................................	699
Government....................................	286
Financial..	988
Others...	1008

In addition to its main business — receiving deposits and making loans — the branch bank has several side lines. For example, there is the Foreign Exchange department, where foreign money is bought and sold. Here you can buy American dollars for a trip across the border; business firms can buy pounds or marks or yen, or have foreign accounts converted into Canadian dollars. The branch bank also offers a variety of financial services to its customers. It buys and sells bonds and, for customers who own bonds, the bank will "clip the coupons" and add the interest to their bank accounts at regular intervals.

Main Branches

Standing between the thousands of ordinary branch banks and their head offices are a number of main branches. Each main branch serves a territory which takes in from fifty to a hundred branch banks and is responsible for supervising the branches in its district. Before making a large loan, the ordinary branch must get approval from its main branch. Only the largest loans are referred to head office.

The main branches also act as a "clearing house" for cheques. Have you ever wondered what happens when you write a cheque? The cheque requires your bank to transfer money from your account to another account, probably in some other bank. Let us say that your account is with the Bank of Nova Scotia. If you write a cheque for $20 and this cheque is deposited at the Bank of Montreal, your bank then *owes* twenty dollars to the Bank of Montreal. In the course of one day's business your bank will become indebted to the other banks as well. At the same time, of course, other banks will be required to honour their own cheques collected by the Bank of Nova Scotia. And since each bank has payments to collect as well as payments to make, it does not need to pay out the full amount of the cheques drawn against it. Only the differences need be settled. This settling of differences takes place at the end of each day when all the cheques are sorted out. It is called "clearing".

If the Bank of Montreal has $50,000 in cheques (including your twenty dollars) drawn on the Bank of Nova Scotia, while Nova Scotia has $40,000 to collect from the Bank of Montreal, the only necessary transaction is the transfer of $10,000 to the Bank of Montreal. And even this transaction may not be necessary. If the Bank of Montreal owes $10,000 to the Royal Bank at the end of the same day, it is simpler to let Nova Scotia pay the Royal. The clearing system is carried through at three levels. Accounts are offset in the local clearing association, then at the district level. Finally, any remaining differences are settled by actual transfers among the nine banks at the national level. In this way a multitude of unnecessary transactions is eliminated.

Head Office

The head office of a bank, like the head office of any large corporation, decides company policies and supervises and reviews the work of the branches. The chief policy decisions concern the use of funds. What part of the bank's funds can be put to work earning profits? And how can they earn the most profit? The activities of the branch bank will reflect the decisions made at head office. Although the branch manager has the authority to make loans he must act within the rules laid down by head office policy. If current policy favours an expansion of loans, then the total of loans approved by the branch manager will grow larger. Borrowers will find loans are easier to get. At another time the branch manager may have instructions to refuse certain kinds of loans and to limit others to the very safest borrowers. Then the branch manager will make fewer loans and turn away many would-be borrowers.

Some part of the bank's funds are invested in stocks and bonds. These investments are made at head office by the investment department. In Canada the bulk of these investments is in government securities. There is also a foreign exchange department in head office which co-ordinates the buying and selling of foreign exchange in the many branches. It buys foreign currencies that are in short supply in the branches and sells excess supplies of foreign currencies purchased by the branches.

The Cash Reserves

Having reached head office our brief tour of a Canadian bank is at an end. We have seen the main features of the banking business: receiving money that people want to deposit, and using that money — in loans and investments — to earn profits for the bank. There is nothing mysterious about this, although one question should occur to you. How can banks lend out money that may at any time be *withdrawn*? If the money that you and I deposit is loaned to the XY Shoe Store, will the bank have our money when we want to draw it out?

The answer is that not all funds go into loans and investments. The banks always keep some cash on hand, and these cash reserves are always large enough to meet the ordinary demands for cash. Let us see why.

Theoretically, the demand for cash could equal the total of deposits in the bank. Since every dollar on deposit can be withdrawn, every dollar on deposit is a potential demand for cash. Thus a bank with a million dollars in deposits would need a million dollars in cash *if all depositors decided to close out their accounts on the same day*. But this does not happen. Individuals and business firms do not close out their accounts all at once. They need only a certain amount of cash for till and pocket money, and any cash over that amount is put in the banks. Thus cash is always flowing into the banks as well as out, and the banks can see to it that the outflow is about equal to the inflow. The banks, therefore, need very little cash in reserve and can put any excess cash to more profitable uses. This is the basis of the business of banking.

How much cash do banks need? Because a bank earns profits on its loans and invest-

ments it is greatly tempted to keep very little cash on hand. At the same time a bank must always have enough cash on hand to meet *all* demands or people would quickly lose confidence in that bank. To be absolutely safe at all times a bank would need one dollar in cash for every dollar of deposits. This is called a hundred per cent cash reserve ratio. But a hundred per cent reserve, as we have seen, is not necessary. In fact, banks could meet the ordinary, day-to-day demand for cash with a reserve ratio as low as 2 or 3 per cent ($2 or $3 in cash for every $100 of deposits)! To be on the safe side Canadian banks prefer to hold more and the Bank Act requires them to hold minimum cash reserves of 8 per cent. Thus a bank with a $100 million of deposits will hold $8 million in cash.

So far we have considered the need for cash reserves under normal circumstances. A "run" on a bank is not a normal circumstance and here the normal assumption — that all depositors will not want to close out their accounts at the same time — will not hold. If depositors believe their bank may *fail*, they will all want their money right away. Thus a run may start with rumours of mistaken investments and large losses by the bank or a bank panic may develop during a severe depression. Whatever the cause, the bank is confronted with demands for more cash than it has got and is forced to close its doors.

The basic trouble in the event of a run is not so much lack of *cash* as lack of *time*. Given time, the bank can convert its loans and investments into cash. Bonds can be sold, loans can be called in and notes and drafts falling due will be repaid. But when a run develops there is no time to convert other assets. A crowd of depositors is waiting, all seeking to withdraw their savings immediately, and the bank, unable to satisfy them all, is obliged to suspend operations.

Since bank failures are rare in Canada the course of events described above is drawn largely from American experience. In the United States some 5200 banks, with deposits of over $4 billion, were casualties of the banking crisis of March, 1933! Through a dozen years of depression no bank failed in Canada. However, this difference cannot be explained on the basis of cash reserves. Canadian banks actually hold smaller cash reserves than American banks! The chief reason why we have fewer failures than the United States is that the Canadian system of branch banking is much stronger than the American "unit" system of thousands of separate companies.

3. BANKS AND THE SUPPLY OF MONEY

In their ordinary everyday business banks supply a fundamental service to the modern community. They collect the savings, large and small, of a great many people and, by lending, channel these savings into productive uses. But this does not explain the peculiar importance of banks. The difference between banks and other lending institutions is that banks can change the supply of money in the community; other lending institutions cannot. You may find this statement puzzling when you recall that banks do not print dollar bills. As we have seen, the Bank of Canada issues all bank-notes and it is not a commercial bank. But the commercial banks do create money in the form of bank deposits, and bank deposits are by far the most important kind of money. To see how the banks create this money we must look at the several ways in which bank deposits come into existence.

How Bank Deposits Arise

When an individual goes into a bank and deposits two ten-dollar bills, bank deposits increase by $20 (see page 112). Clearly, this new deposit adds nothing to the total supply of money available to the public. There is simply an exchange of one kind of money for another: $20 in cash is exchanged for $20 in bank deposits. If, instead of cash, I deposit a cheque for $20, the amount of money available to the public is still unchanged. Although deposits at my bank increase, deposits in some other bank will be reduced by the same amount and so the *total* of bank deposits remains the same.

The second way in which bank deposits come into existence is through bank loans.

When the XY Shoe Store borrows $5000 from the bank the $5000 is credited to the store's account; bank deposits, therefore, increase by $5000. And since no money has been given up by the public, these new deposits *are* an addition to the total supply of money. We say that the bank has *created* money — $5000 worth. The fact that the $5000 does not remain in the bank makes no difference. When the store writes a cheque part — or all — of the new deposit is simply transferred to accounts in other banks. If the store withdraws the whole sum the deposit disappears but the public will have $5000 more in cash. Thus the increase in deposits, however it is used, is an increase in the supply of money.

Bank deposits also increase when the bank buys bonds. This is the third way in which bank deposits arise. If I have a government bond to sell the bank will give me a cheque for a hundred dollars, drawn on itself. When I deposit the cheque in my account deposits are increased by one hundred dollars. There is no *decrease* in deposits somewhere else — as happens with any other cheque — nor have I given up a hundred dollars in currency. Again the increase in deposits represents new money — money created by the bank. The same is true when a bank discounts a bill of exchange, makes personal loans or finances mortgages for the construction of new houses.

Banks Create Money

New bank deposits that arise with an expansion of bank credit transactions increase the supply of money. The explanation is quite simple. It is that banks, and *only* banks, can exchange new money (a bank deposit) for something that is not money (a promissory note, a 90-day draft, a residential mortgage or a government bond).

To illustrate, let us take two loans, one by a bank and one by some other lending institution. If the XY Shoe Store goes to the bank it can exchange a promissory note for $5000 in bank deposits. The $5000 comes into existence on the strength of the promissory note. But if the loan is made by a finance company, the $5000 is simply transferred from one bank account to another. Although the store will have $5000 added to its bank account, the finance company will have $5000 *less*. The total amount of money available to the public does not change. Similarly, when I sell a bond to a trust company the increase in my bank account is offset by a decrease in the trust company's account. In all transactions among members of the public and firms like the finance company and the trust company money simply changes hands. At the bank, however, a few strokes of the pen put money into somebody's account — without taking it away from someone else! This money is an *addition* to the total supply of money.

Banks not only create money but they may also reduce the supply of money. By calling for repayment of loans, the bank requires the XY Shoe Store to pay $5000 either in cash or by cheque. If the store pays in cash the money of the public is reduced by that amount; if it pays by cheque its deposit at the bank is reduced by $5000. In either event the supply of money available to the public is reduced. A reduction in other types of bank loans and investments has the same result. When banks make fewer loans and discounts or cut down on their purchases of securities and mortgages bank deposits decline. A contraction in bank credit causes a contraction in the money supply held by the public, that is, in the money held by individuals, business firms and governments.

4. CONTROL OF THE BANKING SYSTEM

Changes in the Supply of Money

We have now answered the question raised in Chapter 9: where money comes from. Further, we can see that the supply of money will *change* as banks expand or contract their loans. Banks, in pursuit of profits, expand or contract their loans in response to changes in the demand for credit.

The most important source of demand for bank credit is the business community. Their demand, of course, will vary. In Chapter 8 we examined the factors that underlie the fluctuations in economic activity. When these factors are favourable the demand for credit increases; when unfavourable the demand for credit falls. The banking system, however, may over-react. In their enthusiasm for making loans when business is prosperous the banks may expand the money supply too rapidly. Spending then grows faster than production and, as a result, we have rising prices (inflation). When conditions are less favourable the supply of credit and money may contract too rapidly. Then the shortage of bank credit would contribute to the decline in spending which had already lowered sales and destroyed jobs and incomes. For these reasons it does matter whether *more* money or *less* money is becoming available. In a period of inflation more money would make the problem worse; in a period of depression less money would cause more unemployment. In short, the banks may add to our difficulties.

This conflict between the public interest and the profit-seeking activities of banks is the main reason why Canada, like all advanced countries, has a "central bank". Through the government-owned Bank of Canada the government can play a major role in deciding the supply of money because the Bank of Canada has the powers to control the actions of all the banks in our banking system.

This system of control, which was introduced in 1934, does not relegate the commercial banks to a position of minor importance. The banks still have considerable power. They are still the source of the supply of money. The difference is that now the government-owned central bank may call the tune. In other words, the government's bank may *require* the banks to act in a way that increases the supply of money or vice versa.

Neither does the new system mean that inflation and deflation and depressions have

been conquered. Smoothing out booms and slumps requires other remedies in addition to control of the money supply. Nevertheless, when business slumps it is better to make *more* money available for spending by easing credit conditions. At the peak of a boom it is better to restrict credit than to go on adding to the money already in circulation. These are objectives of the Bank of Canada. Fitting this central bank into the picture will complete our survey of money and the banking system.

The Bank of Canada

A central bank is not an ordinary commercial bank like the ones described in Section 2. Neither you nor I can open an account in the Bank of Canada. Nor can we go there to borrow money. The Bank of Canada is a banker's bank. It is the bank where the commercial banks have *their*

Bank of Canada, Ottawa

The façade of the Bank of Canada, the government-owned "central bank" in Ottawa.

accounts. Just as I have an account in the Bank of Montreal, so the Bank of Montreal and the eight other commercial banks have accounts in the Bank of Canada. A few dealers in short-term credit secure loans from the central bank. The federal government also keeps deposits in the Bank of Canada. If you look at federal government cheques you will find that some are drawn on the Bank of Canada — your mother's family allowance cheque, for example.

Another thing that distinguishes the Bank of Canada from the commercial banks is that it is a government-owned corporation. It is not in business to make profits (although it generally does) but to serve the community by promoting a more stable economy. Whether the problem is too much money (inflation) or too little (deflation and unemployment), the central bank's job is to bring about appropriate changes in the supply of money. Its primary function is to implement the government's monetary policy.

In effect, the Bank of Canada can say: "There's too much money around. The commercial banks will have to tighten up on loans and discounts. We will take steps to make sure they do." Alternatively, steps could be taken to encourage the banks to ease credit and increase the supply of money. The details of this process cannot be described in full. The day-to-day operations of the Bank of Canada are in themselves complex and involve other institutions which cannot be described in a single chapter on banking. With this reservation in mind — that several aspects of central banking have been left out — we may look briefly at two ways in which the Bank of Canada controls the commercial banks: open market operations and informal agreements. Until quite recently these were the chief methods of control.

Control of the Commercial Banks

The volume of bank deposits — and hence the supply of money — depends upon the *cash reserves* of the banks (see page 120).

If cash reserves are ample, banks are free to increase deposits (through loans and discounts), but if cash reserves are low banks are forced to "go slow". Consequently, if a central bank can control these all-important cash reserves, it can control the volume of bank deposits.

In its open market operations, the Bank of Canada goes into the market either to buy or to sell bonds. When it *buys* bonds it pays for them in cash and, since this cash flows into the banks, the cash reserves of the banks increase. When the Bank of Canada *sells* bonds it will receive cash in payment. This reduces the cash reserve of the commercial banks. Thus the Bank of Canada may increase or decrease the cash reserve of the banking system, and this will cause much larger changes in the volume of bank deposits.

A second method of control is more direct. Because there are only nine banks, representatives of the Bank of Canada can easily meet with their representatives. Agreements are reached by which the commercial banks carry out the wishes of the Bank of Canada. While such agreements are informal the banks are inclined to accept the suggestions of the Bank of Canada because it speaks for the government.

The effectiveness of the Bank of Canada's control over the policies and practices of the banks was increased in several ways by amendments to the Bank Act in 1954. The legal minimum cash reserve ratio, formerly 5 per cent, was raised to 8 per cent and the Bank of Canada was empowered to raise the legal minimum (by one percentage point a month) to 12 per cent. Thus the Bank of Canada may prevent an increase in deposits by requiring the banks to hold still more cash. Another amendment was designed to increase the effectiveness of "Bank Rate" which is a short-term rate of interest announced from time to time by the Bank of Canada. As a result, the Bank Rate has become an effective influence upon interest rates actually charged in many short-term lending transactions.

Conclusion

The subject of money is a large one. We cannot pretend to have covered every aspect of the subject. But in a bird's-eye view of the whole economy it is enough to see how money and the banking system form part of the pattern. That money is an important part was made clear in Chapter 9 where we learned its several uses and saw the serious effects of changes in its value. In this chapter we have examined the banking system to understand the source of money and changes in its supply. In the next chapter we shall see more clearly the relationship between the supply of money and the well-being of the community.

Any brief sketch of the money and banking system should close with a note on its limitations. Because the sketch has been brief it has also been greatly over-simplified. As with so many relationships in economics, those involving money are highly complex.

To explain the role of a single actor — money — a great many actors have been left in the wings. The causes of inflation and deflation, for example, include many factors other than the lack or excess of money forthcoming from the banks. But lack of money does make recovery from recession more difficult, so government monetary policy in depressed periods is aimed at easing credit, putting more money into circulation. Similarly, the causes of inflation go much deeper than an excessive enthusiasm on the part of the banks in making loans. But an excess of money does add fuel to the flames and government and central bank policies should be designed to absorb surplus money and prevent its further expansion. Monetary policy is never a cure-all but it is one of several policies that may help to keep the economy on an even keel.

QUESTIONS FOR DISCUSSION

1. Explain how a bank earns profits (a) on personal loans, (b) on discounting, (c) on buying and selling bonds.

2. What is a cheque? If you have a cheque for $100 drawn on the Royal Bank and deposit it in the Bank of Nova Scotia, how does your bank collect the $100 from the Royal? As a class project, establish three banks in the room, each with a district manager. Each student will have an account of $1000, and the accounts are divided in approximately equal numbers among the three banks. Each student then writes a dozen cheques, payable to other members of the class (no overdrafts allowed). Cheques received are deposited in the student's account. At the close of these transactions the three district managers come together and "clear" the cheques, recording the *total* and the *net* obligations of each bank on the blackboard.

3. Ask your local bank manager if he would receive a delegation from the class. With his help the group should examine a bank balance sheet issued by head office, with particular attention to (a) the relationship between cash and deposits, (b) the total volume of loans, and (c) the different kinds of loans.

4. Have a second delegation visit a local credit union. On the basis of reports prepared by the two groups compare the business of the credit union and the business of a bank.

5. Explain how banks create money. In your illustration, suppose that a cheque is written against the full amount of the new bank deposit as soon as it is created. Is the supply of money then reduced? Why not?

6. Describe two ways in which banks may supply short-term credit to business firms, and explain why the supply of money will increase. How is the supply of money affected when loans to the public are made by a finance company? Why?

7. In a bank "the chief policy decisions concern the use of funds." How do banks use the funds that are not loaned? What circumstances would favour an expansion of loans, a contraction of loans? Trace the effects upon the community of each policy.

8. Your answer to question 7 can be used to explain why the supply of money changes. Now show why changes in the supply of money may occur too rapidly. What is the primary purpose of a central bank?

Chapter 11

The Changing Price Level

1. PRELIMINARY

Ever since World War II, inflation has been the number one economic problem in all the countries of the West. The same period has also been one of unparalleled prosperity in Canada and Canadians who can recall the depression of the thirties are tempted to regard inflation as a minor ailment. Yet inflation causes great hardships too. For example, the loss of half Mr. Brown's savings, which we described in Chapter 9, was a direct result of rising prices. In an extreme case, as in Germany after World War I, inflation can destroy income as effectively as unemployment and wipe out the value of past savings as well. In Germany, middle-class families suddenly found themselves poor. Old people living on the savings gleaned from a lifetime of work were destitute. In the ordeal the German econ-omy virtually collapsed. Although it was patched up and put in running order again, a great many Germans had lost faith in the kind of system where such catastrophes could happen. Thus the ravages of infla-tion helped to pave the way for Hitler.

More recent history has supplied many new object lessons on the evils of inflation in such countries as Greece, Hungary and China during and after World War II. In this same period, moreover, rising prices became a major problem everywhere. To-day all countries are threatened by inflation.

Why should prices rise? As we have seen, Canada has had periods of rising prices before. Also we have had periods when the level of prices was falling. As far back as the records of prices go, we find that the price level has always behaved in this way:

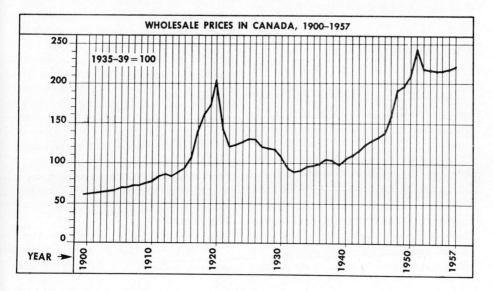

WHOLESALE PRICES IN CANADA, 1900-1957

1935-39 = 100

sometimes rising and at other times falling. A changing price level appears to be unavoidable in our kind of economy. This fact is worth investigation. The study of price movements will help us to understand the current problem of inflation and also shed light on the working of our economic system. Why should the general level of prices move either up or down? Are there reasons for preferring one state of affairs to the other? In the light of what we know about inflation, can we say that it is better to have prices falling? These are the questions that this chapter is designed to answer. To begin with, let us see *why* the price level changes.

2. WHY THE PRICE LEVEL CHANGES

The Price Level

When we say that prices today are high we mean that prices of *most* things are higher than at some point in the past. Some prices, it is true, have risen a great deal more than others, some have hardly increased at all, and a few have fallen. When we say that the price level is rising, we mean that the average of all prices is becoming higher than it was. Prices do tend to move in the same direction at the same time, and so it is possible to speak about a *general* or average level of prices. By inflation we mean simply that prices of most things are rising; deflation means that prices generally are coming down. However, it will be easier to see the reasons for the general movement if we start with a single price. Why does *any* price move up — or down?

A Rise in the Price of Eggs

In Chapter 3, under the heading "The Role of Prices", the reason for an increase in the price of eggs was discussed very briefly. A rising price, we learned, results from a shortage of eggs. When eggs are in short supply the stores will raise the price. Accordingly, if consumers begin buying *more eggs than usual* their extra purchases will create a shortage and so raise the price. Eventually the higher price may bring more eggs to market, but it takes time to increase the production of eggs. Therefore, when people decide to buy more eggs the first thing that happens is a rise in the price.

Total Spending

From this first step in our argument — consumers buying more eggs — it is a simple second step to think of them also buying more meat and shoes, more shirts and socks and goods and services of every kind. This extra spending will push up the price of a great many things at the same time. The explanation for rising prices, then, appears to be an increase in consumer spending. But consumers are not the only ones who may buy more things than they did last year. Business firms may spend more on new buildings and machines; governments may increase their expenditures; foreign customers may decide to buy more Canadian products. A rise in *total spending* will cause the price level to rise.

Increased spending works to push up prices in two ways. One, as we saw with the eggs, is the effect of more buying: when supplies run short prices rise. Second, higher prices mean greater profits for producers. To fill larger orders, many business firms are encouraged to expand, but to get more workers they may have to pay higher wages. But now we are back to where we started: higher profits and higher wages give consumers more money to spend. So it goes in a circle — higher spending, higher prices, higher incomes, still higher spending.

Why Prices Fall

Since more spending makes prices rise it is not surprising that a *decrease* in total spending makes prices fall. When consumers buy fewer eggs the stores find themselves overstocked. To clear their shelves the stores have to lower the price. And when consumers and business firms, governments and foreign buyers all cut down on their spending, surpluses of a great many things appear. Hence a great many prices fall.

Less spending also means lower wages and lower profits. When fewer sales take place business firms not only lower prices but they may also decide to produce less in the future and cut down on staff. Unemployment, lower profits and lower wages mean less money income and still lower spending. We are in the same circle, going the other way.

Changes in Spending

At this point we have an explanation for both a rising price level and a falling price level. In either case the cause is a change in the total amount of spending: an increase in spending pushes prices up and a decrease in spending makes prices fall. If total spending were more stable there would be little change in the price level. Why, then, does spending change?

Some of the reasons were given in Chapter 8. Consumers, for example, will spend more or less as their incomes rise or fall. We have also listed several reasons why exports and the level of investment may increase or decrease. But in Chapter 8 we had not examined the process of credit creation. Now we are able to see that changes in the level of spending may originate with changes in the supply of credit.

Without any raise in salary I can increase my spending by using the instalment plan. Business firms, by borrowing, can spend more on plant and equipment and governments can always increase their spending without waiting for larger tax revenues. Governments can borrow even more easily than the rest of us. In short, an increase in spending can come about because more things are bought on credit. And, as we learned in the last chapter, the banking system may create credit.

To sum up: changes in the level of spending affect prices. These changes may be caused by changes in the level of output and employment. When our incomes go up we spend more and when incomes generally are rising a great many people contribute to an increase in spending. Similarly, when incomes fall, people spend less. It is for this reason that the price level tends to move in the same direction as national income. But changes in the level of spending may also originate with changes in the supply of money. An increase in spending which will push prices up may begin with an expansion of credit; a decrease in spending and a decline in prices will follow a contraction of credit.

Rising Prices at Full Employment

When total spending is on the increase an important question arises. Are production and income really rising? Or is it simply that more money is being spent and only prices are rising? In either case prices will rise, but the two situations are very different.

In the first case, when national income is really rising, the production of goods and services that people want is also rising. Therefore, although the increase in spending will push up prices, the increase in *production* will check the rise in prices. To see why, let us go back to the price of eggs. The reason for a rising price, you will recall, is the shortage of eggs. Accordingly, when more eggs reach the market the price of eggs will tend to level off because there are fewer unsatisfied buyers. Similarly, when more goods and services of every kind pour into the stores, the pressure on prices is checked. As long as production can go on increasing, increased spending cannot push prices up very far.

Now let us look at the second situation — a spending spree financed on credit when resources are already fully employed. If the whole labour force is already fully employed, production cannot increase. We might turn out more cars if we made fewer tractors, but the grand total of goods and services produced must remain near to last year's level. Suppose, then, that governments and business firms borrow from the banks and proceed to spend the borrowed money. Spending will go on rising, but the rising prices cannot be checked by greater supplies of goods and services. This is the problem of "too much money". As the extra money is spent prices must rise. If the expansion of credit continues when production of goods and services cannot be increased, prices will rise indefinitely.

Twenty Years of Rising Prices

What we have said about rising prices can be illustrated from Canadian experience. Going back twenty years — to the late nineteen-thirties — we find an illustration

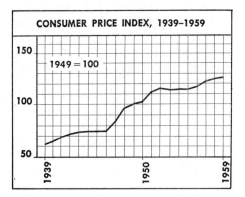

CONSUMER PRICE INDEX, 1939–1959

1949 = 100

of the first case discussed above: prices rising when production and incomes were also rising. At that time the Canadian economy was beginning to emerge from the great depression. More spending meant more jobs and higher incomes, and also higher prices, but as unemployment declined production increased too and prices rose slowly. With the outbreak of war the pace of recovery speeded up. As more and more workers found jobs consumer spending rose. The construction of new plants and factories and conversion of old ones meant large increases in investment spending. And the federal government, to finance the war effort, drew up the largest budgets

to date. Yet in spite of all this spending prices did not rise rapidly through the early war years because production was also increasing rapidly. More goods and services kept appearing to satisfy the greater amount of spending, and so general shortages did not appear. The pressure on prices was not very great.

By 1942 the Canadian economy was in a very different situation. Because the whole labour force was finally drawn into jobs, production could not *go on* increasing at the pace set in 1940 and 1941. And with much of the labour force devoted to the war, either in the armed services or in defence plants, supplies of many consumers' goods began to run short. These shortages on the production side did nothing to abate the demand for goods. Canadian farmers and factory workers, soldiers and sailors, were all earning money and eager to spend. The *attempt* to buy more goods than the Canadian economy could produce could only push up prices. In 1942, then, we moved into the second situation described above — rising prices at full employment. If the government had not stepped in with direct controls on prices, Canadians would have had first-hand experience of a major inflation.

Inflation in post-war Canada is described in Section 4. There we shall find another illustration of rising prices at full employment. Through most of the post-war period our resources have been fully employed and spending has increased more rapidly than production. Of course, production has increased as a new generation joined the labour force, as immigrants arrived in numbers, as new resources were discovered and new techniques applied in production. But the economy could not produce enough goods and services to satisfy the demands of spenders. We have had to look to the government to keep inflation within bounds. Before we describe the fight against inflation we shall learn more about the effects of inflation upon different groups in the community.

3. EFFECTS OF A CHANGING PRICE LEVEL

Is it better to have prices rising (inflation) or falling (deflation)? Either way, a change in the price level has repercussions on the rest of the economy, some of which are good and others bad. Either way, these changes strike the individual in a very vital spot — his income! And since we live in a price system it is well worth knowing what may happen to us when the price level rises or falls. In this section we shall see that changes in the price level may affect incomes in two ways: by changing the *distribution* of income, and by changing the pace of *production*.

Effects on the Distribution of Income

Rising prices mean that each dollar buys less. Yet the effect of rising prices is not, as you might think, to make us all poorer. Nor do falling prices make everybody richer. With rising prices *some* people get poorer, but others get richer. The same is true of falling prices. The explanation is that different *kinds* of income are affected in different ways. The wage earner, for example, fares differently than the man whose income is in the form of profits. Since a change in the price level makes some incomes larger and others smaller we say that it alters the *distribution* of income. If, as a result of inflation, your income increases more rapidly than the national income you are getting a larger share of the national income. If your income increases **less** rapidly your share of the national income is declining.

Who Gains from Rising Prices?

Let us look first at the people who stand to gain from inflation. One of these is the average business man. Because it is *more spending* that pushes prices up, his sales are bound to increase, and with larger sales the average business man can expect larger profits. Indeed, many business men with less than average ability will make larger profits simply by being in business! For example, the XY Shoe Store might order shoes to sell at $6.95 a pair and find, when the shipment arrives, that similar shoes are now selling for $7.95. The store makes an extra dollar a pair, thanks to the rise in price! Business men who make such easy profits are sometimes accused of "profiteering" and many people blame profiteers for rising prices. This is not the case. Prices are pushed up — as we learned in Section 2 — by the increased spending of the whole community. A conscientious merchant who decided to sell his shoes at $6.95 would not affect the price of shoes in general.

A second group which benefits by rising prices is stockholders. Inflation brings larger profits to corporations as well as to individual proprietors. People who have invested in corporation shares will reap the benefit of these larger profits. Investment in real estate also pays well during an inflation because the prices of land and buildings will rise along with other prices. This does not mean, however, that everyone with investment income will favour rising prices. Only *owners* benefit; creditors do not. The corporate bondholder, as we shall see, is in a very different position.

Inflation, then, favours individuals whose incomes depend on *profits*, namely business men and stockholders. Greater profits are the result, in part, of the greater volume of sales, as described above, and also of the fact that costs tend to rise less rapidly than prices. Some costs, such as interest on bonds, mortgages and other debts, are fixed and cannot increase. Wages and salaries, as we shall see, also tend to lag behind the rise in prices. So average revenue rises more than average cost and the difference, which is the average profit margin, widens.

The position of farmers in Canada is a peculiar one. Farm incomes also depend upon profits but farm incomes are depressed relative to urban incomes even in the best of times. Consequently, in periods of rising prices, although farmers as a group are not well off, they are better off than they would be if prices were falling. In periods of falling prices, farm product prices fall much more than the prices farmers have to pay for the things they buy. For this reason farmers are included among those who benefit from inflation.

Before we go on to other kinds of income receivers we must add a third group which stands to gain when prices rise: the people who *owe* money. Thus Mr. Brown, whom we met on page 111, found that his house was easier to pay for than he expected. His mortgage payments stayed the same and he met them with dollars that could buy less and less of other things.

Who Suffers from Rising Prices?

Now we turn the coin over and consider the people who find themselves poorer as a result of rising prices. Heading the list are those who depend upon money incomes that do not rise at all. Bond interest, government annuities, insurance benefits, are all "fixed" incomes. They do not rise with inflation. A hundred-dollar-a-month annuity will yield its owner a hundred dollars a month whatever happens to prices. If prices double the annuity will only buy half as many goods and services. Old-age pensions and other government allowances may be a somewhat better source of income when prices are rising because governments can increase them. But the increases are not likely to keep pace with prices and so these incomes also shrink. When prices are rising one wants an income that will rise as much as prices. Unfortunately, people with fixed or relatively fixed incomes are very often the ones who can least afford to have their purchasing power lowered. Men and women past working age, widows with small children, are examples of people who find it difficult to get new jobs to increase their incomes. Thus inflation is particularly hard on the groups that are least able to protect themselves.

The last group to consider — wage and salary earners — is the largest of all and when prices are rising this group too must be listed among the losers. While some — such as salaried executives and workers in the strongest unions — may manage to keep their incomes rising as fast as prices, average wages are likely to lag behind. Some wages and salaries are particularly "sticky" or slow to change. Most of the "white collar workers" — clerks, ministers, teachers, civil servants and so on — fall into this category.

Do unions cause prices to rise? This charge is often made by sections of the press and public in times of rising prices, especially when big unions go on strike to get raises for their members. Indeed, the unions are more often blamed than the "profiteering" business man. Here again we must remember where the initial pressure on prices comes from. It is extra spending that generates inflation. If governments and business firms and consumers all set out to buy more things, and the banking system creates the money to finance the extra spending, prices will rise whatever the unions do.

Of course, higher wages do add fuel to the flames. The company that is forced to pay higher wages will raise prices if it can do so. Thus big business and big unions together may raise prices to the consumer and, in a period of rising prices, the higher wages won by unions become one more inflationary pressure. But they are not the only pressure. Prices are pushed up and maintained at high levels primarily by the expansion of credit. And when prices are rising it is unreasonable to expect labour to watch wages shrink without attempting to protect themselves. To satisfy their members the unions must seek higher wages. However, only the most powerful are ever in a position to exploit the consumer. When prices rise rapidly the wages of labour as a whole tend to lag behind the rise in prices.

The effects of rising prices on the distribution of income are summarized in Table 8 (p. 133). Column 1 lists the classes of income receivers who receive a larger share of the national income while column 2 shows the ones who get a declining share.

How Falling Prices Change the Distribution of Income

When prices are falling the effects on the distribution of income are quite different. In general, people who gain with rising prices are losers when prices are falling and those who gain in periods of deflation lose in periods of inflation. For a summary of the effects of falling prices you can reverse the headings in Table 8. Now bondholders and pensioners and the others in column 2 appear as winners; the people in column 1 become losers.

crease are also slow to fall. While wage earners may take wage cuts and some pensions may be reduced, these money incomes are not likely to fall as much as the prices of the things they buy. Thus the school teacher, the postman, the old-age pensioner and a host of others will get a larger share of the national income as the purchasing power of their money incomes rises.

At this point the question of rising prices versus falling prices must appear more puzzling than ever. If some people get richer when prices rise while others are better off

---

TABLE 8

Rising Prices and the Distribution of Income

Winners	Losers
Business men and others with income in the form of profits	Bondholders—and other "fixed" income receivers
Most farmers	Pensioners and other relatively fixed income receivers
Owners of stocks and real estate	Most wage and salary earners
Anybody who owes money (debtors)	Anybody to whom money is owed (creditors)

The reasons can be sketched very briefly. Profits fall for two reasons. Falling prices accompany less spending and profits fall because of the decline in sales. The profit margin on each sale also tends to decline because some costs are fixed and others fall more slowly than prices. Even the shrewdest business man cannot maintain profits in the face of lower sales, and for many the loss of sales may be so great that profits shrink to zero and turn into losses. If the fall in the price level persists corporations are forced to lower dividends or even to declare no dividends at all.

Turning to the other side, we find incomes that decline much less than profits or dividends — and some that will not fall at all. Fixed incomes that cannot increase — like bond interest and annuities — cannot decrease either and, since any fixed income will buy more when prices are falling, persons with fixed incomes are better off. Similarly, incomes that were slow to in-

when prices fall, how can we say which is the more desirable for the country as a whole? Your own preference might be influenced by the way you make your living, whether as a business man, an old-age pensioner or as a clerk in an office. It might also depend on whether you had payments to make on a mortgage, or had money owing to you! However, we cannot make a selection at this point because we do not have all the facts. The effects of changes in the price level are not confined to the *distribution* of income — as between profits, pensions, wages and so on. In addition, changes in the price level are usually accompanied by changes in the *size* of the total income to be distributed. Consequently, the level of production and hence the amount of income that is created must be considered. Once we have looked at the relation between rising or falling prices and *production* we will be better able to choose between them.

Effects on Production

We can be enthusiastic about rising prices when there is unemployment in the country because rising prices go with expanding output. The increase in spending that tends to raise prices also stimulates production and employment. Rising prices indicate that more goods and services can be sold and more profits can be made. Such favourable conditions encourage business firms to take on more workers, and produce more goods and services, and this process of expansion may continue as long as more men and materials are available. Except for the special case of full employment, when production cannot be expanded, higher spending and rising prices bring about greater output and higher incomes.

Falling prices, the result of a decrease in spending, have opposite effects on production. Business firms make fewer sales and smaller profits (often actual losses). This leads them to restrict production and employment. The stores place smaller orders with the wholesalers. Wholesalers order fewer goods from the manufacturers and manufacturing firms, in turn, reduce their orders for raw materials. Thus, output grows smaller, fewer workers are needed, and incomes shrink right down the line of production.

Inflation Versus Deflation

Can we say now which is better? Actually the ideal solution is a stable price level with full employment. But if we have difficulty achieving and maintaining full employment a case can be made for a slowly *rising* price level because of its stimulating effect on output and employment. We want the total output of goods and services as large as possible in order to have the highest possible national income. If national income is getting smaller there is less to go around no matter how it is divided up. At anything less than full employment, then, we would choose rising rather than falling prices.

Who might quarrel with this verdict? Let us consult the list of losers in Table 8. With rising prices most wage and salary earners were counted losers because their incomes fail to keep up with prices. However, although they may lose on the redistribution of incomes, wage earners as a whole gain more than they lose if rising prices create jobs and incomes for more people. A man with a job is much better off even if it takes ten dollars from his pay cheque to buy what nine dollars from his unemployment insurance used to buy. Hence wage and salary earners as a group are not losers when rising prices are part of the return to full employment.

What about creditors? They lose in an inflation because they are repaid with dollars that buy less, but the fact that creditors find it easier to collect when employment and incomes are expanding will offset some of this loss. If falling prices mean lower production and employment some creditors cannot collect at all!

There is one other group in the list of losers — people with fixed incomes. They have nothing at all to gain from rising prices. Since incomes from pensions and annuities do not vary with production people living on pensions and annuities do not share in rising production and they lose part of their incomes to rising prices. This group is always better off when prices are falling.

4. THE POST-WAR INFLATION

The case for rising prices, as we have seen, rests on the stimulus they give to production. When there is unemployment the good effects of slowly rising prices can outweigh their disadvantages. But what is the verdict when production cannot be increased? Obviously rising prices must then be viewed in a different light. Then rising prices cannot create jobs and incomes — since everybody is already working — but they can and do change the distribution of income. And redistribution of income through changing price levels does more harm than good. Rising prices at full employment are clearly undesirable.

This kind of undesirable inflation has plagued people and governments all over the world for the better part of two decades. Inflation has seldom been so persistent in the past. World War I was followed by a severe inflation, but by 1921 (that is, within three years after the war) the price level in most countries was declining rapidly. How different the inflation which followed World War II! The upward movement in prices has scarcely paused since wartime price controls were removed. The current inflation is also remarkable in its severity, although, in this respect, Canadians are lucky. Our price level is more than double the pre-war level — in England the increase in the price level is more than three times pre-war, in France twenty times! In some countries even the French inflation appears relatively mild.

Why have prices risen so much? There is not space to explore the facts for every country but we can explain the major reasons for inflation in Canada. Indeed, we have already found the basic trouble in the fact that spending has increased more rapidly than production (page 130). Now let us investigate this post-war rise in spending.

Consumer Spending

To begin with, immediately following the war, there was an immense "backlog" of unsatisfied consumer wants, the porduct of ten years of low incomes through the depression plus five years of wartime shortages. There was also money to spend. Canadians had jobs and incomes and also large savings put aside during the war. So, as soon as the war was over, Canadian consumers set about satisfying their wants. Spending rose sharply. Not only did we want new cars and household appliances but also more and better food, clothing and shelter than we had had in the past. The growth of population added many new buyers. New products — like television and

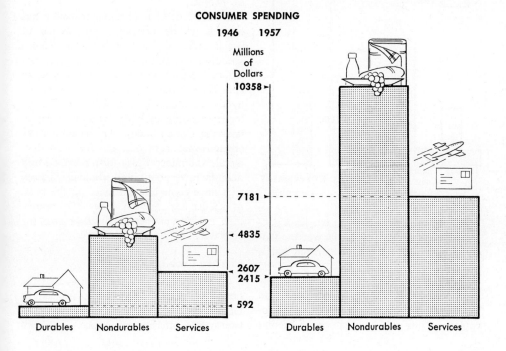

CONSUMER SPENDING

1946   1957

Millions
of
Dollars

10358 ►|

7181 ►

◄ 4835

2607
2415 ►

◄ 592

Durables   Nondurables   Services   Durables   Nondurables   Services hi-fi record players — swelled the list of wants. Only a lack of money could have dammed the flood of spending. But to savings and current income new money was added through instalment buying and other credit arrangements. Thus Canadian consumers spent more rapidly than Canadian producers of consumer goods could increase output.

Business and the Government

In the post-war rise in spending, consumers were not the chief offenders. By greatly increasing expenditures on plant and equipment Canadian business firms played a major role in raising prices. Vast sums went into the expansion called forth by the growth in consumer markets, and other billions went to exploit new resources, such as iron, uranium, oil and gas.

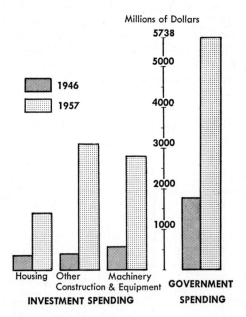

Millions of Dollars

1946
1957

5738
5000
4000
3000
2000
1000

Housing   Other   Machinery
Construction & Equipment   **GOVERNMENT**
INVESTMENT SPENDING   **SPENDING**

A third important element has been government spending. Before the war the federal government spent approximately half a billion dollars a year. In 1958–9 federal expenditures totalled $6 billion. Over the same period expenditures by provincial and municipal governments more than quadrupled. Thus we have a very different

economy in the post-war world. Government spending on such a scale is a new development and a major factor in the post-war inflation.

Government expenditures that are financed by borrowing from the banks are particularly inflationary because they increase the amount of money in circulation. During the war the government could not raise all the funds it needed by taxing and borrowing from the public. It had to borrow from the banks on a large scale. As a result, we started the post-war period with a greatly swollen money supply. More recently the federal government has again been a large borrower from the banks.

How can we account for the tremendous upsurge in activity by governments? At the municipal level the chief driving force has been the growth of population. Year by year, as cities spread across the open countryside, Canadians have built mile upon mile of city streets and sidewalks, new schools by the score. Investment in each and every service that municipal governments supply has had to be multiplied many times to meet the needs of larger numbers of people.

At the federal level a major factor has been a greatly expanded programme of social services. And since 1950 defence spending has put an enormous and persistent pressure on the economy. Here we consider not only the large sums expended by the Canadian government but also defence spending by other nations, particularly the United States. This spending has created vast new markets for Canadian metals and minerals, for farm products and manufactured goods, and whole new industries have come into existence on the basis of defence demand. To a very large degree, then, inflation has been a consequence of the cold war.

Can We Curb Inflation?

So far Canadians have been spared the horror of hyper-inflation as experienced in Greece and the more moderate dose of twenty-fold inflation in France. But with inflation at full employment there is always the danger that rising prices will get out of hand. Because the rise in prices *cannot* be checked by increased supplies of goods and services, the inflation must be controlled through government action.

Several remedies are available. One, which we used in wartime, is to put direct controls on prices. This means that sellers cannot raise prices beyond specified limits. Price controls worked well in Canada during the war, but control of prices by government decree is not as easy as it sounds. Enforcement is difficult and expensive, particularly if people generally do not accept and support the system of price control. In peacetime few Canadians admit the need. Another reason for avoiding direct price controls is that free prices have the job of guiding economic activity. If the federal government controlled prices it would also have to decide the relation between prices. In other words, the job of directing economic activity would be taken over by the federal government. Still another argument against direct controls is that they do not strike at the root of the problem. Price controls can suppress the effect of inflationary spending, for a time, but they cannot solve the problem at its source which is excessive spending based upon the expansion of bank credit. Therefore, as a defence against inflation, they must be regarded as only a temporary expedient.

The direct way to control inflation is to control spending. High taxes are one way to curb spending: the more we pay in taxes the less we have to spend. High taxes also work to reduce inflationary spending by governments. When governments spend more than they raise in taxes they may finance all or part of the difference by borrowing from the banking system. As we have noted, this will increase still further the amount of money in circulation. If they borrow only from the public they add to the

pressure on a limited supply of savings. In a period of inflation, therefore, governments should pay for all expenditures out of tax receipts. Indeed, as we learned in Chapter 8, they should aim at a budget surplus — that is, tax receipts should exceed government expenditures.

Spending may also be controlled by limiting the amount of credit available to persons and business firms. On several occasions in recent years the Bank of Canada has put the brakes on the creation of credit.

Perhaps the most logical place to check excessive spending would be to reduce government spending. However, it is not easy to find agreement on what parts of the programme to eliminate. Less for defence? Fewer social services? Most Canadians support the government's decisions on both social services and defence-spending. Indeed, the change of government in 1957 was followed by an expansion of federal-spending to an all-time record high and the largest peacetime deficit in history. Federal borrowing obliged the banking system to increase the money supply by over a billion dollars in a single year.

At this point we are forced to recognize that the problem of inflation, which we call an economic problem, is not an economic problem at all. Inflation could be curbed if Canadians were prepared to live within their means and to require their government to do the same. Instead, we want to have our cake and eat it too. It is not the fault of the average citizen if he fails to see that there is a choice, but we cannot win the fight against inflation unless governments and the general public come to understand the problem. Given this understanding, and the will to curb inflation, Canadians could agree to the necessary measures: less credit, higher taxes, and less government spending in periods of high production and employment.

QUESTIONS FOR DISCUSSION

1. Why do prices tend to rise in periods of prosperity? Can prices rise when employment and national income are *not* increasing? Explain.

2. Consider the situation described briefly in Chapter 9 in which the government printed a new $10 bill for every Canadian. On the basis of the analysis in this chapter enlarge upon the probable effects upon the community assuming (a) a large amount of unemployment and (b) full employment.

3. Compile a family budget, based on current prices, and convert it to prices of 1980 on the assumption of a rise in prices equal to the rise that occurred from 1939 to 1959 (see chart of consumer price index, page 130).

Look up the median income of an urban family today and calculate what income would be needed to provide the same level of living in 1980 if prices should rise at the assumed rate.

4. Explain why increases in production serve to check a rising price level. In view of the tremendous upsurge of production in post-war Canada how do you account for the continued upward movement of prices?

5. Contrast the inflationary pressures which existed in the early years of World War II (1940-1) and in the Korean war period (1950-1).

6. In our discussion of money we concluded that money would serve us better if its value were the same at all times. Explain why we do not have such an ideal money. Now imagine that all prices were "frozen" at the level prevailing on a given date. Can you think of some of the *disadvantages* which would follow? (Review the role of prices as described in Chapter 3.)

7. In Chapter 10 we studied changes in the supply of money and saw how these changes may affect the economy's performance. Now we find that the causes of inflation may be monetary in their origin, or they may not, while some combine both non-monetary and monetary factors. An upsurge in consumer spending, for example, may be partly due to an increase in employment and higher incomes, but easy credit terms will also help us to spend more. Examine other sources of inflation in this way.

8. "The total supply of money is not easily controlled" (Chapter 10). In theory, the government has considerable power to influence the supply of money yet increases in the money supply have been more rapid than we would like. Why? Prepare a class discussion on this topic.

9. Municipal governments in Canada have spent more than their current receipts in every year since the war. The reasons — and the effects — may be inferred from the discussion in this chapter. From the standpoint of inflation, municipal policy seems misguided. It would be less inflationary if the costs of expanding services had been met to a greater extent from tax receipts. On the other hand, municipal taxpayers believe that taxes have increased too much. Opposition from the voters has prevented local governments from raising more in taxes. In the light of this experience, discuss the question: Is it possible to achieve sound government policies in a democracy?

10. In 1960 the federal budget's provision for defence amounted to approximately $1.5 billion and represented 26 per cent of the federal budget. Describe some of the possible economic consequences of disarmament.

PART III

Chapter 12

The Theory of Price in Commodity Markets: Pure Competition

1. PRELIMINARY

The study of prices is the core of economics because the job of organizing production and assigning incomes is done by prices. To understand how our economy works we must know how prices are determined. We begin with the price of commodities. In this chapter our purpose is to find out what determines price in competitive markets. In the next chapter we shall study pricing of commodities under conditions of monopoly and imperfect competition. Finally, in Chapter 14, we turn our attention to the wages of labour and pricing of the other factors of production.

At times our subject matter will seem far removed from the real world around us. You must keep in mind that our intention is not to describe actual markets. Rather, it is to uncover theoretical principles which explain how a market economy works. In any science we study theory in an effort to explain events in the world around us. The theory of gravity is an example from physical science. The theory of price is an example from economics. But real events are never simple. This problem is solved for the natural sciences in the laboratory. In a controlled experiment the force of gravity, for example, can be measured under ideal conditions. But we cannot pull society into a laboratory to conduct experiments on its economic behaviour. Instead we must imagine how people would behave under ideal circumstances. Then we can introduce the complications that exist in the real world. In this way it is possible to discover the forces which shape our economic life.

Our study of price begins (Section 2) in the market square of any town. Here we are introduced to the two great market forces of demand and supply and we see how, in this particular market, demand and supply determine a price for eggs. The process described in Section 2 is the basis of all price theory. But it is not a complete account of the price of eggs, steak, shoes or any of the things we buy each day. In Section 3 we see why our egg market is a special case which we call "pure competition". In Chapter 13 we shall move a step closer to the real world by considering price in other kinds of markets. We see, first, how price is set under conditions of pure monopoly, then in markets with varying degrees of competition and monopoly. The vast majority of actual prices are determined in markets of the latter kind.

2. DEMAND AND SUPPLY

Why Eggs at 50 Cents a Dozen?

Have you ever wondered how the different prices in a supermarket get to be what they are? Suppose you were asked: *why* are they are? Suppose you were asked: *why* are eggs 50 cents a dozen? You might say, for a start, that this price was set by the manager. On reflection, you might add that it costs something to produce eggs, get them to town, grade and package them and put them on the shelves so that 50 cents probably represents the cost of production, including profit for the store. Yet this is only part of the answer. All these costs enter into the price of eggs but they do not determine it.

To see why, suppose that eggs did cost 50 cents to produce but no one was willing to pay that much. Would the store go on stocking 50-cent eggs? Obviously not. There is no profit in goods that cannot be sold. To sell the eggs the store would have to *lower* their price until they would sell. Thus buyers as well as sellers influence price. Because the price is stamped on the package, the buyers' role is not so obvious, but it is no less important than the role of sellers. Now let us see how the actions of *both* buyers and sellers determine the price of eggs.

Illustration in the Market Square

Our scene is a market square where a great many farmers have come to sell their eggs and a great many housewives have come to buy. As the market opens, buying and selling begin at the price of the previous day. Now suppose that farmers have brought in more eggs today than yesterday although buyers' wants have not changed. Clearly, if yesterday's price prevailed, all the eggs could not be sold. Some farmers, therefore, will try lowering their price. And as word gets around that eggs can be bought at this lower price no one will pay the higher price. Thus the price of eggs is driven down.

In the opposite situation, when the supply is unchanged but buyers want more eggs, the price of eggs will be driven up. To get the extra eggs they want some housewives will pay more and, as this news gets around, the price will change for everyone. The new price will depend upon the pattern of buying and selling — the demand for eggs and the supply of eggs. In other words, demand and supply determine price.

Demand, and the Factors Behind It

Someone has said that even a parrot may become an economist: "all he must learn are the two words Supply and Demand". It is true that both terms are commonly used, but to understand how supply and demand determine prices we must first find out what they mean.

Demand, to begin with, is not only the state of wanting eggs (or bread or shoes). Mrs. Jones may want eggs because her family likes them, but her *demand* is the number of eggs she is prepared to buy. If she has come to market without her purse she has no demand for eggs at all.

The second point about demand is that it *varies* with the price. Mrs. Jones' demand is not a single quantity, such as three dozen. She may be prepared to buy three dozen eggs if the price is 35 cents, but at 25 cents she may buy five dozen and at 50 cents only two dozen. In other words, she is prepared to buy more eggs when their price is low, fewer when their price is high. The reason is easy to see. When eggs are dear a careful housewife will try to substitute cheaper foods for the high-priced eggs, so she buys less. When eggs are cheap she is more likely to bake angel food cakes and serve omelettes as a substitute for meat, and so she buys more eggs.

Another major influence on demand is income. Mrs. Jones has only so much to spend. Out of that income and with a given price she buys some quantity of eggs. With a higher income she could buy more eggs at that same price. So, as a general rule, the demand for eggs will rise with a rise in income.

Not all housewives have the same demand as Mrs. Jones. A few may be so wealthy that their purchases are unaffected by a rise in price. Others may like eggs so little that they buy no more at a lower price. The Smiths may buy more eggs at every price because their family is larger, because their income is higher, or because they are very fond of eggs. Generally speaking, however, most of the housewives in our market will react in much the same way as Mrs. Jones: they will buy *more* eggs when the price is low, *fewer* eggs when the price is high. And so we can think of a *total* demand for eggs which might be as follows:

Price of eggs per dozen	Quantity of eggs that would be bought at each price
15 cents	800 dozen
20 cents	700 dozen
25 cents	600 dozen
30 cents	500 dozen
35 cents	400 dozen
40 cents	300 dozen
45 cents	200 dozen

This table is called a demand schedule. It shows how many eggs would be bought at various prices in a particular market and at a particular time. Underlying this demand schedule and reflected in it are the factors that influence buyers. These include the personal tastes, incomes, and size of all the families who buy eggs. As we shall see later, any one of these factors can change. But for a given time and place — our market square on a Saturday morning — it is quite accurate to think of a particular demand for eggs as described in our schedule. Once we have looked at supply we can put our knowledge of demand to work in explaining prices.

Supply, and the Factors Behind It

The supply of eggs is the quantity which farmers are prepared to sell at each different price. For example, expecting a price of 30 cents a dozen they may bring 500 dozen eggs to market; at 40 cents, 600 dozen and at 25 cents, only 450 dozen. The supply of eggs, then, could be described as follows:

Price of eggs per dozen	Quantity of eggs that would be offered at each price
15 cents	350 dozen
20 cents	400 dozen
25 cents	450 dozen
30 cents	500 dozen
35 cents	550 dozen
40 cents	600 dozen
45 cents	650 dozen

The supply schedule, you will notice, is just the opposite to demand. This time, as the price goes up, the quantity increases, and at a lower price the quantity is smaller. Why? Just as we looked at the individual buyer, Mrs. Jones, to explain demand, so must we turn to the individual seller to explain supply.

Farmer Brown's profit margin is the difference between his cost of producing a dozen eggs and the return he gets per dozen. This return, of course, is the price of eggs. Now if the price should rise Farmer Brown could afford the higher cost of producing more eggs. He could buy more feed, for example, and hire more help to look after the hens. By spending more on the care of his hens he would get more eggs from them. At this point you may object. Why should a higher price lead him to incur the higher costs of producing more eggs? Would his profit not be greater if he kept his costs as low as possible? The answer is *no*. As long as the price of eggs is higher than the cost of producing an extra dozen there is profit in producing more eggs. The price of an extra dozen will more than offset the extra cost of producing it. If Farmer Brown fails to increase his output he will be sacrificing profits. Consequently, a higher price calls forth more eggs. The individual farmer finds that he can add to his profits by producing more eggs. Thus the supply of eggs increases as the price of eggs goes up.

The "Equilibrium" Price

Returning to our market we put together the figures used to illustrate demand and supply.

Demand	Price of eggs per dozen	Supply
(number of eggs that will be bought)		(number of eggs offered for sale)
800 dozen	15 cents	350 dozen
700 dozen	20 cents	400 dozen
600 dozen	25 cents	450 dozen
500 dozen	30 cents	500 dozen
400 dozen	35 cents	550 dozen
300 dozen	40 cents	600 dozen
200 dozen	45 cents	650 dozen

Now we can see what the price of eggs should be. There is only one price (30 cents) where the demand is equal to the supply. We call this the *equilibrium price*. It is a price that can last because, when demand and supply are the same, there is no reason for the price to change. And because any other price would change, only the "equilibrium" price can prevail.

To prove the point, suppose farmers had expected the price to be 40 cents. You can see that there would be eggs in abundance (600 dozen) but not enough buyers (300 dozen would be bought). Accordingly, some sellers would cut their price and the price of eggs would fall. If farmers had expected a price of 25 cents eggs would be in short supply and the most eager buyers would bid up the price. Nor would a price of 35 cents do. Again there are not enough buyers. Indeed, there is only *one price* where neither buyers nor sellers will have reason to raise or lower it. It is the price at which the number of eggs buyers want is the same as the number of eggs farmers are willing to sell. We say, therefore, that demand and supply determine an equilibrium price at the point where the demand is equal to the supply.

Illustration with a Graph

Plotting supply and demand schedules on a graph is a good way of illustrating the process of price determination. In Figure 1 below we have plotted the supply and demand schedules from page 142. The price of eggs is shown on the vertical axis; the quantities of eggs demanded and supplied are shown on the horizontal axis. In this way our demand schedule becomes a demand curve (D), our supply schedule becomes a supply curve (S).

To read the diagram, select any price and draw a horizontal line to intersect the two curves. In Figure 1 a line has been drawn at 35 cents. By dropping perpendiculars from the points of intersection to the horizontal axis you can read the quantities demanded and supplied at that price. At a price of 35 cents the quantity demanded is 400 dozen, the quantity supplied is 550 dozen.

Now notice that the two curves intersect. At a price of 30 cents the quantity demanded is equal to the quantity supplied. This, of course, is the equilibrium price.

Is Our Illustration Realistic?

How do we know that 500 dozen eggs will be bought when the price is 30 cents, or that farmers will bring in 600 dozen at a price of 40 cents? In a real market we do not have such precise information. Nevertheless, buyers and sellers *do* act in the way we have described. At a lower price buyers would be willing to take more eggs; at a higher price farmers would bring more eggs to market. An arithmetical illustration makes it easier to see the general process through which the actions of buyers and sellers determine price. Here we can see clearly that the price is not decided by the manager of a store, nor by a government board, nor by a group of farmers. The price of eggs is worked out as eggs are bought and sold, depending on how many buyers want and how many sellers are offering. In other words, the price is decided by demand and supply.

Changes in Demand and Supply

When we say that our equilibrium price is a price that can *last* we do not mean that the price of eggs is fixed for all time to come. In our illustration the price of 30 cents will last as long as demand and supply do not change. This may be a month, a week, or only a day. Sooner or later demand or supply *will* change. Then a new price will

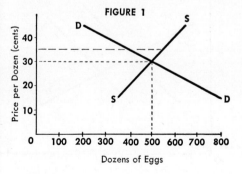

FIGURE 1

Price per Dozen (cents)

Dozens of Eggs

be worked out to fit the new conditions. To see how, let us take a change in demand.

Suppose that incomes in the district rise, or that more people decide to eat eggs for breakfast, so that the demand for eggs is increased. An increase in demand means that more eggs will be bought *at every price*. So we have to draw a new picture of demand. In the demand schedule on page 142 we would substitute higher figures which show a greater demand for eggs. The following table shows a new demand, the old supply, and what happens to the price.

New Demand	Price of eggs per dozen	Supply
(number of eggs that will be bought)		(number of eggs offered for sale)
950 dozen	15 cents	350 dozen
850 dozen	20 cents	400 dozen
750 dozen	25 cents	450 dozen
650 dozen	30 cents	500 dozen
550 dozen	35 cents	550 dozen
450 dozen	40 cents	600 dozen
350 dozen	45 cents	650 dozen

At a price of 30 cents the housewives now want more eggs than sellers will offer and so the price of eggs will be bid up. The new equilibrium price is found at 35 cents where demand and supply are equal again. Thus an increase in demand, when supply is unchanged, results in a higher price.

Similarly, we could see what happens with a decrease in demand. Our demand schedule would show *smaller* quantities at every price and the new equilibrium would be at a lower price.

Supply can also change. Anything that lowers costs — a new kind of feed, say, or a decline in farm wages — means that *at every price* farmers are willing to offer more eggs for sale. This is an increase in supply. Declining prices for other farm products, because they make the egg business more attractive, will also increase supply. On the other hand, higher costs or rising prices of other farm products are likely to bring about a decrease in the supply of eggs. The new supply schedule, whether higher or lower, will give us a new equilibrium price. But unlike changes in demand, which cause price to move in the same direction, changes in supply cause inverse movements in price. In other words, an increase in supply results in a *lower* price, a decrease in supply *raises* the price.

Illustration with a Graph

The influence of changes in demand and supply is more readily seen in a diagram. Take an increase in demand. This means that more eggs are bought at every price and so the demand curve shifts to the right. In Figure 2A the demand curve shifts from D_1 to D_2.

The effect upon price is easily seen. At the old equilibrium price (P_1) the quantity

FIGURE 2

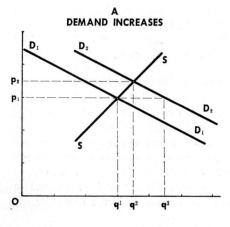

A
DEMAND INCREASES

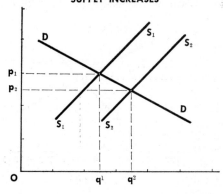

B
SUPPLY INCREASES

demanded (q_3) greatly exceeds the supply (q_1). The price will therefore rise. With higher prices farmers bring more eggs to market. We move up along the supply curve from P_1, the old equilibrium price, to P_2, the new and higher equilibrium price. The quantity supplied increases from q_1 to q_2.

Now turn to Figure 2B, where we illustrate the effects of an increase in supply. An increase in supply means that larger quantities are supplied at every price. And so the supply curve shifts to the right, in Figure 2B from S_1 to S_2. Moving down the demand curve we go from P_1, the old equilibrium price, to P_2, the new and lower equilibrium price.

In these two figures we see how an increase in demand raises price, how an increase in supply lowers price. Similarly we could illustrate the effects of a decrease in demand or a decrease in supply. In either case our curves would shift to the left. As an exercise, draw the curves and trace through the changes in the price and quantities that would follow a decrease in demand or supply.

The Influence of Time

When we consider changes in supply and demand we must add a new element: time. The response of producers to a change in the price of eggs depends upon the *period of time* during which this response is measured. While a higher price will lead them to produce more eggs, the supply cannot be increased immediately. Similarly, it takes some time before a lower price results in a smaller supply of eggs.

In a very short period — say a single market day — there can be very little response. The supply brought to market will be a *fixed amount* determined by what farmers expected the price to be. A higher price could not add to this amount. Nor could a lower price decrease the supply when farmers are unwilling to take any eggs back to the farm. In this situation price will depend upon the relationship between demand and the *fixed* supply.

Over longer periods of time supply *will* respond to the prevailing price level, and changes in the quantities supplied will influence the price. If the market price is higher than expected, farmers will be induced to expand egg production. The initial expansion will not be great because it is limited by the existing number of hens, but an increase in supply will occur and this will work to lower price.

If the increase in demand is not large a new equilibrium may be reached very quickly. On the other hand, if the increase in the demand is large the price will remain at a high level, calling for still further increases in supply. Then, as time passes, flocks can be increased and the egg supply further expanded. Assuming no other changes in demand, price would move to a new equilibrium position where the larger quantity lowered price still further.

Economists commonly distinguish three supply situations: the immediate market situation, in which supply is relatively fixed; a short-run period, when expansion is limited by existing resources in the industry (the number of hens, in our illustration); and the long-run, which is a period long enough to allow additions to resources of every kind employed in the industry. The same treatment of time is followed when we consider contraction of the supply in response to an unprofitably low price.

When we take account of time on the supply side we have a better understanding of the equilibrium price. If changes in supply could come about *immediately* then an equilibrium price would always prevail. This cannot be true in fact because producers do not have perfect knowledge of all future market conditions and they cannot immediately adjust their output to current demand. However, the important thing is that actual prices do tend to move to their equilibrium level. Although a *particular* equilibrium price may never be reached, at all times price is moving to an equilibrium position. The equilibrium will change as often as there are changes in demand and supply.

3. AN IDEAL PRICE SYSTEM

In Section 2 our purpose was to show how the forces of demand and supply determine a single price. To make the task easier we chose a particular market situation, a "purely competitive" market. Now we must define pure competition. What are the conditions in our market square that make it a special case?

If we look at the world around us we will find few markets which meet the essential conditions of pure competition. The prices which are determined in most actual markets are *not* purely competitive prices. Nevertheless, in *all* markets we find demand and supply at work. A study of purely competitive markets, therefore, is a first step toward understanding the actual markets in our economy. It is also a way of estimating the shortcomings of our price system. A price system where *all* markets were purely competitive may be called an "ideal price system", and the study of its advantages will help us to understand the shortcomings of our own.

Pure Competition

The distinguishing characteristic of pure competition is that no individual buyer or seller can influence the price. Suppose that one giant firm supplied half of the eggs in the market. By holding back supplies that one seller *could* affect the price. Similarly, on the demand side, if a supermarket was buying a large part of the available supplies, its actions could affect the price of eggs. In purely competitive markets this kind of control is ruled out because there are a great many buyers and a great many sellers and no one of them is big enough to dominate the market. Farmer Brown makes a negligible contribution to the total supply of eggs; therefore, he cannot force the price up by refusing to sell. Buyers would simply go to the next stall. Nor can Mrs. Jones expect to buy her eggs for less than the going price.

It is true that if all the sellers got together and agreed to restrict the supply they could keep the price of eggs above the equilibrium price. But in a market with a great many sellers, each one contributing a small part of the total supply, such an agreement is most unlikely. The fact that there are also many buyers makes control on the buyers' side unlikely too.

Now suppose that Farmer Brown's eggs are a little better than those of his neighbour, or that some housewives think they are better. Then Farmer Brown could charge more for his eggs. In purely competitive markets this kind of control is also ruled out because the product is a *standardized* product. All products moving through the market are the same. Thus, grade A large from Farmer Brown are indistinguishable from grade A large produced by Farmer Smith. Therefore they sell at the same price. Mrs. Jones may choose to buy grade A or B (their prices will be different) but, wherever she buys, the price of each grade will be the same.

In markets of pure competition there is no control of any kind. Neither sellers nor buyers, as individuals, have any power to influence the price. And so it is the *sum of their actions* — how much they sell and how much they buy — that decides what price must be.

Advantages of Pure Competition

In the last section we looked at the *conditions* of pure competition. Now let us turn to the *results*. What are the advantages of having prices decided in this way? These were listed in Chapter 3 under the heading *Advantages of a Price System*. Now that we have some understanding of the price-making process we can see that actually these are the advantages of a *purely competitive* price system.

(1) *Lowest possible prices for consumers*

This guarantee applies to all prices. For each thing he buys the consumer pays a price just high enough to cover the cost of production, including a reasonable profit for efficient producers. To see why this must be so, you have only to look at the alternatives. If the price of eggs is *higher* than this minimum level, farmers must be making more than a reasonable profit. Large profits will attract other farmers into the egg business and, as the supply of eggs increases, the price will be pushed down. The process will go on as long as profits in producing eggs are higher than profits in alternative occupations; that is, until the price of eggs just covers the cost of production including an average profit. The fact that producers *prefer* the higher price is of no consequence. No one of them can keep price high by restricting output. The higher price, in fact, encourages all of them to produce more eggs, which will work to push price down.

The other alternative, a price so low that it fails to provide a reasonable profit, cannot last either. Farmers would simply switch to pigs or turkeys and the price of eggs would have to rise to call forth the eggs consumers want. In the long run, then, price can be neither higher nor lower than the minimum level defined above, and consumers get their eggs at the lowest possible price.

(II) Consumers plan production

The people who do the buying decide what goods and services are produced and in what quantities. We need not express our wants by writing letters to farmers, store-keepers, or factory managers; our wants are made known through prices. If we want to have more eggs we show it by *buying* more eggs. This pushes up the price and the higher price calls forth more eggs. If we decide to eat less pork our failure to buy up existing supplies will cause the price of pork to fall. Farmers will respond by producing less pork. What is produced, therefore, depends on what people buy. When our buying habits change, prices change to inform producers. In this way our new wishes set a new pattern of production.

It is true that we do not share equally in this process, and wants that cannot be expressed in buying do not count at all.

Nevertheless, consumers do plan production and each shares in the plan to the extent of his income.

(III) The consumer is king

The ideal price system assigns a high place to consumers. As we have seen, consumers plan production and buy all goods and services at the lowest possible prices. This concern for the consumer is worth emphasizing because, as consumers, we all share a common interest. We do not meet on common ground as producers. The interests of the farmer and the factory worker and the shareholder in large corporations very often conflict. But whatever our interest as producers we must all buy consumer goods and services. For that reason free enterprisers and socialists agree that the first step in achieving economic welfare is to subordinate the interest of producers to the interest of consumers.

(IV) Most efficient use of resources

Compared with the unlimited wants of people, the resources of land, labour and capital everywhere are scarce. All economic resources, therefore, should be used to best advantage. No economy, however wealthy, can afford waste. Here again the ideal price system earns high marks. Competitive prices help to make sure that resources are used to best advantage. If land is abundant and other factors scarce, then land will be cheap and other factors dear. Hence the farmer will use as much as he can of the cheap land, as little as he can of the labour and capital whose supply is more limited. If coal is expensive and water-power cheap, producers are compelled by the price system to generate electricity from water resources. In their search for profits producers in every field of production are led to economize on scarce factors, rely more on the cheap factors. Thus limited supplies of economic resources are used in the most efficient way possible within the framework of a price system, and this assures a maximum flow of goods and services to consumers.

Conclusions

When we look at the advantages of an ideal price system we are bound to ask: why is it that only an *ideal* price system can claim these desirable results? To find out, we must venture forth from the confines of pure competition and see *how price would differ* in other kinds of markets. This we shall do in Chapter 13. Before going on, however, we should recognize that pure competition is not ideal in every respect.

Pure competition is the best among the various ways to *organize production* within a free price system. But it is not the best way to distribute national income. An ideal price system would permit a large measure of inequality, much larger than Canadians would accept. Nor is this the only limitation of a purely competitive price system.

A system based upon the pursuit of profit by individuals cannot achieve all the economic objectives of a society because, inevitably, there are conflicts between the interests of individuals and the community as a whole. A profitable policy for the individual firm may be harmful to the community. Thus the waste products of industry may pollute streams and rivers; fumes or smoke from factories can lay waste the surrounding countryside. These are illustrations of the *social* limitations of a competitive price system. In a chapter on price it is enough to note that such limitations exist. Later, in our discussion of government (Chapter 15) and of alternative economic systems (Chapter 17) we shall estimate their importance.

QUESTIONS FOR DISCUSSION

1. Make a study of the price of eggs in your community. See whether a local grocery or dealer could supply you with the average price paid to suppliers, week by week, over the past year. (If you live in the West your local Farmers' Union would have such a record.) Plot your prices on a graph and discuss the possible reasons for the fluctuations.

2. In Chapter 6 we considered the major determinants of consumer demand. Prepare a list of possible changes that would bring about an *increase* in demand.

3. Illustrate with a graph: (1) an increase in the quantity demanded, (2) an increase in demand. (Remember that the first is shown by movement *along* the curve. Larger quantities will be bought at lower pieces. The second case represents an increase in the quantities which will be bought at *each* price.)

4. Reproduce the demand and supply curves from Figure 1. Using the following figures, draw a new supply curve.

Price of eggs per dozen	Number of eggs offered for sale
25 cents	200 dozen
30 cents	300 dozen
35 cents	400 dozen
40 cents	500 dozen

What does the new supply curve illustrate? How does it differ from the shift in the supply curve in Figure 2B? Explain what happens to the price in both cases and why.

5. The following graphs are used to illustrate three supply situations. Can you interpret them?

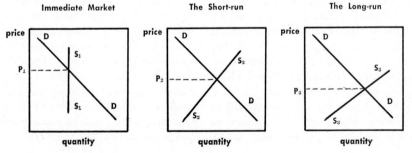

Chapter 13

The Theory of Price:
Monopoly and Imperfect Competition

The world of pure competition exists only in the economic textbooks. With a few exceptions, most of our markets are imperfect and our price system is a long way from the ideal price system. You may wonder whether it is worth studying the ideal price system at all. Would it not be more practical to see how prices are decided in the real world around us?

In fact, we have learned a great deal about real prices because all prices are determined by demand and supply. Tastes, incomes, costs of production: these and many other factors behind demand and supply shape prices in the real world as well as in our market square. The difference is this: in an ideal price system all are factors which individual buyers and sellers cannot control. Therefore, we can imagine a particular demand and a particular supply and we can say, as we did on page 143, *this* is what the price must be. When we consider the real world we shall have to take account of new factors, factors which do permit an element of control. And so the results are different. In this chapter we shall see how price will differ.

1. A PURE MONOPOLY

We begin with the case of a single seller or monopolist. The result, in terms of price and of quantities supplied and consumed, will enable us to contrast the disadvantages of pure monopoly and the advantages of pure competition.

Demand from the Standpoint of a Monopolist

In pure competition the seller cannot influence the price. He may sell more, he may sell less; but changes in the quantities supplied by any one seller are too small to affect the price. The monopolist, however, controls the whole supply. By putting more or less of his product on the market he can control the price. He will not charge the highest price possible, but neither will he charge the lowest price possible, the price which prevails in pure competition. To see why, we must follow the calculations which determine the price and output for a particular monopolist.

For illustration we use a municipal power company. The first table shows the company's demand schedule — that is, the quantities consumers would buy at different prices. The table also shows the revenue which each different point in the demand schedule would yield.

You will notice that this demand schedule has the same general appearance as the demand schedule for eggs. There is the same inverse relationship between sales (demand) and price. The lower the price the greater the sales. The third column, total revenue, is simply price times sales, and from this we derive the *extra* revenue from additional sales. (See column 4 in Table A.) Before we can say what price and output our

An electric power corporation is usually in a near-monopoly position. Pictured here is a generating station on the Ottawa River.

A

Municipal Power Company: Demand and Revenue

(1)	(2)	(3)	(4)
Sales in kilowatts per week	Price per kilowatt	Total Revenue	Extra Revenue from additional sales
(millions)	(cents)	($000's)	($000's)
10	5.0	500	....
11	4.8	528	28
12	4.7	552	24
13	4.5	585	21
14	4.3	602	17
15	4.1	615	13
16	3.9	624	9
17	3.7	629	5
18	3.5	630	1
19	3.3	627	−3
20	3.1	620	−7

monopolist will choose we must know something about his costs. These are shown in the following table.

For any producer the position of greatest profit can be defined as follows: it is the output at which the extra *revenue* from an additional unit of sales just offsets the extra *cost* of an additional unit of sales. If he

	B		
	Municipal Power Company: Output and Costs		
(1)	(2)	(3)	(4)
Production in kilowatts per week	Average Cost	Total Cost	Extra Cost from additional production
(millions)	(cents)	($000's)	($000's)
10	4.6	460	16
11	4.3	476	16
12	4.1	492	16
13	3.9	508	16
14	3.7	524	16
15	3.6	540	16
16	3.5	556	16
17	3.4	572	16
18	3.3	588	16
19	3.2	604	16
20	3.1	620	16

(Note: Average cost is rounded to nearest tenth of a cent.)

produces *more* the extra cost will be greater than the extra revenue. If he produces *less* he sacrifices profit because an addition to output would add more to revenue than to cost.

Our municipal power company would choose a level of output somewhere between 14 and 15 millions of kilowatts per week. At 14 million the extra revenue from the last million of output is $17,000 (Table A) and the extra cost is $16,000 (Table B). If the company expands to 15 million the additional cost is again $16,000 but the extra revenue is only $13,000. To expand output by a full million kilowatts would entail a loss. The best position is an output somewhat above 14 million but below 15 million. At this point the extra revenue from the additional sales would just equal the extra cost of these sales. To avoid small fractions we assume that the best output occurs at 14.5 million kilowatts with a price of 4.2 cents (see Column 2, Table A).

This price is not the highest possible price and for a very good reason. Higher prices yield lower total profits. (This is apparent in Table C below which combines Tables A and B.) Nor does our monopolist choose the price which yields the highest total revenue. That price is 3.5 cents (Table A) but here the extra cost more than offsets the extra revenue and total profits are smaller (see Table C). Our monopolist will charge 4.2 cents because that price yields the most profit. This is a higher price than would prevail with pure competition.

Note that a price of 4.2 cents is well above the average cost of production (3.65 cents) at that particular volume of output. The difference is 0.55 cents per kilowatt. And since average cost includes a *normal* profit, this difference represents an extra profit. Now consider what would happen in a competitive industry. Extra profits attract new firms into the industry. Thus supply increases and the price is driven down. This process would continue as long as the price was high enough to permit extra profits. So price would be driven down until profits were no larger than the normal profits in other industries. With pure competition, therefore, the long-run equilibrium price will equal the minimum average cost of production (in Table C, a price of 3.1 cents).

With pure monopoly, however, there are no other sellers. The monopolist can choose the price-output combination that yields the greatest profit, and although the price is

				C		
			Municipal Power Company: The Profit Position			
(1)	(2)	(3)	(4)	(5)	(6)
Sales in kilowatts per week	Total Revenue	Total Cost	Monopoly Profit	Average Cost	Price per kilowatt
(millions)	($000's)	($000's)	($000's)	(cents)	(cents)
10	500	460	40	4.6	5.0
11	528	476	52	4.3	4.8
12	552	492	60	4.1	4.6
13	585	508	77	3.9	4.4
14	602	524	78	3.7	4.3
15	615	540	75	3.6	4.1
16	624	556	68	3.5	3.9
17	629	572	57	3.4	3.7
18	630	588	42	3.3	3.5
19	627	604	23	3.2	3.3
20	620	620	0	3.1	3.1

above average cost, supply will not increase. Price can *remain* high. This higher price permits profits that are larger than the normal profits in competitive industries. In Table C we subtract total costs from total revenue to show the monopolist's profit position at different levels of output (Column 4).

The Disadvantages of Monopoly

From this single illustration one can easily see the disadvantages of having price decided under conditions of monopoly. The first disadvantage is obvious: consumers are forced to pay higher prices. In our example they would pay approximately 4.2 cents per kilowatt instead of 3.1 cents which would yield the normal profit of a competitive industry. When price is 3.1 cents monopoly profits are zero. Our monopolist, with a price of 4.2 cents, will earn monopoly profits somewhat higher than $78,000.

A second disadvantage of monopoly is that quantities produced and sold are smaller that the quantities produced and sold in competitive markets. While our monopolist would sell between 14 and 15 millions of kilowatts per week, total output in a competitive market would expand to 20 millions. Monopoly, therefore, lowers consumption.

Considering price and output in a monopoly market, we conclude that the consumer is no longer king. Consumers do not pay the lowest possible price as they do under pure competition. Production is not planned to satisfy consumers' wants as fully as possible. Production is planned to enrich the monopolist.

The restriction of production by the monopolist also means a less efficient use of resources. This is the third disadvantage of monopoly. The municipal power company in our tables would have a lower average cost if it raised the level of output. (The reason is that overhead and other fixed costs could be spread over greater quantities of output.) Average costs are lower in pure competition because competition compels each firm to expand output to the point where the average cost of production is a minimum. Monopoly production is higher cost production. This means that we are not getting as much production as possible from our scarce economic resources. The monopolist enriches himself at the expense of the rest of the community.

2. PRICE IN THE MODERN WORLD

We have seen the advantages of pure competition and, in contrast, the ill effects of monopoly. Our own price system cannot claim all the advantages of the one, but neither is it burdened by all the ill effects of the other. Pure monopoly, like pure competition, is rare. When monopolies are inevitable, as with some public utilities, they are generally controlled by the government. The majority of Canadian markets fall somewhere between the two extremes. They lack one or more of the conditions of pure competition and yet are not thoroughly monopolistic. To illustrate, we shall take three common market situations.

Price in Markets with a Few Large Sellers

In the first a few producers sell a standardized product. The monopoly element is the small number of sellers. For illustration we may go to the newsprint industry, or to the producers of pig iron or steel ingots. There are many others.

In each of these markets a few large firms account for most of the production in their industry. As a result they do have some control over price. Smaller companies cannot force them to lower price because the smaller companies do not produce enough to satisfy the market. And the few large firms prefer to keep their prices uniform. Although they compete with each other they seldom compete on the basis of price. Each company knows that if it lowered price in the hope of larger sales the other large companies would follow suit. *All* companies would be worse off. If a competitive lowering of price continued the results would be disastrous all round. So all companies fear the "price war". All companies have an incentive to avoid price competition, to hold the price at the most profitable level for **the**

Consolidated Paper Corporation Limited

Paper mill at Three Rivers, Quebec. In this industry, as in many others, production units tend to be very large, and a few large firms contribute a high percentage of total production.

Toothpaste, soap, cosmetics — these are some of the industries in which competition tends to centre on advertising rather than on price.

group as a whole. In other words, the group may act as a single monopolist.

In the second market situation, like the first, the number of sellers is small but now each firm is also selling a slightly different product. This situation is so common that examples come easily to mind. Automobiles, matches, sugar, cigarettes, soap, agricultural implements, petroleum products and glass are but a few we could name. Here the "differentiated product" is another source of control over price. Because some people prefer A brand toothpaste, Company A can go on selling toothpaste at its old price even if Company B lowers the price on its brand. Similarly, Company B and Company C have their special markets. All companies choose to compete on the basis of advertising rather than price. Thus, selling costs are added to production costs and the consumer pays these extra costs in the higher price of the product.

In any market where the number of sellers is small, individual firms have some power

to set their own prices. On the other hand, such a market is not a case of pure monopoly. Company A is always in danger of losing customers to Company B and so cannot move its price too far out of line. The chief danger is that sellers will *agree* to avoid price competition. If they set their prices on an agreed basis they are acting like a monopoly and the results are similar to those of pure monopoly described above. Moreover, the agreement need not be a formal one. As we have seen, these companies dislike price competition and may choose to keep their prices uniform without an explicit agreement. Where one large firm dominates an industry it often happens that this firm sets the price and all other firms fall in line.

Price with Many Sellers and a Differentiated Product

To have pure competition it is not enough to have many sellers in the market. Whenever the product of each seller differs slightly from that of the others, monopoly elements creep in. Retail markets are a good illustration. In any city the retail market contains a great many sellers but their "products" are not the same. Thus the corner grocery store can charge more than its competitors because of location. Some people will shop there, in spite of its higher prices, because it

City of Toronto Planning Board

The corner grocery store is in a partial monopoly position.

is inconvenient to walk the extra distance to the chain store, or because they can buy on credit at the corner store, or enjoy free delivery service. Here we have a seller who has higher prices than his rivals but who does not lose all his customers as a result.

If we compare this particular market situation with the two described in the previous section we find a very important difference in the end result. In a market with many sellers higher prices do not yield monopoly profits. Prices are high at the corner store because the business, being small, is not as efficient as a larger one. But the corner store does not make monopoly profits like so many of our big manufacturing companies. The reason is that in an industry like retail trade there are no barriers to

entry. New firms can easily enter the field and they do so. As we noted in Chapter 4, this particular field is always crowded even though the typical small store may earn less than normal profits.

Imperfect Competition

We use the term "imperfect competition" to cover all markets where sellers have some control over price. This term will help to explain a puzzling question. If it is the lack of competition that makes most actual markets differ from the world of pure markets, why do we still hear so much about competition? The independent grocer claims that competition from the chains is ruining him. The second-hand car dealer cuts his price below cost in an effort to outdo his rival up the street. There appears to be competition in abundance and very keen competition at that! The answer is that this is not the *kind* of competition the economist has in mind when he speaks of the pure competition that will result in the lowest possible prices for consumers. To see the difference let us look again at a purely competitive market.

Suppose we have 100,000 farmers selling No. 1 Northern wheat in a market with many buyers on the demand side. What does the individual seller have to say about his price? Clearly he has no influence at all. The individual producer cannot *raise* his price for he would sell nothing. Nor will he *cut* his price. Because he can sell all he produces at the going price he has no incentive to cut price in an effort to increase sales. He is not conscious of "competing" with other sellers. Consequently, the individual farmer takes the going price for granted. To maximize profits he simply produces as much as he can at the lowest possible cost.

Under these conditions price is determined by the actions of all the buyers and sellers in the market. This means there is just one price for No. 1 Northern and it will be the lowest possible price. It is a price that just covers the costs of production, including a reasonable profit, of efficient producers. Thus the fact that individual sellers cannot influence the price assures consumers that *all* producers must sell at the lowest possible price.

Higher Prices

Imperfect competition is different. The seller does have some control of his price. One grocery store can raise prices without losing all its customers and it may also lower prices in an effort to attract customers from its rivals. Thus prices become a matter of deliberate policy. All sellers need not sell at the same price and prices need not be as low as possible. Prices may be higher than necessary at both the chain store and the independent. And the price for A brand toothpaste and for B brand toothpaste may also be higher than necessary.

In imperfect competition sellers fear price competition. Indeed, most business firms abhor price competition. As we have seen, the typical company is reluctant to seek

temporary gains at the risk of the certain losses of a price war. It is true that the consumer may pick up bargains in the occasional price war. But this is a far cry from the guarantee that we pay lowest possible prices for all products every day of the year. This guarantee does not exist when individual sellers, for one reason or another, have the power to set their own prices.

When competition is imperfect prices will depend upon the conditions in each individual market. Degrees of control vary. In most markets the individual seller has a *partial* monopoly — of his groceries, of his toothpaste or of whatever he is selling — but his control over price is far from perfect. At some price his customers will go elsewhere for their groceries or switch to B brand toothpaste. Prices, therefore, although higher than competitive prices, are likely to be lower than the monopolist's. But where sellers have agreements to restrict competi-

Toronto Star Syndicate

During a gasoline war in Toronto, competing service stations used large, brightly painted signs to advertise the low cost of their gasoline.

tion price policies will resemble those of a pure monopolist.

Waste of Resources

Imperfect competition not only fails to secure the lowest possible prices; it also represents a misuse of resources. The small retail store is one illustration. There are so many small firms in retail trade that many of them do not provide a reasonable living for their owners. In a world of pure competition the inefficient would be driven from the field. With imperfect competition, capital and labour, which could be used to greater advantage elsewhere, tend to remain in uses where they cannot make a maximum contribution.

Some part of the expenditure on advertising must also be counted as a waste of resources. It is legitimate to pay for information which assists us in making choices, but advertising and other promotional activities designed to establish monopoly power for individual companies are not in the interests of consumers.

Controlling Monopoly

Monopoly is a pressing problem in our modern world. Fifty years ago we were closer to achieving the advantages of the ideal price system because, except in isolated rural markets, there was more price competition. The typical business firms were relatively small and in most industries there was room for many sellers. Advertising and other forms of sales promotion were in their infancy. Thus a great many commodities were bought and sold in markets where individual sellers had very little control over price. Today very few markets approach this standard. Imperfect competition is the rule. In consequence, a modern price system tends to produce more of the ill effects of monopoly, fewer of the benefits of competition. There is no easy solution.

Many, but by no means all, of our giant firms can produce more efficiently than small ones. Accordingly, when this is true, it would not mean lower prices if the big companies were forced to split into a number of small competing companies. On the other hand, when sellers are few, consumers do not have the guarantee that prices are as low as possible. We want large-scale units when they are the most efficient but we want them to produce at the most efficient level possible and to sell at prices equal to their average costs of production. The problem is still unresolved. We can neither establish the conditions of pure competition nor have we devised a substitute. However, we can and do place limits on monopoly practices. This is the purpose of our anti-monopoly laws which we study in Chapter 16.

Conclusions

In this and the previous chapter we have described the principles which underlie our price system. Having reached the end, can we relate what we have learned to the world around us?

First, we should recall that prices direct our economy. Decisions in production are made by individual producers and choices in consumption are made by individual consumers but all these individuals are guided by prices. At the same time the actions of all concerned determine what prices will be.

Second, we must keep in mind that the ideal price system is not a blueprint of our economy. Nor is pure monopoly. They are both models which show how prices would be decided under certain conditions. In our real world most markets fall between the two extremes of pure competition and pure monopoly. Understanding the two limiting cases helps us to understand our own price system and at the same time illustrates the need for constant vigilance to prevent monopoly practices and achieve as much price competition as possible. Control of market prices by big business leads to a waste of economic resources and to a distortion of income distribution. Monopoly practices result not only in a smaller national income (because of waste of resources) but in the owners of monopoly power getting a disproportionate share of the national income.

To conclude, — let us go back to our starting-point — demand and supply. A little economics, like any kind of learning, may be a dangerous thing. We often hear pronouncements predicting the dire results if government action interferes with the "law" of demand and supply. Now we know that this is not a natural law, like the law of gravity. Monopoly prices as well as competitive prices result from the operation of demand and supply. Demand and supply are simply convenient names for a great many forces that influence prices — tastes, incomes, costs, profit-seeking, market power. Any one of these may be changed, with or without help from the government. Advertising, for example, may change tastes. And government action can limit the market power of combines. As we shall see in Part IV, much of the so-called interference from government is designed to make our price system do a better job.

QUESTIONS FOR DISCUSSION

1. The monopolist, by definition, has no competition. Yet the price selected by the municipal power company in our illustration was not 5, 6, or 10 cents but only 4.2 cents. Why?

Consulting Table A we find that total revenue is greatest at a price of 3.5 cents. Show why the price that yields the highest total revenue is not the price a monopolist would choose. Define the best profit position.

2. Both a monopolist and a firm in a competitive industry have precisely the same objective: both seek the best profit position. Explain why the monopolist's price differs from the price which would prevail in a competitive industry.

3. Public ownership is one solution to the problem of monopoly. Notice that the monopolist selected for our illustration is a publicly-owned corporation. Is there any reason to expect that a municipal company might charge less than 4.2 cents? If it does charge 4.2 cents does it matter whether the company is publicly — or privately — owned? Discuss this issue from the standpoint of the consumer and of the community as a whole.

Class discussion: the pros and cons of regulation of rates and public ownership as means of controlling prices charged by "natural" monopolies.

4. The monopolist may keep his price above average cost because there are no other sellers of his product. But we may also find prices that are higher than competitive prices in industries with *several* sellers. Explain. What are some of the factors which may keep new companies from entering a field where profits are high? Over a ten-year period (1949-58) the prepared breakfast food industry in Canada showed abnormally high returns on investment, yet only one new firm entered the industry (Report of the Royal Commission on Price Spreads of Food Products, 1959). Discuss.

5. Are there real differences in the product among different brands of tooth paste, margarine, cereals, soap, pain killers, canned vegetables? One housewife may have decided preferences for certain brands; another will tell you she can't tell one brand from another. A top American executive is quoted as follows: "Advertising is no longer just a neat little description of your products' merits . . . you want the customer to fall in love with your product and have a profound brand loyalty when actually content may be very similar to hundreds of competing brands." (*The Hidden Persuaders*, page 39)

(a) Why do firms choose to compete on the basis of advertising rather than of price? Which would better serve the interests of consumers?

(b) Compile a list of advertising slogans for twenty products. See if you can detect the appeals (rational and irrational) made to potential buyers. Compare prices of different brands in the following products: electric stoves, toasters, tooth paste, ketchup, razor blades, cigarettes, and soap.

6. Public hearings of the Royal Commission on Price Spreads of Food Products (1959) revealed the chief complaint of consumer groups to be premiums, trading stamps, and other promotional devices employed by the chain stores. In its study of prices the Commission found that the cost of a basket of groceries would be much the same at any chain grocery in a given area. Show how these facts fit the conditions of imperfect competition as described in this chapter.

7. Conduct a public opinion survey in your neighbourhood on the question of trading stamps. Be sure to include both shoppers and merchants. Ask if they favour the Commission's recommendation that, if stamp plans are used, the retailer be required to give the customer the alternative of a specified cash discount.

8. In this chapter and in Chapter 4 we posed the problem of weighing the benefits of large-scale organization against the danger of monopolistic practices. The same problem is considered by the Royal Commission on Price Spreads of Food Products. On the one hand, the Commission notes the technical advantages of size and credits the large firms with "many and substantial achievements". On the other, the Commission denies that the chain groceries are low-cost, low-price firms and shows that they feature competition in service rather than in price. In the absence of purely competitive forces, can such firms be made to pass on the gains of efficiency in the form of lower prices?

One suggestion of the Commission is that the government could limit expenditure on promotion or eliminate certain kinds of promotional activity altogether. As one of its principal recommendations the Commission advocates that buying and selling practices of large firms in the food industry be investigated under the Combines Act and given full publicity. Comment on these two suggestions. Do you think that actions of this kind may lead to the development of effective substitutes for purely competitive forces?

Chapter 14

Prices for the Factors of Production

1. PRELIMINARY

This chapter continues the investigations begun in Chapter 12. Here we are concerned not with the price of commodities but with the price of labour and of the other factors of production. These prices are of particular interest because of their bearing on our incomes. The income of a carpenter will depend upon the price, that is, the wage rate, that carpenters command. Other incomes will reflect other prices — wages of bricklayers, salaries of civil engineers, or the fees charged by doctors. Property which is used in production also has its price, and the incomes of people with property — land or capital — reflect its price. Our task in this chapter is to see how prices are determined for the services of labour, capital and land used in production.

To simplify the problem we may think of wages as the price of labour, rent as the price of land and interest as the price of capital. Actually there is a price for each individual service and the different services are too numerous to list. There are as many kinds of labour as there are occupational groups and there are also many kinds of capital and natural resources. But if we keep in mind the great variety of prices it will be safe to talk in general terms about prices for the factors of production.

Factor prices are expressed as rates. The wage of a particular kind of labour service is generally stated as so much per hour, salaries as so much per year. Land rent is expressed as so many dollars per acre per year. Interest, which is the price paid for the use of borrowed money, is stated as a percentage per unit of time, for example, 5 per cent per annum.

Profit is another kind of earning of property owners. "Normal" profit (which we mentioned in the last chapter) is simply the interest earned on the investment of capital. Earnings in excess of this amount are true profits. In consequence, true profit is any earning over and above the competitive rates of return to land, labour, and capital.

By studying the pricing of factors of production we gain a better understanding of the distribution of national income. In a price system the amount of income each individual earns depends upon two things. One is the *price* of the factor (or factors) he can offer in the market. The other is the *amounts* of each factor that he can provide. In other words, what kind of labour service does he offer; how much, if any, land or capital does he own? The first part of the equation — factor prices — is considered in Section 2. The second part — the distribution of skills and ability among members of the labour force and the distribution of ownership of property — is left to Section 3.

There is another important reason why we study the pricing of the factors of production. This same pricing process governs the use of economic resources. Employers, seeking profits, study the prices of factors to find the combination of factors that will produce their output as cheaply as possible. Individuals who work and provide the services of capital and land also study the prices of factors, seeking the opportunities that pay the most. As a result, factor prices allocate the services of labour, capital and land among the different industries and among the production units in each industry.

2. DEMAND, SUPPLY, AND FACTOR PRICES

What determines factor prices? In Chapter 12 we saw how prices of eggs and of all other commodities were determined by the actions of buyers and sellers. We summarized these actions in terms of market demand and market supply. Now let us see how these same market forces determine prices of the factors of production. Again we shall begin with a simple case — the price of a single factor, the wage rate of carpenters.

Illustration: The Carpenter's Wage

On the demand side we have the individuals and business firms who employ carpenters. On the supply side are the men who offer their services as carpenters. In a particular market at a particular time demand and supply might be as follows:

Demand	At Wage of	Supply
Number of Carpenters Wanted		Number of Carpenters Willing to Work
1000	$1.00 per hour	700
950	$1.50 per hour	750
800	$1.85 per hour	800
700	$2.00 per hour	900

Here the carpenter's wage rate *must* be $1.85 an hour because no other wage would equate the supply and the demand. At any wage *below* $1.85 demand is greater than supply. Hence, the most anxious employers would offer more and other employers would have to fall in line or have no carpenters at all. Thus the carpenters' wage would be driven up through the competition of employers. At any wage *above* $1.85 the supply of carpenters would exceed the demand. Many of those looking for jobs would be willing to work for less than the going wage rate. Employers would be delighted to hire them. Thus the wage rate would be driven down through the competition of the carpenters.

Only one wage rate would not change: the one wage rate where demand and supply

are equal. This is the equilibrium wage rate. So long as the conditions of demand and supply described by our schedules remain unchanged the equilibrium wage rate for carpenters would be $1.85.

In this illustration demand and supply are described in a particular way. The demand for the services of carpenters is small at a high wage rate and becomes larger as the wage rate declines. On the other hand, supply is large at a high wage rate and becomes smaller as the wage rate declines. To understand the price-making process we must see why this is so.

Demand for a Factor

The basic reason for the inverse relation on the demand side is productivity. Carpenters (or any factor) are wanted for what they will contribute to production, and this contribution must be balanced against their cost — or wage. Since builders need carpenters to build at all, it obviously pays to employ some carpenters. But it does not pay to go on hiring more and more carpenters indefinitely. After a certain number are hired, the value that extra carpenters can add to the product begins to decline.[1]

So long as the value added to the product by extra carpenters exceeds the cost of employing them, it pays builders to hire more carpenters. But when the value added is equal to the wage, employers will not demand more carpenters unless the wage rate is lowered. Thus, the lower the wage rate, the more carpenters demanded.

We should notice that the demand for a factor is not governed by its physical productivity alone. The employer is interested in the *value of the finished product* which depends upon the price as well as the quantity. The contribution of extra workers is

---

[1] This fact reflects a physical law which underlies all production: the law of diminishing returns. For example, the yield of a given field can be increased by applying fertilizer, but as a farmer applies more and more fertilizer the extra product attributable to the fertilizer will decline. Eventually more fertilizer would fail to add anything to his crop. This law holds for any factor of production when it is combined with fixed amounts of the other factors.

measured by what they add to the employer's revenue. Thus the price of the product plays a part in the demand for the factors which are used to make it. As more carpenters are hired by the industry and more houses are built the price of houses will tend to fall. So for this reason too there is an inverse relation between the wage rate and the number of carpenters demanded.

A Change in Demand

When we studied the demand for commodities we saw that the whole demand schedule could *shift*. This meant that housewives were prepared to buy more eggs at each price (an increase in demand) or less eggs at each price (a decrease in demand). The same is true of the demand schedule for

a factor. To illustrate, suppose that population is growing and national income rising and that people want more new houses. The increase in the demand for houses will raise the price of houses. Then builders would be willing and able to pay higher wage rates to carpenters. When this happens we say the demand for carpenters increases. More carpenters are demanded at every wage rate.

The demand for any one factor of production is also influenced by the principle of substitution. A given amount of any product can be produced by many recipes. For example, one can produce a hundred thousand bushels of grain using a great deal of land and capital equipment, very little labour and no fertilizer, as farmers do in Saskatchewan. One can also produce a hundred

Royal Danish Ministry of Foreign Affairs

In Denmark, about half the farms are less than twenty-five acres. Contrast this harvest scene with the Saskatchewan farmer on page 11 using combines on over 2,000 acres.

thousand bushels of grain using very little land and equipment and much labour and fertilizer, as farmers do in Denmark. The recipe chosen will depend upon the prices of the factors. In Denmark land is dear and labour cheap so they economize land. In Saskatchewan labour is very expensive relative to land and farmers economize by using little labour and much land. Everywhere, and in every kind of production, it pays to combine larger amounts of the cheaper factors with small amounts of the factors that are dear. Consequently, if any one factor becomes cheaper relative to other factors, producers will substitute the cheaper factor for the expensive factors. The demand for the expensive factor falls. This has happened in Canadian agriculture. As the price of capital equipment, such as tractors and combines, became cheap relative to the wages of labour the demand for labour declined.

Finally, there are changes in productivity. Changes in technology may so increase the productivity of some factors that the demand for other factors will decline. The demand for carpenters would decline if technological advances made it possible for unskilled workers using new mechanical methods to do the job of skilled carpenters. The skill of carpenters would become obsolete. This has happened to many kinds of skilled workers in the past as a result of the introduction of mechanical methods.

Demand for Other Factors

This brief survey of demand has been limited to the demand for a particular factor — carpenters. Demand for any of the factors of production can be described in similar terms. Although a carpenter differs greatly from an accountant — and even more from an acre of wheat land — all the factors have one thing in common: all are wanted by business firms in order to produce. The building contractors and all other employers must have land and capital and many kinds of labour; how much they want of each depends on their price, their productivity, the price of possible substitutes, and the price of the product — just as described in the demand for carpenters.

Supply of a Factor

The supply schedule on page 161 shows that the supply of carpenters will increase with an increase in the wage rate. The reasons are not hard to find. At very low wages some carpenters will work as carpenters but many will look for jobs in other lines and so the supply of carpenters will be small. Higher wages will attract local carpenters from other occupations and more carpenters may be drawn into the local market from other areas. Retired carpenters may reappear upon the scene. Thus the supply of carpenters will increase in response to a higher price. The effective supply can also be increased by paying higher rates for overtime.

A similar analysis explains what happens when wages move in the opposite direction. When wages in the local market fall, the local supply of carpenters will fall as carpenters move to other towns and to other industries.

The response of the supply to a rise (or fall) in the wage rate depends upon the period of time over which the response is measured. It takes time for men to move from one job to another, and much longer to train new workers. What we can say about the supply of labour, therefore, depends upon the time period. In the immediate market situation the number of carpenters is relatively fixed and offers of higher wages cannot increase their numbers. More labour can be supplied by overtime work but there are limits to this source of additional labour. Given more time, however, more carpenters will come into the market. Here again we think of a "short-run", a period long enough to allow for movement of carpenters from one job to another and from place to place, and of a "long-run", a period sufficiently long to allow for the recruitment and training of new carpenters. As a general rule, the longer the period of time, the greater the response of the supply to change in price.

The supply picture differs greatly for different kinds of labour. The supply of carpenters, for example, will increase more slowly than the supply of unskilled labourers, and an expansion of the supply of university professors takes much longer than expansion of the supply of carpenters. Among many factors that explain this are differences in personal abilities, in the time and difficulty involved in acquiring different skills, and in opportunities. In Section 3 of this chapter we examine the conditions governing the supply of different occupational groups.

Eventually the supply of labour of all kinds runs into limits imposed by the size of the population, its age composition and traditions affecting hours of work, age and sex of workers. These limits change as population grows and old customs give way to new. Such changes take place gradually. Canada's wartime experience was a dramatic exception. The labour supply expanded rapidly as more women took jobs in industry, as older people came out of retirement, and as workers generally consented to work longer hours.

As with demand, our study of the supply of carpenters can be extended to other occupational groups and to other factors of production. Supplies of capital and land in particular markets respond to changing rewards in the same way as the supply of labour. High rates of return attract capital to expanding industries; low rates repel it. Land is physically immobile but it can be shifted from one use to another and the supply will generally increase in uses where the return is high. Thus capital and land, like labour, tend to move to their most profitable opportunities. The total supply of capital and land, like the total labour force, tends to grow gradually but the study of economic growth is beyond the scope of this chapter.

Unions and the Price of Labour

In the foregoing discussion of factor prices we used the carpenter's wage as an example but we ignored the carpenters' union. Our illustration assumed a purely competitive market where a large number of employers competed for the supply of carpenters. Such markets are rare. In the real world the prices of factors may be higher or lower than purely competitive prices.

In purely competitive markets wages will rise whenever some employers offer higher wages in order to get more carpenters. Wage increases, then, are the result of some new circumstance which *makes it profitable* for employers to take on more carpenters, even at a higher price. The new circumstance may be higher prices for houses, an increase in the cost of bricklayers, or a change in method that adds to the productivity of carpenters. These are events that no individual firm or worker can control. The price is driven up through the actions of all.

In imperfect markets the same forces are at work but there are also elements of control. In consequence, wages do not always rise to competitive levels. Employers attempt to pay less than competitive wages to increase company profits at the expense of labour. It is here that the unions fulfil their major function. If employers have the power to pay less than competitive wages, workers need a union to win wage increases. In many labour markets, therefore, we find elements of control on both sides. The actual wage will depend upon the relative bargaining power of the employer and the union.

The strength of the union depends upon its control of the supply of labour. Strong and socially responsible unions would obtain wages at but not beyond the equilibrium level. Very strong unions may obtain higher wages. To do so, however, the union must restrict the supply of that kind of labour. And to restrict entry to a particular occupation is to act as a monopoly. Employed members of such unions benefit as long as the restriction lasts but, like all monopolists, they benefit at the expense of the rest of the community. When the employer is also in a strong monopoly position there is the danger that both higher wages and monopoly profits will be shifted to the consumer by raising the price of the product.

At the same time there are very definite limits upon the power of even the strongest union. Barriers to entry to an overpaid occupation are not easily maintained. Also the substitution effect, described above, is always at work. If wages are unduly high employers substitute machines for labour, thereby reducing demand. Finally there is public opinion. Government may always intervene to check an abuse of power by a strong union.

Again we find our economy has characteristics of both competition and monopoly. But all these elements of control in labour markets do not alter our conclusion that supply and demand determine wages. All operate through supply or demand. Control on the seller's side will change supply, control on the buyer's side will change demand, but supply and demand determine wages.

3. INEQUALITY OF INCOME

When we looked at the incomes of Canadian families (Chapter 6) we did not attempt to say why incomes differ so greatly. Nor could we say why so many families are in the lower-income brackets, why wealthy families are comparatively few. The inequality of income distribution in Canada was described but not explained. Now that we have studied the pricing of the factors of production we can begin to account for the pattern of income among Canadian families. To do so we distinguish between *investment income* and *wages and salaries* and explain the sources of the inequality characteristic of both.

Investment Income: the Income from Property

All property used in production in the form of land or capital has its price. The distribution of investment income therefore reflects the distribution of the ownership of property. Although property income accounts for a much smaller part of the national income than labour income, there is much greater inequality in its distribution. In this unequal distribution of property we find the reason for the extreme range in incomes in Canada.

In our study of business organization in Chapter 4 we found a wide diffusion of ownership of corporate securities combined with concentration of large blocs of securities in the hands of a few. The same pattern holds for property as a whole: a multitude of small owners and a minority of big ones. This pattern is reflected in the distribution of rents, interest and dividends. To illustrate, let us look at the distribution of tax returns of individuals whose major source of income was investment income. For the year 1951 the Department of National Revenue lists a total of 48,000 tax returns in this category.

TABLE 9			
Distribution of Incomes in which Investment Earnings Predominate, Canada, 1951			
Income Class	Number	Income Share	Average Income
	%	%	$
Under $10,000	87.5	48.2	3,200
$10,000–$15,000	5.0	10.3	12,000
Over $15,000	7.5	41.5	35,000
	100.0	100.0	6,300

Source: Taxation Statistics, Department of National Revenue.

The group as a whole reported $300 million of income. The average income was $6300 — which is above the average for *all* income receivers. However, this does not mean that the typical property owner belongs in the upper-income brackets. Within the group the average income of the vast majority is considerably lower. The 42,000 individuals with incomes below $10,000 (87.5 per cent of the group) received less than half the $300 million of income. Their average income was $3200. The 7.5 per cent with incomes over $15,000 received 41.5 per cent of the total and had average incomes of $35,000.

INCOME CLASS	PERCENTAGE OF INCOME RECEIVERS	AVERAGE INCOME
UNDER $10,000	🚹🚹🚹🚹🚹🚹🚹🚹🚹	💰
$10,000–$15,000	🚹	💰💰💰
OVER $15,000	🚹	💰💰💰💰💰💰💰

Each 🚹 represents 10% of total.   Each 💰 represents $5000.00

Comparison of the pattern of investment income shown in this table and the pattern of all incomes shown in Table 2 (Chapter 2) shows that the degree of inequality is more extreme in investment income than in all income. Thus we can infer that the degree of inequality is less in wages and salaries — which we study in the next section — than in the investment component of the total.

There are two ways to acquire property: to save and to inherit. Both are easier for the rich. Without government intervention, therefore, the inequality of investment income would tend to become greater and greater. For this reason governments tax inheritance. In Canada succession duties are levied on estates exceeding $50,000; the rate depends upon the size of the estate and the relationship of the successor to the deceased. On very large estates passed on to children the duties may take up to 40 per cent.

Occupational Differences

The other basic reason for the difference in incomes is the difference in rates of pay in different occupations. As we have seen, these rates of pay are governed by demand and supply. And since the conditions of demand and supply vary greatly from one occupation to another, the prices of different kinds of labour service vary too. Thus the price system may assign a return of $50,000 a year to one kind of service, $5000 to another, and $1000 to still another.

The services which earn a high return are ones for which the demand is very great relative to the supply. The services of the National Hockey League star, the highly skilled surgeon, and the corporation executive are good examples of high-priced labour. On the other hand, where the supply is large relative to the demand, as with the service of unskilled labour, the price will be low. Between these two extremes lies a sequence of different rates of pay, ranging from the low levels to the high, and reflecting at each level differences in the underlying conditions of demand and supply.

High school students planning their careers should give some thought to these conditions. Any service the community wants very much, particularly if few people can supply it, is bound to earn a high return. The jobs that require little ability or training and involve no risk or responsibility can be filled by a great many people; in consequence, these jobs are poorly paid. Of course, you cannot reach the higher-income brackets simply by choosing the right occupation! The entertainment field takes in the Hollywood extra and the fourth-rate musician as well as the high-priced stars. But it does pay to consider carefully the conditions which govern the price in the occupation of your choice.

Behaviour of Supply

If we consider different jobs and the different rewards that go with them, it is not difficult to recognize the influence of demand. For example, take the carpenter and the unskilled labourer. The productive efficiency of the carpenter is greater than the productive efficiency of an untrained worker. For that reason the former is *worth* more to his employer. Similarly, a highly-trained engineer may add more to the value of the final product than the carpenter and so the employer can pay more to the engineer.

Now let us think about supply. The higher earnings of engineers reflect not only a strong demand but also a relatively small supply. In other words, engineers are *scarce* relative to the demand for them. This small supply is a determining element in all the high-priced jobs. Here is a fact that calls for explanation. Since high rewards should attract large numbers the question arises: what keeps supply small? Since the medical profession pays well why don't more men and women become doctors? Since clerical workers are not well paid why do so many crowd their ranks?

The answers to these questions will explain much of the inequality of income. If more people offered their services in the better paid occupations, rates of pay would fall in these occupations — and rise in the occupations that people were leaving. Wage differences would be greatly reduced. It is necessary, therefore, to account for the behaviour of supply.

Differences in Ability

The first explanation that comes to mind is that people differ in native ability. Some have rare talents. Few hockey players can match Maurice Richard or Gordie Howe, and no one can play the violin just like Menuhin or sing like Marian Anderson. The supply of their services must always be small. If we exclude the uniquely gifted and look at the rest of us, we still find great differences in abilities. Not everyone is born with the manual dexterity of the skilful surgeon or the intellectual equipment of a top-flight mathematician.

But this explanation of differences in earning power cannot be pushed too far. It

is not only differences in ability that govern the supply of labour in different occupations. If it were, we would have to believe that the people of little ability greatly outnumber people of superior ability because the number of people in low-priced jobs is large and the number in high-priced jobs is small. But studies of *ability* show a very different pattern. There are relatively few people with little ability as well as relatively few with great ability. Most of us are somewhere in between. Therefore, while the need for superior ability restricts the number of entrants to certain occupations, lack of ability does not explain the excessive numbers in the low-priced occupations. The majority would not be destined for humble jobs if innate ability were the only determinant.

Education and Training

Lack of training is a more important explanation. A great many people do not have the education or training for the better jobs. But this explanation raises another question: why are skills and special knowledge not more widely acquired? It can easily be demonstrated that the costs of greater training are more than compensated by the higher earning power of a trained individual. It *pays* to finish high school, it *pays* to take university training, and it *pays* to acquire skills in any expanding trade. Why, then, do not more people take advantage of these opportunities?

One reason is that the opportunities are not available to everybody. Many people cannot afford the money costs and the time involved in extra training. A second reason is ignorance. Many people can afford the time and cost but do not know the benefits of training. Third, there are people who have the opportunity and understand the benefits but who lack the qualities of initiative and self-discipline required to take advantage of their opportunity. For all these reasons the supply of unskilled and semi-skilled labour remains large; the supply of highly trained persons continues to be small.

In an ideal price system every individual would *know* the advantages of education

TABLE 10

Employment of Saskatchewan Students on Withdrawal from School (1948)
(percentage distribution)

Girls	Personal Service	Sales and Office	Transport and Commerce	All Other	Unemployed
Grades 7 and 8............	81	2	0	6	11
Grade 9........................	61	11	0	16	12
Grade 10......................	50	23	0	17	10
Grades 11 and 12........	31	34	8	16	11
Graduates*..................	27	40	4	29	0

Boys	Labour	Primary Industry	Sales and Office	Trades	All Other	Unem-ployed
Grades 7 and 8..........	22	50	2	5	10	11
Grade 9........................	11	60	7	7	12	3
Grade 10......................	12	45	9	16	12	6
Grades 11 and 12......	16	32	16	12	20	4
Graduates*..................	8	29	31	15	17	0

* excluding graduates who went on to further training.

Source: Saskatchewan Report of the Royal Commission on Agriculture and Rural Life, Vol. 6: "Rural Education," p. 243.

and technical training and all would have equal opportunities. Thus the supply of trained persons would increase. The increase in supply would lower their wages and salaries until their extra earning power was equal to the extra costs of their training. Under these circumstances, where every individual developed fully his native capacities, the distribution of wages and salaries would be much more equal and the average would be higher. In the lack of opportunity and the lack of knowledge which prevents this full development we find both a major source of inequality and a defect in our price system.

Why Finish School?

The connection between income and education is a topic that interests most high-school students. Many are tempted to take jobs without finishing school because the prospect of earning money is always alluring, while the value of education — in terms of future income — may seem uncertain and remote. The issue is the more puzzling when you can point to a business man with a grade eight education who makes $30,000 a year and the university instructor with three degrees who earns only $7,000! But indi-

vidual cases do not make a general rule. Our successful business man may have had a helping hand of another kind — such as luck or inheritance — and the university instructor could earn more if he chose to give up teaching. In any event, the vast majority of men and women with little education are in the lower-paid jobs. Education *does* increase your earning power because it makes you eligible for the better paid jobs. Although the high school does not train you for a particular job it does provide the necessary foundation for the training and responsibility better jobs require.

Immobility of Labour

The expense and time and hard work required to get an education are *barriers* which restrict the movement of labour from one occupation to another. They are not the only barriers. Many social and economic forces conspire to keep certain kinds of workers in the lower-paid jobs. Women, for example, are not well represented in the best-paying occupations. Although few are actually closed to women not many women workers reach the top positions, whether in the professions, business or the government. A person's race may also count against him.

In the United States, Negroes earn considerably less, on the average, than their white compatriots. In both the United States and Canada immigrants from eastern Europe and from Asia are often restricted to the lowest-paid jobs. Wherever barriers exist, whenever labour cannot move, we say that labour is "immobile".

Labour cannot move freely from one occupation to another or even from place to place. This lack of movement explains regional differences in wages. If carpenters in Halifax make $1.50 an hour while the going wage in Toronto is $2.00, some carpenters should move. Then, as the supply of carpenters became smaller in Halifax and larger in Toronto, wages in the two cities would be equalized. Of course, some workers do move; but the movement is not great enough to wipe out differences in wages.

In an ideal price system wage differences between two cities would not be greater than the cost of moving. In our price system much greater differences persist. Again, one reason may be lack of knowledge. Very often workers do not know the going wage rates elsewhere. But immobility of labour between places is not wholly explained by limitations of our price system. People have attachments for a particular place, for friends and for a familiar job. All things considered, a carpenter may feel better off in Halifax even though he could earn more money in Toronto. We are not wholly economic men. However, when wage differences do reflect ignorance of opportunities our aim should be to eliminate them.

Increasing Mobility

If labour had perfect mobility — between occupations and between regions — differences in incomes would be very greatly reduced. Also, we would achieve a more efficient use of our labour force because high prices show what kinds of labour are needed most and where. But very often labour cannot move. As we have seen, the costs of training keep many individuals of ability from shifting to better paid occupations. The cost of moving, inertia, and lack of knowledge may limit movement from place to place. Perfect mobility is an impossible goal. Nevertheless, the more that *artificial* barriers can be broken down the better.

Governments can help to break down barriers. For example, the National Employment Service, with offices across the country, supplies up-to-the-minute information on job opportunities in different places. As more and more employers and workers take advantage of this service, ignorance of opportunities should cease to be a cause of immobility. Canadian governments also increase the mobility of labour through special training and placement programmes. By far the most pressing need is an attack on the inequality of opportunity in education. Although education has long been a responsibility of government, we do not offer every Canadian child the same education. Many with high ability cannot afford to finish high school. Many are handicapped by the lower standards in poorer school districts.

In recent years public interest in education has undergone something like a revival. Federal government subsidies to universities have been initiated and may point the way to higher expenditures on all levels of education. Such expenditures are not extravagant. Because they would help to increase the quality and mobility of Canada's labour force, they are public investments in which the return would far exceed the cost.

QUESTIONS FOR DISCUSSION

1. On a graph draw the demand and supply curves for the schedules on page 161. Indicate the equilibrium wage and the number of carpenters who will work. Give two reasons why the demand curve slopes downward to the right.

2. What is meant by (i) an increase in the number of carpenters demanded, and (ii) an increase in the demand for carpenters? Illustrate both on a graph. List four factors which could bring about an increase in the demand for bricklayers.

3. When demand increases the wage is likely to increase, particularly in the short run when the supply is relatively fixed. Over longer periods the wage is also influenced by the behaviour of supply. Draw a graph to show (a) the wage resulting from an increase in demand, and then (b) an increase in supply and the equilibrium wage determined by the new supply.

4. List as many factors as you can that influence wages in different occupations. How do the factors described in Section 3 affect the price of particular labour services?

5. Why do we say that the pattern of *investment* incomes shows more inequality than the pattern of other incomes? Using Table 2 and Table 9, complete the following table and write a commentary on your results.

Income Class	Per cent of Income Receivers		Per cent of Total Income Received	
	All income receivers	Investment income predominates	All income receivers	Investment income predominates
Under $10,000				
Over $10,000				
	100.0	100.0	100.0	100.0

6. The National Employment Service has published a series of pamphlets describing a wide variety of occupations open to students including building trades, mechanics, social work, mining, hospital work, teaching, meteorology, etc. Ask your local NES office to send the whole series (45 in all) to the school library and then have each member of the class prepare a short paper on the career of his or her choice.

7. The following figures are average wage rates in selected occupations at October 1958, as compiled by the Department of Labour. The figures are averages of all wages and therefore higher than the usual starting wage.

	Hourly Wage Rate
Domestic help	$ .85
Section men, railways	$ 1.32 - 1.39
Miners, gold	$ 1.84
Miners, iron	$ 2.45
Tool and die-makers (agricultural implements)	$ 2.18
Tool and die-makers (motor vehicles)	$ 2.36
Welders (agricultural implements)	$ 1.73
Welders (motor vehicles)	$ 2.03
Carpenter (Halifax)	$ 1.90
Carpenter (Vancouver)	$ 2.68
Motor mechanic, truck transportation (Toronto)	$ 1.79
Motor mechanic, truck transportation (Vancouver)	$ 2.13
Senior Stenographer, female (Halifax) per week	$47.19
Senior Stenographer, female (Vancouver) per week	$59.11

Can you explain the regional and occupational differences in wage rates shown above in terms of what you know of the concepts of supply and demand?

8. On the basis of a 40-hour week, calculate approximate monthly and annual wages from the hourly wage rates listed above. Compare them with the following average salaries (1958 in all cases except teachers—1958-59—and professors—1959-60):

nurses in hospitals, per month	$ 175 to $ 275
elementary school teachers, per annum	$2400 to $3900
high school teachers, per annum	$3600 to $6000
university professors, median salary	$12,175

Annual earnings of self-employed professionals:

accountant	$10,879
dentist	$10,234
lawyer	$13,244
doctor	$13,978

Find out the length of training and approximate cost required for the following occupations: stenographer, welder, motor mechanic, teacher (first-class certificate), registered nurse, professor, accountant, lawyer. Can you explain the differences in wages and salaries shown above on the basis of the time and cost involved in training for each? If not, what other reasons are there to explain the differences?

9. For many years Canadians have been hearing about the shortage of teachers. In an ideal price system a shortage of any labour service would lead to a higher price and the higher price would increase the supply. In Canada teachers' salaries have risen but still the shortage of teachers persists.

What are some of the special factors which explain: (1) why teachers' salaries lag behind those of many other occupations with shorter and less expensive training requirements, and (ii) why the increase in salaries of teachers has not yet resulted in the desired increase in the supply?

10. In the United States it is estimated that 10 per cent of the population of college age graduate from college. In Canada the comparable figure is 6 per cent. The Department of Labour reports the following *starting* salaries offered by Canadian employers in various fields in February 1959:

	Monthly median
Social work	$315 — female
	$335 — male
Pharmacy	$375
Education	$350
Civil engineering	$400
Mining engineering	$415
Geology	$415

How do these compare with beginners' earnings in a bank, in a store, as a carpenter? Do you think that Canada should raise its percentage of college graduates? In your opinion, how should this be done? If the proportion of college graduates were to increase rapidly, what effect would you expect to find upon the earnings of college graduates?

11. In 1952 the Department of Labour conducted a survey to determine the employment prospects of university graduates. Canadian universities reported an increasing demand for the services of most graduates and they predicted that supplies were likely to fall short of demand. The following were among the major reasons for the expected shortages: limitations of available teaching facilities (medicine and dentistry), the high cost of university education, competition from high-paying occupations that do not require a university degree, lack of information on university courses and employment opportunities, and a failure in the high schools to encourage an interest in university training.

Evaluate each of the reasons given from the point of view of your own experience and judgment.

(Since 1952, the NES has been publishing a special bulletin called "The Supply and Demand Situation in Regard to University Graduates". In these bulletins one can find the size of the graduating class in each professional field each year, the difficulty or ease of placing graduates, predictions of future demand, etc. Write to NES for a copy of the latest bulletin and compare the prospects for students in different kinds of training. Attempt to explain the reasons for the different outlook in the different fields.)

PART IV

Chapter 15

The International Economy

1. PRELIMINARY

Among the nations of the world Canada takes fourth place in terms of total trade. Only the United States, the United Kingdom and Western Germany trade more. In terms of trade *per capita* Canada leads all countries. Our trade per capita is four times the American and seven times the world average. To a much greater extent than most countries Canada lives by trade.

In Chapter 7, as part of our bird's-eye view, we saw that trade is the very basis of our high level of living. Canadians look to other countries for the things they cannot grow or make themselves — or cannot make as efficiently as others can. In exchange they offer Canada's specialized products. Our purpose now is to explain how the exchange takes place. We cannot ship wheat to Brazil to pay for their coffee but, in the final analysis, it is our exports that pay for our imports. In Section 2 we shall see why. Here too we shall look at some of the major problems in international payment.

In Section 3 we examine the case for and against international trade. When we study the economic principles, which explain why trade benefits all countries, we are led to expect that each country must trade as much as possible. But in the world around us international trade is deliberately held in check. Every country, including Canada, restricts the flow of trade by devices such as the tariff. Why? Every future voter should know why we have tariffs and how they affect our economy.

For further light on trade and tariffs we make a brief journey back to the nineteenth century when "free trade" was the rule. We will see that nations have not always sought to throttle trade. Tariffs and other restrictions on trade are essentially modern problems and are among the major problems of the twentieth century. In the last part of Section 3 we seek to explain the decline of "free trade". Today most nations are agreed that more trade is desirable and the ailing patient — the international economy — is being treated with a variety of cures. Some of these treatments are described in Section 4.

2. THE BALANCE OF PAYMENTS

Exports and Imports

Canada's major exports, all staples, are shown on page 175. Together, they accounted for 60 per cent of total export sales in 1957. The remaining 40 per cent covered a great many smaller items: barley, farm implements, whiskey, flaxseed, fish, flour and machinery, to name but a few.

Imports into Canada are not so easily described because our imports are not concentrated on a few major items. Almost *any* article you can think of, even if it is "made in Canada", depends in some way upon imports — perhaps for raw materials or parts, perhaps for the machinery and equipment used in making it. We are particularly

Eight Leading Exports, 1957	$ Millions
newsprint and woodpulp	1007
*aluminum, nickel, copper, zinc (primary and semi-fabricated)	704
wheat	380
planks and boards	282
iron ore	152
petroleum, crude and partly refined	141
uranium ores and concentrates	128
asbestos, primary	108

* Could be called non-ferrous metals, primary and semi-fabricated.

dependent on imports for the so-called heavy goods — automobiles and household appliances and machinery and equipment of all kinds. These heavy goods, or their component parts, surpass any other group of imports.

To list the various countries with whom Canada trades would require well over a hundred names. However, an overwhelming proportion of our trade is with two countries: the United Kingdom and the United States. The United States is by far the more important. Americans buy well over half our exports; the United Kingdom takes less than one-sixth! The rest of Europe buys less from Canada than Britain does, and we sell more in the rest of Europe than we do in Asia and South America. Our dependence on the United States for imports is even greater. About seventy per cent of all Canada's commodity imports are American. Only nine per cent comes from Britain. The remainder is distributed among many countries.

The Problem of Payment

Trade between countries is not the same as trade within a country for a simple and obvious reason: each country has a different money. The Canadian wheat farmer has little use for British pounds; the British textile mill cannot pay its staff in Canadian dollars. Exporters in every country want to be paid *in their own currency*. In normal times such payments are easily arranged. Canadian exporters earn pounds, American dollars and other foreign funds and exchange these earnings at their banks for Canadian dollars. The banks can then sell foreign funds to Canadians who want to buy from other countries. In this way exports pay for imports. As our exports create a supply our imports create a demand for foreign exchange.

Invisible Trade

Imports and exports of commodities are not the only transactions which create a demand for and a supply of foreign exchange.

Ten Leading Imports, 1957	$ Millions
machinery and parts	632
petroleum, crude and refined	306
automobile parts (except engines)	260
electrical apparatus	249
rolling mill products (iron and steel)	221
pipes, tubes and fittings (iron and steel)	148
tractors and parts	128
engines	124
automobiles	106
aircraft and parts (except engines)	94

THE INTERNATIONAL ECONOMY

176

The services of a British ship which carries Canadian wheat to Liverpool must be paid for just as surely as an order of British bicycles. Foreign owners of Canadian bonds and stocks must be paid interest and dividends. At the same time, of course, similar payments are made to Canadians. Canadians who hold securities in foreign companies receive interest and dividends from abroad. Tourist travel also works both ways. Canadian tourists need foreign money to travel in other countries; tourists coming to Canada must have Canadian dollars to buy from Canadians. These are the major "invisible items" in a country's trade.

Canada's Balance of Payments

Let us look at Canada's account with the rest of the world. Table 11 presents a simplified version of Canada's "balance of payments" on current account. This is a summary statement of the trade in goods and services between Canada and all other countries for a given year. It shows the total payments made to other countries by Canadians and the payments that foreigners made to us on all current transactions in 1957.

ports of goods, interest and dividends paid to foreign owners of Canadian securities, freight and shipping charges of foreign ships, and spending by Canadian tourists in other countries.

In 1957 the payments we had to make to other countries were greater than our receipts from trade. Total payments exceeded total receipts by more than a billion dollars. Before we ask what this means let us see how it happened.

In part, the explanation lies with the invisible items, which always show a net debit balance. Canadian tourists abroad spend more than our own tourist business earns; the services of foreign ships cost more than our merchant fleet takes in from foreigners. Much more important, Canadian companies and provincial and local governments look to the United States for a very large portion of the capital funds they need. In consequence, their interest and dividend payments to Americans far surpass the earnings of Canadians who have invested in other countries.

Canada does not always have a deficit in its commodity trade. Very often we have a surplus of commodity exports. In some

---

TABLE 11

Canada's Balance of International Payments (current account)

1957

(millions of dollars)

Receipts		Payments	
Exports of commodities	4909	Imports of commodities	5488
Major invisible exports	1067	Major invisible imports	1746
Other receipts	649	Other payments	791
Total receipts	6625	Total payments	8025

Source: Canadian Balance of International Payments, 1957, D.B.S.

On the credit side we find all transactions in goods and services which result in payments to Canadians: export of goods, interest and dividends from foreign securities held by Canadians, earnings of Canadian ships, tourist expenditures in Canada, and other smaller items. The debit side covers similar payments that Canadians must make in other countries. These result from im-

years the surplus is large enough to offset the deficit from invisible trade. But when, as in 1957, there is a surplus of commodity imports the *total* deficit in the balance of payments will be large.

A Debit Balance of Trade

When total payments exceed total receipts we say that a country has a *debit* balance of trade. The opposite situation, where receipts are larger, is called a *credit* balance. On the face of it, a credit balance sounds more desirable and some people cling to the terms "favourable" (for a credit balance) and "unfavourable" (for a debit balance). However, a debit balance is not necessarily a bad thing. Let us see what it means.

A country with a debit balance is buying more goods and services than it can pay for with its own sales. To make up the difference it must *borrow* the money. A debit balance, therefore, means that a country is *borrowing* from others.

Foreign "borrowing" requires an explanation. When Canadian business firms and governments sell bonds and stocks to foreigners, when foreign firms in Canada borrow directly from their parent companies, Canada obtains foreign funds without giving up goods and services in return. In this way Canada has been borrowing on a large scale since 1945. Viewed in this light our debit balance does not seem alarming. The excess of payments means only that we have been shopping on the instalment plan — buy now, pay later!

The same process of borrowing is also a source of Canada's debit balance. When Canadian business firms and governments have extra funds to spend they buy from other countries as well as from Canadians. Further, a larger volume of spending at home raises incomes so that consumers order more imports. In post-war Canada, therefore, the influx of borrowed funds raised imports, but also provided the means of paying for the extra imports. The result of debit balances has been more goods and services, both for producers and consumers, and a higher rate of economic growth.

The case for a debit balance can be seen more clearly if we look at Canada's experience in the early years of this century. A wealth of resources lay waiting but the tools of production were lacking. To acquire them, quickly, Canadians turned to the instalment plan. They borrowed vast sums of money in London and New York and used the borrowed funds to buy equipment

and materials from other countries. For ten years, from 1903 to 1913, Canada's imports greatly exceeded exports. Far from doing us harm, the debit balance of trade speeded the pace of economic development. Had imports been limited to the level of exports the Canadian economy could not have grown as rapidly as it did.

A debit balance of trade, then, is often a sign of economic health. But a debit balance cannot be maintained forever. Unless a country can borrow *indefinitely*, sooner or later it will have to pay its way out of receipts from trade. It must arrange to pay for imports, for interest and dividends on borrowed funds, and, eventually, it must repay much of the money it has borrowed. This can be done *if exports grow*. An expanding economy may safely borrow if a large share of growth takes place in export industries.

A Balance of Payments Problem

Under other conditions a debit balance is an index of trouble. If it persists year after year in a country that is not expanding rapidly, a debit balance can lead to an economic crisis. Such a country is buying more than it can pay for now *or* in the future. On the day of reckoning — when the supply of foreign capital disappears — the country will be forced to scale down imports to the level of its current means. This can be disastrous. In any country industry needs some foreign materials and consumers rely on imports to add to the stock of goods available for consumption. Any large cut in imports, therefore, will bring dislocation of industry and a decline in the level of living. In the post-war period this danger has confronted many countries where essential imports depended upon American loans. To avoid a "balance of payments" crisis such countries have given a high priority to increasing their exports.

The Dollar Shortage

A balance of payments problem arises when *total* receipts from trade are less — and will continue to be less — than total payments. Another kind of difficulty may occur when receipts *from a particular country* are less than payments to be made to that country. In other words, a country that buys more in the United States than it sells there may run into a shortage of American dollars.

This has seldom been a problem for Canada although we buy considerably more from the Americans than we sell to them. The extra American dollars we need are supplied by American capital movements and also by conversion of other currencies. Our trade with many countries results in a surplus of exports and, traditionally, our surplus pounds have been converted into American dollars. In the past other countries have done the same. In a world of freely convertible currencies there was no dollar problem.

Freely convertible currencies, however, were among the casualties of the great depression and World War II. Faced with the complete disruption of international trade most nations sought to conserve their supplies of gold and scarce currencies, such as American dollars. To do so they placed strict controls on foreign exchange. In recent years the demand for American dollars has greatly exceeded the supply and even Canada experienced a dollar shortage. During the war and in the early post-war period we had to limit imports from the United States and ration American exchange. For much of the world the dollar shortage is still a problem. Many countries are short of Canadian dollars as well. We shall see why in the next section.

A Credit Balance of Trade

The "favourable balance" was once an aim of government policy. The theory, which was widely accepted in the seventeenth and eighteenth centuries, was this: if exports were greater than imports, payment would have to be made in good, hard money (gold). Thus a country with a surplus of exports would grow rich. This theory, we know now, is quite mistaken. It is *not* gold or money that makes a country rich but goods and services of every kind. Imports bought more cheaply than they can be produced at home increase the total quantity of goods available. Of course, a credit balance may be preferable for other reasons, but it is no more a certain road to riches than a debit balance is invariably the road to ruin. Let us see what a credit balance means.

Creditor Countries are Lending Money

Canada had a credit balance in the years 1946 to 1949 and again in 1952. In each of these years we sold more to other countries than we bought from them. At the same time there was more capital moving out than foreign capital coming in. Canadians were paying off large sums they had borrowed earlier and the Canadian government was making loans to other countries. A credit balance, therefore, means that a country is reducing its debts and *lending* money.

A creditor country actually finances its surplus of exports. It sells more to other countries than it buys from them and the outflow of capital enables its customers to pay for the difference. If the loans stopped, other countries could not buy as much. Indeed, they would have to cut their purchases until they were no larger than their earnings from trade. Thus exports in the lending country would fall until they were no greater than its imports.

The United States as a Creditor Nation

In the past fifteen years we have heard a great deal about American loans and gifts to other countries. Now we can see why. The basic reason is that other countries cannot earn the dollars to buy all that they would like to buy. All the world is eager to buy the products of American industry, but the United States, with its great and varied resources and advanced technology, has less need for the products of other countries. A tradition of high tariffs also keeps imports small. So it is that American exports generally exceed American imports. Loans and gifts to other countries provide the extra means of payment.

Britain as a Creditor Nation

The international economy has not always needed American loans and gifts to smooth the path of trade. Through most of the nineteenth century, when Britain was the workshop of the world, the international economy fared much more successfully than it does today. One of the main reasons for this success was Britain's trade pattern.

created a plentiful supply of British pounds and the world heard very little about balance of payments problems.

In the twentieth century the centre of the international economy has shifted to a country which is more reluctant to import. Our era also lacks the confidence and optimism of its predecessor and, as faith in peace and progress have been shaken, private investors

Morris Motors (Canada) Ltd

The sale of English cars in Canada is one way for Britain to earn dollars to pay for Canadian wheat.

Shunning tariffs, the British bought from other countries on a large scale and the large volume of British imports enabled other countries to buy the products of British industry. Further, British investors were quite prepared to invest in Canadian or Indian railways, plantations in Ceylon or ranches in the Argentine. Together, British imports and British foreign investments

are more reluctant to put their money into foreign enterprises. So it is that dollars are difficult to earn. Today many countries find it hard to arrange payment for their imports. Americans and Canadians are slow to learn that international trade is a two-way street. We cannot expect other countries to buy from us unless we provide them with the means of payment by buying from them.

3. TRADE AND TARIFFS

Why Nations Trade

Any Canadian can answer this question without studying economics. How else could we have tea and coffee, cotton shirts, enough oil and gasoline, or any one of a thousand things we use each day? And what would we do with our newsprint, wheat and minerals which we produce in much greater quantities than we can use? Yet international trade is more than an *exchange* of products, like wheat for coffee. It is a way of having *more* products, hence a higher level of living.

The reason is that trade permits the nation to reap the benefits of specialization. Every region has *some* advantage — in its

we buy in other countries. Other countries — indeed all countries — have made the same decision. As a result, the amount of international trade is much less than it could be. Now we must ask: why do nations not trade as much as they could? Is there some flaw in the argument that a nation grows rich through specialization and exchange? Or is it a case of good advice going unheeded? We shall attempt to answer by examining the most popular device for restricting trade — the tariff.

The Protective Tariff

A tariff is simply a tax or duty collected on goods coming into a country. It can be

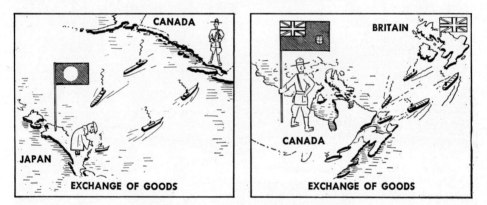

THE MORE WE BUY, THE MORE WE CAN SELL!

natural resources, or its people, or its technology — and the nation's total output will be greater when it specializes in producing things in which it has a comparative advantage. When these specialties are exchanged for things produced more cheaply elsewhere, the nation's income is increased. All nations can have more goods and services when they engage in specialized production and then trade freely with one another.

Canada, as we have seen, puts the principle of specialization to good use. Yet Canada is far from achieving the advantages of international trade in full measure. We have chosen *to limit* the quantity of things

viewed as a source of revenue for the government but if this is its *only* purpose the amount of the tax must be small. More commonly the revenue element in the tariff is incidental. Its main purpose is to raise the price of goods imported from other countries so that high-cost home industries are *protected* from the competition of more efficient foreign producers. The duty is collected from the importer, but when the goods go on to the wholesaler, the retailer and the consumer, the amount of the duty is included in their price. Thus a tariff on British sweaters raises the price of British sweaters to Canadian consumers. As a result Canadian manufacturers can compete. Canadian tariffs are of this protective type and have been so for eighty years.

From an economic standpoint protective tariffs are undesirable. First of all, the consumer pays higher prices. Because prices are higher the consumer's dollar buys less. Tariffs therefore lower our level of living. An extra dollar or two on a sweater or a cent on a pound of sugar may seem very little, but several hundred dollars on a new car or fifty or sixty dollars on an automatic washer is obviously a great deal of money! Also, a few extra cents on a great many items add to a total that is worth worrying about. A recent study of the Royal Commission on Canada's Economic Prospects placed the cost of tariffs to Canadian consumers at one billion dollars a year!

The second undesirable effect of the protective tariff is the misuse of economic resources. Instead of concentrating on industries in which it has a comparative advantage, the nation with a protective tariff puts men and materials to work producing things that could be bought more cheaply elsewhere. The nation as a whole produces less, which means that tariffs lower the national income.

The misuse of resources not only lowers income; it also affects its distribution. Overexpansion of industries with no comparative advantage raises property income originating in these industries. On the other hand, property in industries which do have a comparative advantage is under-utilized; hence property income in these industries is reduced. Thus, in Canada, protected manufacturers benefit at the expense of agriculture and other export industries. The tariff, therefore, both reduces the national income and distorts its distribution.

Why Have Tariffs?

Since trade increases wealth — and tariffs have the opposite effect — why have tariffs at all? The chief reason is that many producers want them. Whatever the effect upon the Canadian consumer, the Canadian textile firm makes larger profits when British textiles are made more expensive. Indeed, if it were not for the tariff, many industries would cease to make profits at all! If something can be made much more cheaply somewhere else, a tariff is needed to keep the home industry in business.

Why the controlling interests in protected industries *want* tariffs is easy to see. It is more difficult to see why we allow them to have tariffs. Somehow those who profit from the tariff have convinced the rest of us that tariffs are good for the country as a whole. But if we look at some of the popular arguments we shall see that the logical case in favour of tariffs is really very weak.

(1) *Protecting Canadian Wages from the Competition of Foreign Labour*

This argument runs as follows. Countries with cheap labour have a competitive advantage. If Canadian producers are forced to compete with Japanese producers, for example, the wages of Canadian workers will be driven down to the Japanese level. Tariffs, therefore, protect Canadian workers from the competition of cheap foreign labour.

In fact, Canadian wages would *not* be lowered by an increase in imports from Japan. Suppose we lower our tariff on Japanese toys. The lower tariff would put some Canadian firms out of business, but these firms could not solve their problem by wholesale cuts in wages. Their workers would move to other industries! They could find jobs in the industries where Canada does have a comparative advantage because the demand for these products would rise. As a direct result of Canadians buying more from Japan, Japan could buy more from us!

Nor is there any danger that the Japanese could undersell us in every line of production. Every country has advantages in producing certain things. Where labour is cheap it is also less productive than the relatively high-priced labour in Canada. It is less skilled and has fewer machines to work with. Thus the competitive advantage in many lines is found in countries like Canada, in spite of their high wages. If, in some industries, we cannot produce as cheaply as the Japanese we would do better to buy from them — and sell to them in exchange the things we can produce most cheaply.

In short, it is not the tariff that keeps our wages high. It is our technology and our combination of economic resources.

(2) *Keeping Money At Home*

This argument asks us to believe that in buying Canadian goods we help our fellow citizens, while money spent on foreign goods goes into the pockets of foreigners. No Canadian should take this argument seriously. As every western farmer knows, the money we spend on British goods comes back as income for Canadian farmers. Britain does not want our money for its own sake. She wants it for what it will buy — our wheat. To buy from us she must earn dollars by selling to us. So the more we buy in Britain the more Britain can buy from us. Money spent in other countries, far from being lost to us, creates markets for Canadian products and new money incomes here at home.

(3) *Making Jobs*

Are tariffs useful in reducing unemployment? It is perfectly true that tariffs *can* create jobs. If the tariff were high enough almost any industry could be established in Canada and offer employment to Canadian workers. At the same time, however, the higher tariffs would *destroy* jobs. With

the products of other countries kept out of Canada other countries could not buy from us. The loss of jobs which followed the decline in exports would have to be deducted from the new job opportunities artificially created by the tariff. On balance Canadians would be worse off because productivity is higher in our export industries.

Tariffs, therefore, are not a good way of combatting unemployment. If making jobs were the only aim we could shut out the goods and services of every country and the whole nation could be kept busy making things which are made at half the cost elsewhere. But our standard of living would sink to a much lower level. It would make as much sense to create jobs by junking power equipment in construction. Let everyone use a shovel! Better still, by junking the shovels and digging by hand we could employ even more workers. Instead of using tariffs to relieve unemployment we are better advised to look to exports, which also create jobs but give us the advantage of international specialization.

(4) *Establishing Industry in Under-developed Countries*

Here (at last) is one argument for tariffs to which economists lend support. The case is this. In a country that has not developed industrially new firms find it hard to get started. Although they have the economic resources and a sufficient market for profitable operations they cannot, at the outset, meet the prices of established foreign firms. By eliminating foreign competition, a tariff gives the new industry the time to become established. This is the "infant industry" argument. Eighty to ninety years ago it was used in the United States and Germany to justify their tariffs and Canadians were not slow to follow suit. In the twentieth century the same argument is advanced by most underdeveloped countries.

If we accept this one argument, however, we must recognize that it applies only in particular cases. Only for those industries which have a reasonable hope of standing on their own feet eventually can the "infant industry" argument justify a tariff. If the protected industry can and actually does meet foreign competition at some later date, the tariff will have no long-run ill effects. The trouble with this argument is that the "infants" do not always grow up. Too often industries are established which should not have been established in the first place; industries, that is, that *never* reach the point where they can compete with foreign firms. A long list of Canadian industries have had tariffs for seventy years or more and still show little sign of being able to survive without protection.

(5) National Security

One other way of justifying tariffs is to go beyond the ordinary boundaries of economics. The economist can point to the effect of tariffs on our level of living (which is almost always to lower it) but governments must also consider national security.

pockets. Their effect is precisely the reverse. And while tariffs may create additional jobs when there is unemployment there are much more effective methods of combatting unemployment.

This is not to say that tariffs already in existence can be eliminated, or even greatly reduced. The jobs of many thousands of Canadian workers depend upon the existing tariffs which protect their industries. Large tariff reductions would throw many of them out of work. Eventually new job opportunities would appear, but meanwhile there would be severe social dislocation and much suffering. If we are to lower tariffs the change must come slowly so that the people affected can be absorbed into other industries.

The Rise and Fall of Free Trade

Because of the advantages of specialization any nation can grow richer by trading *more* with other nations. This principle, per-

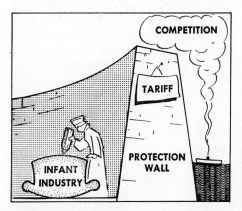

For example, it may be wise to encourage certain home industries as a precaution against loss of essential supplies in wartime. Thus Britain nowadays is attempting to produce more food at home. Tariffs are one way of doing it.

The Case Against Tariffs

Apart from the "infant industry" argument, which applies under very special circumstances, there is no economic case for tariffs. They do not protect Canadian wages; they do not put money in our

ceived by Adam Smith in the late eighteenth century, at one time exerted a powerful influence on government policy, particularly in Britain. Between 1850 and 1914 the world's foremost trader had no tariffs. Other countries, including the new Dominion of Canada, remained lukewarm to the merits of "free trade" but their tariffs were moderate and other restrictions on trade were seldom used. It was, therefore, an era of expanding trade. Within the orbit of British trade the wealth of all nations increased. After World War I the international economy entered a new era. Now the nations who had prospered with expanding trade in the nineteenth century set a new course aimed at keeping trade within limits and encouraging production at home. The results, as you would expect, benefited none. How, then, can we explain this folly of the twentieth century?

The decline of free trade cannot be traced to any one factor. Balance of payments problems created by the war were one cause. The nations in Europe had less to sell and other earnings — from shipping or foreign investments — had been greatly reduced. As a result, they could not pay for all their imports. To check imports was one way to narrow the gap between receipts and payments. Another factor was the world-wide depression in the 1930's. As exports everywhere collapsed mass unemployment became the chief concern of every government. To scale down imports seemed to serve the two-fold purpose of conserving foreign currencies and creating jobs in home industry.

In the 1930's the flight from free trade gained momentum. The British abandoned free trade (1931) and the Americans imposed the highest tariff schedule in their history.

The Canadian and other governments followed the trend to higher tariffs. Many nations also placed controls on foreign exchange and introduced quotas and prohibitions on imports. There is no need to describe the whole battery of restrictions which inventive governments devised. All had the effect of restricting trade.

Unquestionably, the problems of this era went much deeper than the remedies which individual governments could apply. But the new philosophy contained a second fundamental weakness: no country was prepared to give up trade altogether. Although doing everything possible to limit imports each nation still aimed to increase its exports! The two ends, of course, are incompatible. The less a country buys the less it can sell. Thus restrictions on trade prolonged the depression they sought to banish. This fact was soon apparent. But reducing tariffs and other restrictions is a slow and difficult process. The international conferences which tackled the problem in the nineteen-thirties produced few results and the end of World War II found the nations seeking new ways to chop through the barriers and increase trade.

CANADA'S TRADE IN 1957

PERCENTAGE DISTRIBUTION

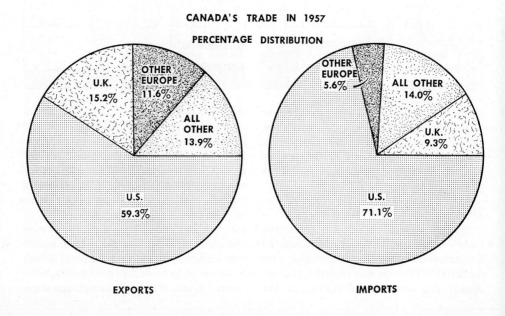

EXPORTS   IMPORTS

4. BUILDING A NEW WORLD ECONOMY

In recent years we have heard a great deal about new international institutions: the International Trade Organization (I.T.O.), the International Monetary Fund (I.M.F.), the International Wheat Council and many others. Each is designed to solve some particular problem in world trade. Taken together, this is our answer to the problem of increasing trade. But why must complex institutions be established? Why not go back to "free trade"? Couldn't the nations simply do away with restrictions and automatically restore the golden age? Unfortunately, the solution is not that simple. Let us look at some of the reasons why it is difficult to eliminate controls.

The Real Barriers to Trade

One factor is fear of depression. It would be fine, we say, to do away with controls if the international economy always worked at high levels of production, income and employment. But the experience of the inter-war years is not easily forgotten. If depression strikes *one* country, unemployment and declining incomes may spread to all its trading partners. A depression in the United States would be disastrous to countries with large exports to the United States and to countries which depend upon American loans. Every nation wants the power to control its imports should the need arise. If governments sign agreements which prohibit restrictions, no country can attempt to insulate itself against depression in other countries. Today most governments prefer to have that power. They choose a lower but more stable level of national income.

The fear of war is another reason for trade controls. The industrialized countries of Europe protect a high-cost domestic agriculture rather than import cheaper food because overseas supplies could be cut off in wartime.

Difficulties of still another kind are found in underdeveloped countries. A few export staples tie their economies to the advanced countries in which they sell and a falling price for a single product may bring on full-scale depression. The low-income countries want the higher standard of living which a more balanced and developed economy would confer. Taking a leaf from the notebook of the West they can reasonably conclude that tariffs are one way to establish new industries.

In advanced countries the opposition to freer trade is rather one of vested interests. Industries that can only flourish behind the shelter of tariff walls assert that the livelihood of their employees and the interest of the nation depend on tariffs. Our own country supplies abundant examples. While Canada is willing to work with other countries towards a gradual reduction in tariffs we are careful not to push the idea of free trade too far. The interests of industries which still need protection are held always in view by the Canadian government.

Another type of opposition to freer trade is best illustrated by the United States. Although the American government has played a leading role in the war on trade restrictions, it does not apply the principle to the trade in agricultural products. The reason is political. The politically powerful farm bloc in the United States secured a rigid structure of government subsidies, and this policy has had the effect of pricing many United States agricultural products above world prices. It is therefore necessary to restrict the import of lower-priced farm products from Canada, New Zealand, Denmark and other efficient producers.

The trade pattern of the leading creditor nation is another twentieth-century problem. As we learned in Section 1, dollars now are relatively harder to secure than were pounds in Britain's heyday. And nations with a dollar shortage cannot safely relinquish controls.

For all these reasons free trade cannot be restored with the stroke of a pen. The relative freedom of trade in the nineteenth century may well have been a by-product of special circumstances. If the modern world is to have more trade, the nations must tackle the problems one by one and work out new arrangements to meet the new conditions. Against this background let us look briefly at some of the new international institutions.

I.T.O. and G.A.T.T.

An International Trade Organization was one of the first post-war proposals. Negotiations, which began in 1945, involved the representatives of a great many countries and two divergent points of view. The original aim of the United States was a thoroughgoing multilateral trading system in which exporters are free to sell in any market whatsoever and importers are free to buy from any country. Governments would not attempt to balance exports and imports with *each* country as under bilateral trade. Prices, not government control, would govern the flow of trade. Such a system would naturally favour a strong economy like the United States. Less developed countries felt that the American proposals would not meet their special needs, and advanced countries such as the United Kingdom were unwilling to expose themselves to the full blast of American competition. In the end the I.T.O. was not set up. Although the United States made concessions in the negotiations, the concessions were rejected by the United States Congress. The negotiations did lead, however, to the General Agreement on Trade and Tariffs.

G.A.T.T. is an agreement under which many countries, including Canada, extend tariff concessions to one another. There are now thirty-four countries participating. Under the first agreement, in 1947, Canada reduced the tariff to other G.A.T.T. members on five hundred and ninety items and undertook not to increase rates on another four hundred and sixty items. Other countries made similar concessions. The list was extended in later agreements in 1949, 1951 and 1955.

In spite of the failure to establish I.T.O. the free trade cause has made some progress under G.A.T.T. But the pace is slow. Lower tariffs do not always mean more trade.

When a tariff is high to begin with even large reductions may leave it high enough to keep out foreign competition. Meaningless concessions can also be made by doing away with tariffs on goods that need no protection. The greatest weakness in the Agreement is the acceptance of so-called waivers. That means that the terms of the Agreement are waived or suspended in particular cases. While the Agreement subscribes to the objective of multilateral trade, waivers provide exceptions to this general rule and these have become numerous.

The European Economic Community or Common Market

Failure to re-establish free trade among nations has been accompanied by several less comprehensive international schemes. Among the most important is the European Economic Community, established in 1957. The six founding members, West Germany, France, Italy, Belgium, Holland and Luxembourg, had earlier established a free-trade area in steel and coal. Now, over a period of twelve to fifteen years, they will eliminate the tariffs charged to each other so that within the community there will be a common free-trade market for commodities and also the free movement of people and capital. At the same time they will erect a joint tariff wall against the rest of the world. The plan also creates a new area of preferential tariffs between the six and their overseas possessions. In this and other respects E.E.C. is incompatible with G.A.T.T., to which the six are parties, but, as we have seen, the principles of G.A.T.T. are not wholly binding on its members.

The United Kingdom urged a larger free-trade area. This counter-proposal was rejected by the members of E.E.C. Subsequently (1959) the United Kingdom, Norway, Sweden, Denmark, Switzerland, Austria and Portugal initiated the European Free Trade Association. The seven members agreed to abolish within ten years tariffs and other obstacles to their own trade in industrial products. Each member will retain its own tariffs and other restrictions against non-members.

The Fund and the Bank

These two institutions have a longer history. They began operation immediately after World War II. The first, the International Monetary Fund, is designed to deal with problems in foreign exchange. It has forty-six member countries. Each contributes to the Fund's resources (a quota paid partly in gold and partly in its own currency) and is eligible for the services the Fund supplies. The Fund acts as a storehouse of foreign currencies which can be loaned to members in time of need. To illustrate, suppose Britain is temporarily short of Canadian dollars. Instead of re-stricting imports from Canada or taking other drastic action, Britain could *borrow* Canadian dollars from the Fund. Later, when Britain's accounts were favourable again, the loan would be repaid. This procedure would not work in every situation. Because the Fund must have a ready supply of foreign currency on hand at all times there are limits on the amount which can be borrowed and on the time allowed for repayment. The Fund cannot solve the problem of a large or continuing shortage of foreign currency, but it is useful in meeting the temporary difficulties of a member with its balance of payments.

The International Bank for Reconstruction and Development is designed to increase the flow of international investment, par-

Information Service of India

The Canada-India Atomic Reactor at Trombay, near Bombay — built with aid provided under the Colombo Plan.

ticularly to underdeveloped countries. Its capital resources, like those of the Fund, were subscribed by member countries. They are used in making loans for long-term developmental projects which cannot attract capital through ordinary commercial channels. Loans are also made from borrowed funds and private loans may be encouraged by the Bank's guarantee. Over the past twelve years the Bank has financed electric power projects in South America, flood control and irrigation in Thailand, railways in the Sudan and similar projects in many parts of the world.

Yet the Bank is far from solving the capital problems of underdeveloped countries. Compared with the *need* for funds the Bank's resources are far from adequate. Nor has a solution been found in other international lending projects such as the Colombo Plan and the American Export-Import Bank. An overwhelming proportion of the capital resources in advanced countries is still devoted to increasing productive capacity at home. To the rest of the world the new institutions appear as little more than a step in the right direction.

The International Wheat Agreement

One of the major problems of international trade in the past has been the instability of the prices of primary products. Price fluctuations cause hardship for both importing and exporting countries. A high price for coffee hurts the Canadian consumer just as a high price for wheat harms the consumer in Britain. A low price for wheat is undesirable for exporting countries. When the price of wheat falls the value of Canadian exports and incomes are lowered. So it is that bumper crops are not always cause for rejoicing. If Canada and other wheat exporters were to sell their current surpluses the price of wheat would fall to disastrously low levels. Both exporters and importers, then, prefer price stability, and this is the goal of international commodity agreements. The I.W.A. is such an agreement.

Forty-two countries signed the first I.W.A.

in 1949. Four, including Canada, were wheat exporters; the rest were importing countries. All members, importers and exporters, bound themselves to marketing policies designed to limit fluctuations in the price of wheat. If the price dropped below a certain minimum, importers would buy a fixed quota from member exporters at the minimum price. These purchases would bolster the falling price. If the price rose above a certain maximum, exporters would sell a certain quota to member importers at the maximum price. These sales would help to check the rising price. Thus importers would forego the temporary advantage of a price below the minimum, exporters would forego the temporary advantage of a price above the maximum, so that both sides might reap the greater advantage of long-run price stability.

In the early years of the I.W.A. the quotas were large and fifty-five per cent of the world's trade in wheat moved under the terms of the agreement. As a result, the agreement stabilized the average price of wheat. Since the free market price was high the advantage of price stability went to the importing countries. In 1951, for example, Canada was selling wheat at $2.40 a bushel on the free market but most of our exports went to I.W.A. members at $1.80, the maximum I.W.A. price in that year. Our compensation was the prospect of maintaining farm incomes when the price of wheat fell. But when the break came in 1953 and the price of wheat began to fall the United Kingdom, who is the leading importer, declined to enter the second I.W.A. signed in that year. For the next six years quotas were smaller, importers were not obliged to take up the guaranteed quantities, and the I.W.A. was much less effective. Canada and the United States prevented the price from falling to the minimum by accumulating large stocks of wheat at home.

The outlook for the fourth I.W.A. signed in 1959 is much more hopeful as the United Kingdom is once again a member. The new agreement provides a minimum price of $1.50 a bushel and a maximum of $1.90. It also establishes the principle of percentage buying. Each importer agrees to buy a fixed percentage of its wheat imports from the exporters who are members of the agreement, so long as the price is *within* the price range (that is, between the minimum and the maximum). At the same time the nine exporters are obliged to offer wheat to meet all their requirements. Since the agreement covers seventy per cent of total imports of the thirty importing countries, the bulk of the wheat moving in world trade will be subject to the stabilizing influence of the agreement.

QUESTIONS FOR DISCUSSION

1. This chapter began by noting that Canada is one of the world's foremost trading nations. Now suppose we exclude trade *within North America*. The relationship between overseas trade and production in Canada is not unlike that characteristic of the United States. In other words, Canada's great dependence on trade results largely from the large volume of trade with our neighbour. Does this mean that Canada would benefit by the establishment of a free-trade area in North America?

Describe the possible effects of free trade between Canada and the United States in terms of the economic interests of the following groups in Canada: consumers, the automobile industry, the newsprint industry, the livestock producers.

2. A Canadian firm places an order for British woollens and buys an order to pay in English money. Explain why Canadian banks have English money to sell. Can your answer be applied to the supply of all foreign exchange? Explain.

3. The fact that exports pay for imports should not lead us to suppose that exports to a particular country must equal imports from that country. In 1953, for example, our imports from Venezuela amounted to $155 million, while our exports to that country were valued at less than $40 million. How was it that Canada could arrange payment for all the imports from Venezuela?

4. Our exports to Latin America have always been a small proportion of our total exports (less than 5 per cent) and, apart from oil in recent years, imports from Latin America have also been very small. Yet Canada cannot grow tropical products and must buy West Indian sugar, Brazilian coffee, bananas from Central America, etc. On the face of it one would think that a *high* proportion of our trade would be with tropical countries. Can you think of reasons why it is not?

5. A simplified version of Canada's balance of payments on current account in 1952 is given below:

Receipts		*Payments*	
(millions of dollars)		(millions of dollars)	
Exports of commodities	4339	Imports of commodities	3850
Mutual aid to NATO countries	200	Official contributions	
Tourist expenditure	275	re: NATO, etc.	216
Interest and dividends	145	Tourist payments	341
Freight and shipping	383	Interest and dividends	413
All other receipts	516	Freight and shipping	375
		All other payments	499
Total	5858		5694

Compare this with Canada's balance in 1957 as shown in Table 10. What change do you find in the "invisible items"? Will this change account for the over-all debit balance in 1957?

Notice that the difference between the small credit balance in 1952 and the large debit balance in 1957 is more than $1½ billion. Show where most of the change took place. What can you infer from the change in Canada's international accounts between 1952 and 1957?

6. The table above shows a "favourable" balance of trade. Is this evidence that the Canadian economy was healthier in 1952 than in 1957? Justify your answer. Why may a debit balance of trade be desirable under some circumstances and, under others, a cause for grave concern?

7. In World War II Britain lost 18 million tons of shipping. A high proportion of her overseas investments was sold to pay for wartime imports (the value of these lost investments plus increased overseas debts is estimated to be roughly 3 times the total war damage in Britain). British exports were reduced as manpower was diverted to war industries and the armed forces.

With these facts in mind, examine Britain's pre-war trade pattern, given below, and explain why a serious balance of payments crisis was a recurring threat through the early post-war years.

Pre-war earnings from trade (average 1936-1938, in millions of pounds)

Exports	496
Overseas investments	203
Shipping services	105
Banking and miscellaneous	44
Total	848
Pre-war cost of imports	884
Deficit	36

8. In Chapter 2 we noted that some regions of the world are much more favourably endowed than others. From this it is often mistakenly inferred that the poorest regions cannot gain by specialization because they do not have an absolute advantage in any field of production. Actually, all regions have the opportunity to specialize, because even the most fortunate region has greater advantages in producing some products than in producing others. It will pay to concentrate on those lines in which its comparative advantage is greatest. Less fortunate regions will concentrate on those in which their comparative disadvantage is least. As a result, all regions will be better off.

Evaluate Canada's wheat industry and pulp and paper industry, on the one hand, and our automobile, iron and steel, and textile industries, on the other, in terms of the theory of comparative advantage.

9. A prominent Canadian industrialist (R. W. Todgham, President of Chrysler Corporation) stated in a public speech that Canada imports more fully-manufactured goods than any nation in the entire world. Does this fact make Canada any poorer?

Comment on the following three factors which Mr. Todgham holds responsible for the difficulties confronting Canadian manufacturers: soaring labour costs, a comparatively small home market, and Canadian preference for imported manufactured goods.

Notice that the speaker did not mention the basic reason why a high proportion of manufactured goods is imported, nor what would happen if, as he advised, Canadians made it a rigid policy wherever possible to "buy Canadian". Discuss this thesis: that the interest of a particular group like Canadian automobile producers may differ from the interest of the country as a whole. (When you read the newspaper make a habit of noting how frequently the spokesman for a particular group will identify his own group's special interest with the national interest.)

10. Canadian tariffs on cotton textiles and industrial machinery are now very much lower than they were in 1928. In both, however, Canadians import the same proportion of their total requirements as they did thirty years ago. What conclusions could you draw about Canadian tariff policy?

Current tariffs on cotton textiles (average rate of duty, 13 per cent) and on iron and steel machinery (average rate of duty, 20 per cent) cannot be called low. Both items have been protected since the 1880's. Comment on the relevance of the "infant industry" argument for these Canadian industries.

11. Discussion topic: Canada's interest and the increase in tariffs on imports from Japan in the federal budget of 1960. Consider the different points of view of the following: wheat producers, workers in cotton textile factories, the owners of these factories.

12. The growth of the Canadian automobile industry is reflected in the following figures:

Imports as a percentage of total requirements	1928	1953
motor vehicles	25	11
parts	80	46

What are the advantages and disadvantages of this development? The automobile industry supplies jobs for thousands of Canadians (35,000 in motor vehicles in 1956) but the price of Canadian-made cars is well above the American. Prepare a class debate on this topic.

13. "Free trade cannot be restored with the stroke of a pen." Comment briefly on the difficulties of removing trade restrictions. Have each member of the class prepare a report on one of the new international institutions: G.A.A.T., E.E.C. and the Outer Seven, I.M.F., World Bank, Colombo Plan, and I.W.A. Be sure to consult additional references. Reports may be obtained from provincial or public libraries and by writing the Department of Trade and Commerce in Ottawa.

Chapter 16

Government and the Economic System

1. PRELIMINARY

To the average person "government" means *taxes* and reluctance to pay taxes is a firmly rooted tradition. Of course, the modern taxpayer has less reason than the English barons who refused to pay their taxes to King John. Since we have a voice in spending taxes, why should we object to paying them? One answer is that we do not always see what taxes buy. This is one of the differences between paying for government services and paying for the goods and services we buy directly. Accordingly, the many useful services performed by Canadian governments are listed in Section 2.

A second difference between taxes and other kinds of spending is that taxes are compulsory. You are not obliged to buy a new car; you can buy a second-hand car or do without. But you do have to pay — we all must pay — the taxes levied by governments. Consequently, a first principle of government taxation policy is that taxes be *fair*. In other words, the share of the cost of government borne by each individual should be proportionate to each individual's capacity to pay. With this principle in mind we shall look at the different *kinds* of taxes used in Canada.

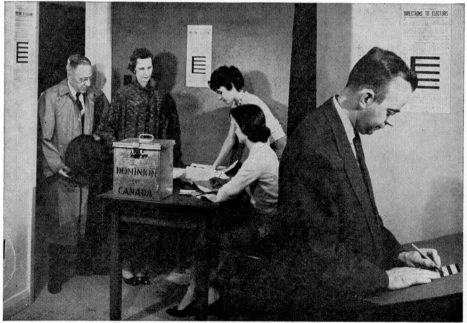

National Film Board Photo

Canadians express their views at the ballot box.

These topics should interest every citizen. Not only will you be called upon to pay taxes; as a voter, you will also have a voice in determining how much tax you pay, what kind of taxes, and how taxes are spent. If you own property you will vote on money by-laws to determine whether or not your town will have better schools. In provincial and federal elections — where all adults vote — you may choose between a party that promises lower taxes and one that promises more services (although it is not uncommon for parties to promise both!). Consequently, along with every voter, you will need to know something about the way governments raise and spend money.

In Section 3 we turn to the larger role of government. This was sketched in Chapter 3 and almost every chapter which followed has filled in some of the details. In this chapter we pull all the threads together.

2. GOVERNMENT EXPENDITURES AND REVENUES

To see where our tax dollars go we must look at the services supplied by the three different levels of government. Under the British North America Act certain services must be performed by the federal government, others by the provinces or delegated by the provinces to the municipalities. Some overlapping exists, but by and large the responsibilities of each government level are different.

Spending by Local Governments

For the rural municipality and city council alike, the greatest single expense is education. Local governments must provide schools and, although provincial governments help to meet the cost, a high proportion of the cost falls to the local taxpayer. In the field of health and welfare we find public health services, hospital care for people who cannot pay, relief for needy families and for men who are unable to work. The local government is also responsible for police and fire protection, local roads, sidewalks and sewers, street lighting, water supply and garbage collection, parks

GOVERNMENT EXPENDITURES

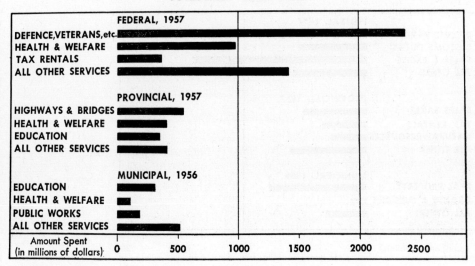

FEDERAL, 1957						
DEFENCE,VETERANS,etc.						
HEALTH & WELFARE						
TAX RENTALS						
ALL OTHER SERVICES						
PROVINCIAL, 1957						
HIGHWAYS & BRIDGES						
HEALTH & WELFARE						
EDUCATION						
ALL OTHER SERVICES						
MUNICIPAL, 1956						
EDUCATION						
HEALTH & WELFARE						
PUBLIC WORKS						
ALL OTHER SERVICES						
Amount Spent (in millions of dollars) 0	500	1000	1500	2000	2500	

and libraries. And many city governments have gone into business to supply gas or electricity and urban transportation.

Provincial Expenditures

Provincial governments build most of our highways and bridges. Taking the ten provinces together, almost one-third of total provincial expenditure goes for roads. Education is another major item. Grants to local school boards, administrative expenses, vocational training and provincial universities: these provincial expenditures must be added to the cost of schooling which we all take for granted. Then there are the welfare services. Mothers' allowances (which should not be confused with the federal family allowance) are paid in cases of need. Old-age assistance, again on the basis of need, is paid to persons in the age group 65 to 69, the five years before they are eligible for federal old-age pensions. (Part of the cost of old-age assistance is borne by the federal government.) There are many other provincial welfare services. Provinces also share the costs of hospital care and provide special programmes for T.B. and mental illness.

These are the chief expenditures in all provinces: highways, education, health and welfare. Of course, the emphasis varies from province to province. Saskatchewan, for example, has the most extensive health programme. The scheme provides hospital care to all Saskatchewan residents. It is financed in part by a special tax (up to $40 a year for a family) and in part from the general revenues of the province. As a result Saskatchewan, which spends much less than the national average on roads, spends double the national average on health.

Federal Expenditures

Almost 40 per cent of the budgetary expenditure of the federal government goes for defence. If we include the interest on the national debt, which is largely a result of the cost of past wars, and payments to veterans, war and defence account for close to half of the total expenditure of the federal government. Pensions and family allowances are the next major item. Old-age pensions are paid to every Canadian over the age of 70 and family allowances involve expenditures for every child under the age of 16. The cost of the two programmes together is just over 40 per cent of the cost of defence. Less expensive, at least at the present time, is the federal unemployment insurance plan, which is financed very largely by contributions

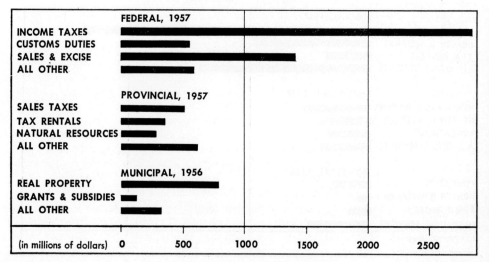

GOVERNMENT REVENUES

FEDERAL, 1957
- INCOME TAXES
- CUSTOMS DUTIES
- SALES & EXCISE
- ALL OTHER

PROVINCIAL, 1957
- SALES TAXES
- TAX RENTALS
- NATURAL RESOURCES
- ALL OTHER

MUNICIPAL, 1956
- REAL PROPERTY
- GRANTS & SUBSIDIES
- ALL OTHER

(in millions of dollars)   0   500   1000   1500   2000   2500 from workers and employers; a smaller contribution is made by the federal government. Other federal services include public works, national parks, communications in the north, Indian affairs, radio broadcasting, television and a national film board.

Government Revenues

While these lists are not complete for any level of government they do cover the major services our governments supply. These services are what we buy with our taxes: schools and roads, bombers and tanks, police protection, old-age pensions, family allowances, and all the rest. Now let us see how governments raise the money they need.

The different levels of government rely on different sources of revenue. Each had particular tax fields assigned at Confederation, and the original pattern, with a few adjustments, holds good today.

Local Government Revenues

The property tax is the chief source of revenue for local governments. Some tax personal property, such as furniture and watches, but nearly everywhere the property tax is levied only on land and buildings. This one tax bears a high proportion of the cost of schools, libraries, sanitation, and all the services which local governments supply! Revenues from other local sources, such as business licences, building permits, and parking meters are relatively small. Consequently, local governments look to their province to keep the tax burden upon property owners within reasonable limits. Provincial grants are generally the second most important form of municipal revenue.

Revenue of the Provinces

The revenues of provincial governments are more varied and somewhat less obvious. While the property owner knows his local taxes to the last cent he is not always aware how much he contributes to his province. The reason is that provincial governments raise much of their moneys through *sales taxes*. These are taxes added to the purchase price of something we buy — like gasoline — so that the price we pay includes a payment to the government as well as to the company. All ten provinces have a sales tax on gasoline and in most this is the largest single source of revenue. Quebec, British Columbia, Saskatchewan, and three of the Maritime Provinces also have a "general" sales tax which applies on every kind of retail sales (with the exception of food and certain other essentials).

The next item in provincial finance is the tax rental payment from the federal government. These payments represent a return to the provinces under agreements which give the federal government the exclusive right to levy direct taxes on income and succession duties. Most of the provinces have leased their right to levy succession duties, personal income taxes and corporation income taxes.

Other sources of provincial revenue include timber leases, mineral rights, car licences, and profits from provincial liquor control boards. As with expenditures, there are important differences among the provinces. Alberta, for example, has not used a general sales tax because its oil leases produce so much revenue. Quebec, which has both a tax on income and a general sales tax, raises more in taxes than any other province.

Federal Revenues

The *income tax* is a major source of revenue for the federal government in Ottawa. Each year the tax on personal incomes extracts well over a billion dollars from the pockets of Canadians and the tax on corporation income yields only slightly less. All told, federal income taxes produce more revenue than the revenues of all ten provinces combined. Yet income tax does not pay the whole cost of the federal government. Ottawa has "hidden" taxes too. Federal sales taxes are called excise taxes. The large tax on cigarettes is a federal excise tax and there are many others. They are levied on a wide range of the things we buy, including cars, radios, and television sets. In addition, there are the customs duties described in the last chapter. Few goods enter Canada duty-free. Almost every time we shop we are bound to contribute to federal revenues, either through excise taxes or customs duties. Together, these taxes yield slightly more than the tax on personal incomes.

Are Taxes Too High?

Canadians are called upon to pay an impressive array of taxes. Although we receive in return an equally impressive array of services, a great many people believe that taxes are too high. Going over the list of things that governments do, can we find some things that could be eliminated? Even the most hardened critic of government spending accepts the need for schools, sewers, roads and, indeed, most of the services supplied at the local or provincial level. Perhaps our governments could spend *less* on each item. But can we say our schools are so good that governments should economize there? Can we let traffic problems multiply to save the cost of better highways?

The advocates of economy in government usually concentrate their fire on the welfare services. "Cut these frills," they say. But the majority disagree with them. Few Canadians would return to the days when private charity and the individual family shouldered the whole burden of caring for the aged, the sick and the unemployed. Welfare services exist because most Canadians *do* approve of them as welfare measures and also because expenditures on welfare help to stabilize our economy.

Granting that we cannot dispense with welfare services, what is left? Defence costs are the biggest single burden on the Canadian taxpayer and their justification raises military and political issues that would take us well beyond the bounds of economics. Eventually, we may hope, defence costs will be lowered; but apart from defence how could government spending be curtailed? In spite of the arguments we hear against taxes it is difficult to find the services that we would be willing to do without. And, unless

Photographic Survey Corporation Limited

The 401 – a major new highway in southern Ontario which is already suffering from serious traffic congestion.

we find such services, there is no prospect of a significant cut in taxes.

Different Kinds of Taxes

Since it is clear that we must pay taxes let us take up the second problem: what taxes are best? The income tax, the sales or excise tax and the property tax are all used in Canada and so it is worth asking: what are their relative merits?

The *income tax* arouses the most hostility. Yet a progressive income tax has one great advantage: it is adjusted automatically to the different capacities of individuals to pay. Thus Canadians with the largest incomes pay the most income tax while Canadians with low incomes pay little or none at all. At 1958 tax rates, a man with a wife and two children and an income of $2500 a year paid no income tax. A man with the same number of dependents but an income of $5500 paid $480, while a man with $15,000 a year paid $2890 in income tax. The tax rate rises with the level of income. In 1958 the rate was 17 per cent on taxable incomes from $3000 to $4000 (that is, on income after the deduction of legal exemptions). The rate rose step by step to 78 per cent on taxable incomes in excess of $400,000 a year. With this "progression" of the rate, the tax is apportioned in the fairest way: the largest contributions come from the people who can most easily afford to pay taxes, smaller contributions from the less well-to-do, and nothing from those whose incomes are below a certain minimum amount.

The *sales tax* has been called the painless way of paying taxes. There is neither the bother of filling out tax forms nor the inconvenience or embarrassment of paying a large sum of money all at once. We pay sales taxes in bits and pieces and most of the time we are not aware that we pay them. Over the year, however, they mount up to a large sum and, aware of them or not, our incomes are that much lower.

The worst feature of the sales tax is that it is *not* progressive. A rich man will not greatly feel the loss of the hundred dollars which he pays in cigarette taxes over the

year. The man with a low income may pay the same although he can ill afford it. Thus sales taxes bear more heavily on low incomes. Customs duties are the same because, like sales taxes, they are added to the price of the article. Low-income families pay as much tax on a pound of sugar, a British suit, or a Volkswagen as does the millionaire. From the standpoint of fairness, sales taxes and customs duties must be ranked well below progressive income taxes.

The *property tax*, the mainstay of local government, also has shortcomings. For one thing, it taxes only one kind of wealth. A hundred years ago a man's house and land were a good measure of his total wealth but today stocks and bonds are a more important source of income. Furthermore, the property tax is not always fair. The rich man who lives in a hotel makes a modest contribution to the tax when he pays his rent, while the owner of a small house often finds his property tax a real burden. Finally, the higher property tax paid by the rich is, at best, proportionate to the higher value of their property. Property taxes do not assure that a *more* than proportionate share of the costs of government will fall on the rich as do modern income taxes. This is the basic criticism of the property tax.

Problems in Public Finance

If fair taxes are the goal, the income tax is the best way to finance the costs of government. Yet Canadian governments do not use the income tax exclusively. Even the federal government, which has an almost exclusive power to tax earned incomes, continues to raise money by other means. Why? How can we explain the tax policies of our senior government?

One explanation is that federal sales taxes arouse little opposition. People complain bitterly about their income tax but pay customs duties and sales taxes with hardly a murmur. A gradual replacement of some hidden taxes by direct income tax is possible. But were the government to throw out all sales and indirect taxes and add another billion dollars to the income tax, the party in power would almost certainly be turned out of office at the next election.

A second reason for some sales taxes is that they yield a very steady revenue. Because people go on buying cigarettes in hard times as well as good the government can count on this source of tax revenue at times when receipts from income tax are drastically reduced.

There are also economic limits to the income tax. For example, high taxes may destroy incentives to work. This view is widely held but the danger can be exaggerated. After a certain income level is achieved, extra income is not itself an important incentive. Status, power and the desire to excel are much more important. Entertainers such as Bob Hope and Bing Crosby and a great many less famous people in the world of business continue to work at top pitch even though they are already extremely wealthy and the bulk of their income goes to income tax. The greater risk is that higher income taxes may reduce investment. A reduction in retained income (income after taxes) lowers the savings both of individuals and corporations. And savings are the source of investment to expand capital. Consequently, changes in income tax have to be carefully designed in the light of all the effects such changes may have on the operation and growth of the economy.

Dominion-Provincial Relations

In provincial finance we find a different set of problems. Sales taxes appeal to the provinces for the same reasons they appeal to Ottawa, but income taxation worked poorly for most provinces in the past. To see why provincial governments have preferred to give up the income tax in return for federal "tax rentals", we must look at the problems which arose with income taxation before the war.

One problem was double taxation. The Canadian taxpayer paid two income taxes, one to his province and one to Ottawa. Moreover, since rates differed among the provinces, income was taxed more highly in some provinces than in others. A more serious defect was that the greatest share of taxes on corporation income went to two provinces, Ontario and Quebec, where the head offices of most large corporations were situated. Naturally the other provinces protested. Why, the prairie provinces argued, should taxes paid by Massey-Harris go only to Ontario when sales to prairie farmers were a major source of Massey-Harris profits? Because their income taxes were less productive, seven provinces had to choose between a lower standard of provincial services or a greater reliance on sales taxes.

Overshadowing every other limitation of provincial income taxes was the basic weakness of provincial finance revealed by the great depression of the thirties. Unemployment relief and all social welfare programmes were then a provincial responsibility. The combination of huge expenditures on relief and falling revenues from taxes put an intolerable burden on provincial treasuries. One province (Alberta) suspended interest on its bonds and all provinces found themselves in serious difficulties. In contrast, the federal government was better able to weather the depression. It too, faced falling revenues but it had fewer responsibilities and greater taxing and borrowing powers than the provinces. So it was that the depression called into question the distribution of responsibilities and taxing powers between the provinces and the federal government.

The whole issue of federal-provincial relations was the subject of an intensive study by a Royal Commission and its report was followed by prolonged negotiations between the Dominion and the several provinces. As a result relations between the federal government and the provinces were established on a new basis. Although the new approach is still in the process of evolution we can summarize some of the major changes.

First, there has been a shift in responsibilities. The federal government has assumed more responsibility for unemployment insurance, relief, pensions and other welfare services. It has also undertaken to maintain reasonable levels of employment. Second, there has been a realignment of taxing powers. Eight provinces have agreed to give up both income taxes and succession duties. They receive in return annual tax rental payments. Ontario retained its right to levy succession duties and corporation income tax. Quebec has not yet entered into an agreement. The transfer of responsibilities and tax rights is effected through agreements between the Dominion and individual provinces. The terms of the agreement are re-negotiated every four or five years.

A trial period of ten years cannot tell us whether this new approach is the best solution for provincial governments, but clearly there are some major advantages. The Canadian taxpayer outside of Quebec has a single income tax to pay, instead of two, and

the tax rates are the same from St. John to Victoria. The same is true of corporations outside of Ontario and Quebec. Also the new arrangement strengthens the revenue position of the federal government and so increases its powers to combat depression. Nevertheless, points of friction between the Dominion and the provinces remain. The problem of federal-provincial relations is likely to remain a major issue at each renewal of the agreements until a more permanent solution is achieved.

Distress at the Local Level

How to pay for the services of local governments is another major question in public finance. The income tax cannot be used and, if it could, thousands of municipal income taxes would be even less desirable than ten provincial ones. Yet the tradi-

Hunting Survey Corporation Limited

Don Mills, Ontario, a burgeoning suburb of Toronto, is typical of the new communities which require extensive municipal services. In May 1953, development of Don Mills was begun, on 2036 acres of farm land. Today almost 22,000 people live there, with another 3000 expected upon its completion about the end of 1961. Additional lands being developed within the general area will eventually bring the total to 35,000.

tional method of financing local services through the property tax is far from satisfactory. In addition to the disadvantages already listed (page 197) the property tax is particularly vulnerable in depressions. A collapse of real estate values greatly reduces the willingness and ability of property owners to pay property taxes. Yet during depressions municipal costs can be reduced only with difficulty and the taxes levied are never collected in full. In the nineteen-thirties, when prairie farmers went for years without net income, many rural municipalities went into bankruptcy. Cities and towns were little better off. Tax collections fell everywhere, while relief costs, which the municipalities shared with the provinces, reached record levels.

Today, although local governments have less to fear from depressions, their problems are not solved. They would again be forced to cut essential services if receipts from property tax should decline. At the present time, however, their chief problem is not declining income. Rather, it is rapid growth combined with inflation. To meet the needs of a rapidly growing population, local governments have had to extend their services — schools, streets, sewers and other community services — at a time when inflation has greatly increased the cost. It is a common belief that the municipalities are in trouble once more. To some extent, the crisis exists only in the mind of the property owner. Property taxes have increased greatly, but the income of the average taxpayer has increased as much or more. Nevertheless, local governments do have a problem. As we have seen, the property tax scores only a passing grade from the standpoint of fairness and a very low grade as a dependable source of revenue. Now we see that it is inadequate to meet the financial needs of local governments in periods of rapid expansion. For these several reasons it is clear that municipal revenues need to be broadened.

The search for new sources of revenue has not been very successful. The senior governments have already staked out the most lucrative sales-tax fields (cigarettes, liquor and gasoline), and cities and towns are reluctant to experiment with a general sales tax through fear that shoppers may seek new places to shop. Other sources such as parking meters, business and amusement taxes do not yield enough revenue to permit a substantial reduction in property taxes.

Federal Aid to Education

One popular suggestion is federal subsidies to municipalities distributed through provincial governments. The federal revenues required could be obtained by an increase in income taxes. A strong case can be made for federal aid to education. Under the present system, in which local taxpayers bear most of the cost, school expenditures vary with the wealth of the district. Although provincial governments attempt to equalize educational standards by making relatively larger grants to poorer districts, the difference between richest and poorest districts within a province continues to be large.

The gap between the poorest and the richest province is even more remarkable. For every dollar spent per student in Prince Edward Island in 1951-52, Quebec spent $1.57, Ontario spent $2.15, and British Columbia spent $3.30! These differences

TABLE 12
Expenditure per Student, by provinces, 1951-52 expressed as ratios to P.E.I. expenditure

	($)
Prince Edward Island	1.00
Nova Scotia	1.36
New Brunswick	1.73
Quebec	1.57
Ontario	2.15
Manitoba	1.89
Saskatchewan	2.21
Alberta	2.24
British Columbia	3.30

Source: *School Finance in Canada, 1955* (Canadian School Trustees' Association).

are the more alarming when we consider that, even in the provinces with the highest expenditures, the schools fall short of a reasonable standard for a country as wealthy

Metropolitan Photos, Toronto

A modern city school in Ontario, spacious and well equipped.

as Canada. Equality of opportunity in education is accepted as a desirable goal by the majority of Canadians. But hitherto we have not agreed that the greater taxing power of the federal government should be used to establish a minimum national standard in all provinces.

In summary, we may note that Canadians are far from having an ideal system of tax-ation. We rely too heavily on the property tax to pay for services of local governments. Provincial governments are too dependent on taxes on sales, and, with Ottawa also in this field, "hidden" and indirect taxes of all kinds run to some $4 billion annually. These taxes, that bear more heavily on the poor than on the rich, raise more revenue than the direct taxes on income which bear

National Film Board Photo

This small schoolhouse in northern Canada provides a vivid contrast to the fine buildings available to students in some of our more prosperous city and suburban areas.

evenly on rich and poor. (In 1958 the personal income tax yielded $1.5 billion and the corporate income tax $1.3 billion.) However, the present era of high taxation has a short history and among the major developments the high income tax is comparatively new. As more Canadians gain understanding of the nature of the different taxes we may expect changes in the tax structure with a shift in emphasis to direct taxes on incomes and a decline in hidden taxes.

3. THE ROLE OF GOVERNMENT

Have we "too much government"? Some people say that we do. Business, they claim, has been robbed of initiative, labour spoiled with special privileges, and everybody looks to the government to provide security from the cradle to the grave. According to these critics, we should restore "the good old days" when governments limited their activities to justice, defence and the post office, and left the management of economic affairs to a free price system.

But did the free price system do its job so well? Certainly labour would not say so. From the earliest years of the free market workers have organized to secure higher wages and better working conditions. The co-operative movement among farmers shows that results of a price system were unsatisfactory to farmers. Business has also reacted against the free market. The price system, which business men profess to admire, demands what they individually hate, that is, *real* competition as defined in Chapter 13. To gain a privileged position in the market is always the goal of every firm. Mergers, combines and price fixing, tariff lobbying and other practices described in Chapter 4 reflect the efforts of business to protect itself against the impact of market competition.

We are forced to conclude that producers of *all* kinds were not really satisfied with the free market system. Agriculture, business and labour have all appealed to government to alter conditions in the market to favour their individual interests. And the special privileges won by producers have weakened the market forces which guarantee the best possible results for consumers. Therefore, consumers have also appealed to government. Clearly, it is not true that government destroyed the free market. Each new commitment of government — whether tariffs for industry, anti-monopoly laws for consumers, minimum wages for labour, or price supports for farmers — has been in response to demands from one or another group. There is more government today because people have demanded that the government do specific things. And we have asked for so many things that government now shares with the price system the job of directing our economy.

Anti-Combines Legislation

Under Canadian law it is illegal for a group of firms to agree to set prices and restrict output. Such an agreement is called a combine. Members of a combine are guilty of a criminal offence and can be punished by the courts.

Let us look briefly at the process of prosecuting a combine. Under the Combines Investigation Act an investigation may be launched at the request of any six Canadian citizens or on the initiative of the Department of Justice. The first step is a thorough study of the industry. Then, on the basis of the evidence assembled, the Director of Investigation and Research (Department of Justice) decides whether further action should be taken. If his decision is to proceed, the case is brought to the three-man Restrictive Trade Practices Commission. The Commission then "hears" the case in private and a report is prepared for the

Minister of Justice. The report is tabled in the House of Commons. At this stage the Minister of Justice must decide if there is sufficient harm to the public interest to warrant legal action. If the decision is positive the companies are brought to court and charged. The guilt or innocence of the companies is then determined by normal judicial procedures.

Just how effective Canada's anti-monopoly policy has been is difficult to judge. Investigations reported and convictions secured have not been numerous. On the credit side, however, we must allow for combines that were dissolved under pressure of preliminary investigation, and also for potential combines that, because of the law, did not come into existence. On the other hand, not all combines are exposed, nor are convicted firms necessarily cured. Major weaknesses in the government's attack have been the cumbersome and costly procedure and the mildness of penalties. To illustrate, take the combine in the fine papers industry. From beginning to end this one case took almost ten years! Three years were consumed by preliminary investigations as the files of 45 companies were searched for evidence. Then there were 2 years of private hearings and another 4 years during which the case was brought to trial, the companies convicted, and an appeal lodged with the Supreme Court. The case was finally closed when the Supreme Court upheld the verdict of "guilty" but after so much time and effort the penalties imposed were mild indeed. The total fine, spread among 27 companies, was $242,000, an average fine of $9000 per company!

Before 1953, the maximum fine the law allowed was only $10,000. Heavier penalties can be imposed now as a result of a change in the Act which removed the limit on fines. Other possible penalties are removal of tariff protection and loss of patent rights. The courts may also issue a restraining order which prohibits the continuance of specific monopoly practices.

In recent years the war against combines has been waged more vigorously than ever before. But much more could be done if the Department of Justice had more staff and a larger budget for the job. However, the government is not the only party that can be charged with lack of enthusiasm. We do not often hear of consumers demanding a more intensive attack and it is the consumer who must pay the price of combines. For example, a recent investigation revealed that Canadians had been paying $15.00 for eyeglasses which cost $5.80! In spite of many similar revelations the general public shows little interest in the problem. To end the toll of the monopolists on their pocket-books consumers need to press for greater action under the Combines Investigation Act.

Another step designed to help consumers by increasing competition is the law which prohibits "resale price maintenance". Under this law manufacturers are not allowed to specify the prices that retail stores place on their products. Before this Act was passed (1951) retailers were often obliged to accept the manufacturers' price. This meant that the product of a particular company had the same price tag in every store. Thus Mrs. Housewife was denied the chance to save a few dollars by shopping around for the most efficient retailer. Many stores approved the practice because they disliked price competition and resale price maintenance effectively eliminated such competition. But it was very much against the interest of consumers. Since resale price maintenance was prohibited consumers have saved through lower prices on appliances, brand name foods, cigarettes and drugs.

The result of intervention on behalf of consumers is not the ideal price system of Chapter 12, but a price system in which consumers are spared some of the losses which result from the power of business firms on the supply side. The laws against combines and resale price maintenance do assure us that *some* prices are not as high as they would be if sellers were perfectly free to set prices as they wished.

Aid to Labour

Government intervention on behalf of labour has been described in an earlier chapter. Minimum wage laws, compensation benefits for individuals off work through injury, unemployment insurance, the national employment service, conciliation services and collective bargaining legislation are among the important services supplied by governments to strengthen the position of workers.

Stabilizing Farm Prices

Farm family income in a price system leaves much to be desired. The farmer, who must bear the uncertainties of weather, also faces the risk of abrupt changes in the prices of farm products. A collapse in farm prices can destroy his income just as surely as a crop failure.

In the 1930's both nature and the price system conspired against the farmer. In addition to drought, grasshoppers and other natural disasters, the Western farmer saw the price of wheat fall to 30 cents a bushel. For the thirteen years from 1929 to 1941 the average farm income in Saskatchewan was $57 a year! Among the rest of Canada's farm population the average income from farming was $104, while the average among other Canadians was five times the average for farmers. Admittedly, those years were the worst in the history of Canadian agriculture but as recently as 1954 per capita income in the wheat economy fell by 75 per cent. In Canadian agriculture as a whole per capita farm income that year was only 31 per cent of the non-farm average. It is not surprising that Canadian farmers have long sought government policies to raise and stabilize farm incomes.

The desire for stable prices and incomes does not make farmers unique. Storekeepers, manufacturers, indeed most business firms have precisely the same goals. But in many industries producers do have some control over price because, in one way or another, they can control supply.

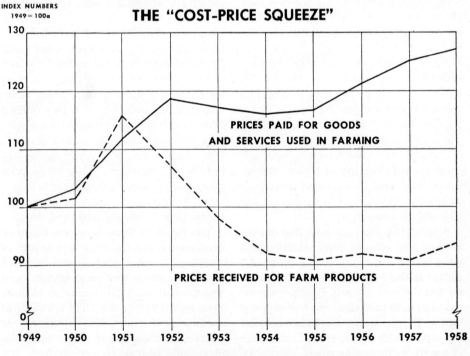

INDEX NUMBERS
1949 = 100a

THE "COST-PRICE SQUEEZE"

PRICES PAID FOR GOODS AND SERVICES USED IN FARMING

PRICES RECEIVED FOR FARM PRODUCTS

1949   1950   1951   1952   1953   1954   1955   1956   1957   1958

a—Base shifted from 1935-39 = 100 by recalculation.

Source: *Report of the Royal Commission on Price Spreads of Food Products, Vol. II, page 13*

The farmer's position is more difficult. It is almost impossible to control supply in an industry where thousands of individual producers sell standardized products. No. 1 Northern wheat on one farm is indistinguishable from No. 1 Northern on another, and grade A eggs are the same whoever sells them. The farmer, unlike the storekeeper and the manufacturer, sells his product under conditions of pure competition. If he is to gain control over price he must turn to the government for help.

In the United States, where farmers have more political power, the government has done much more to stabilize farm prices than has the Canadian government. The free market prices — of wheat, corn, hogs and many other farm products — are deliberately raised by means of government subsidies. In 1958 these subsidies accounted for 40 per cent of American farm income! In Canada the aims of Western farmers have been partially met through the activities of the Canadian Wheat Board. This federal government agency buys the wheat, oats, and barley grown in western Canada. Farmers receive an initial payment when they deliver their grain and additional payments as the grain is sold by the Wheat Board. The initial price is set by the government. The farmer can share (through additional payments) in a rising world price and he is protected, in any one crop year, against a fall in price. This does not mean that the price of wheat cannot be lowered but it need not fall *automatically* if the world price declines. If the government wants to prevent another disaster like that of the nineteen-thirties it has the power to maintain the price of wheat.

In recent years the Canadian wheat farmer has had a fairly stable price, but stability of price has not stabilized farm income. Because the Wheat Board does not guarantee to take *delivery* of grain the crop may and does pile up on the farm. When the farmer cannot sell his wheat a stable price does not raise his income.

Under the Agricultural Prices Support Act (1944) the government may support the prices of other farm products. This it can do by buying part of the crop or by making payments directly to farmers when prices are low. Products which have received support include potatoes, apples, milk powder, butter, eggs, cheese, hogs, and cattle.

Other government measures improve somewhat the supply of capital to agriculture. There is also government insurance against crop failures. Other organizations, such as co-operatives and provincial marketing boards, also help to stabilize farm prices. Nevertheless, the large gap between farm and non-farm welfare in Canada shows that much remains to be done to solve the farm problem.

Redistributing Incomes

Although government does influence many prices, Canada is still primarily a price system economy. Most prices are still largely determined by the actions of the buyers and sellers in each market. The government may be viewed as referee, stepping in to correct the worst abuses in the production system. In the field of income distribution, however, the government plays a role which goes far beyond its influence on prices (such as setting minimum wages and minimum prices for major farm products). Government changes the pattern of incomes set up by the price system. Through progressive taxation combined with education and social services, government in effect raises incomes at the lower end of the income scale and reduces the incomes of the rich. The goal is not complete equality of incomes but rather less inequality of opportunities.

We are still a long way from equality of opportunities. Some people, therefore, favour more redistribution of income, but others claim that the government has already gone too far. It is difficult to make comparisons between countries, but it is safe to say that the United Kingdom and the Scandinavian countries have gone farther in the direction of equality than Canada. Social services are more comprehensive, university education is more heavily subsidized, income taxes take more of the rich man's income and death duties take more of his estate.

Whether or not Canadians will come to favour greater equality they are not likely to turn back the clock. It is not only a sense of justice and humanity that supports redistribution of income. The whole economy benefits from the process. For example, education and welfare services increase the supply of labour for the jobs our system *values* highly. Consequently, these services increase our economic resources and thereby contribute to the national welfare as well as to the welfare of the individuals who benefit directly.

Increasing Stability

When we studied the price system in Part III, the problem of economic stability was not mentioned. This does not mean that an "ideal" price system would be blessed with greater stability than our own. Even an ideal price system would not be free from the business cycle. Nineteenth-century England suffered periodically from depression and at other times inflation played havoc with savings and fixed incomes. In any price economy there has always been a large measure of economic instability. To deal with problems of depression and inflation, therefore, we must look beyond the price system.

As we have seen, the government can check inflation. It can oblige the banks to tighten credit, it can raise taxes; and it can cut down on its own programme of spending. In periods of depression the government can make spending increase. It may start a large public works programme; it may lower taxes and increase welfare payments, and it may stimulate exports and investment. Through deliberate deficit spending in bad times and surpluses and repayment of debt in good times — a process called cyclical budgeting — government can provide the balance wheel to make the economy more stable.

QUESTIONS FOR DISCUSSION

1. Secure a copy of your town's most recent financial statement. Study the summary of revenue and expenditure. Calculate the percentage of total expenditure for each major service: schools, works department, social services, parks and so on.

List the sources and amounts of the municipality's revenues. What proportion of total expenditure, including schools, is met from provincial grants? from surpluses earned by public utilities? from the property tax?

(If a financial statement is not published, a delegation from the class could make an appointment at City Hall and prepare a report on this topic for the rest of the class.)

2. What is the mill rate? How is it determined? Assign a member of the class to consult back copies of your local newspaper for the last municipal election campaign. How many candidates stressed the need to keep the mill rate down? How many urged that taxes be increased to meet the need for more municipal services and to raise the standard of services?

Conduct a public opinion survey (each member of the class might query five citizens) on this question: Do you think that rising local taxes are chiefly the product of (a) extravagance in government, (b) inflation, (c) rising population or (d) better municipal services?

3. Using the most recent budget speech made in your provincial legislature, prepare a statement of the ways that your provincial government raises and spends money. In what respects does it diverge from the general picture of provincial finance presented in this chapter?

4. Write briefly on *one* of the following services provided by the federal government: unemployment insurance, the National Film Board, health and recreation services, provision for Indians and Eskimos, northern development, old-age pensions and family allowances, assistance to under-developed countries. Data, and also references to other government publications, may be found in the *Canada Year Book.* Be sure to add your own comments on the purpose, adequacy, and value of the service balanced against the cost.

5. Year after year municipal governments press for ever-increasing provincial grants to education. Do you think that they are acting irresponsibly? After all, schools are paid for by the people, whether they pay taxes to the province or the municipality. Can you justify more provincial aid? more federal aid?

When you argue for more money from the senior governments remember there is another side to the problem. Canadians have always insisted that their schools be run at the local level. If some other government supplies the money would local school boards retain the same authority? What are the advantages— and disadvantages—of local control?

6. The federal tax on cigarettes equals 16 cents per package of 20 cigarettes. Calculate the tax paid in a year by a man who smokes a package a day. On page 197 we compared the income tax paid by three men with different incomes. Assuming each buys a package of cigarettes a day, calculate the proportion of income the cigarette tax takes in each case. Compare with the percentages for income tax. How may the cigarette tax be justified?

Evaluate the following excise taxes (per cent of manufacturer's sale price): cars, 20 per cent; candy and gum, 20 per cent; phonographs, 25 per cent; cameras, lenses and film, 10 per cent; radio and television sets and parts, 25 per cent; tires, 10 per cent; furs and luggage, 10 per cent.

7. Most people agree that from the standpoint of fairness the sales tax is less acceptable than the income tax. Why do provincial governments use the sales tax? Why do they not tax incomes?

8. Although high-level income taxes are a relatively new development, the income tax itself has a long history. It was applied in England during the Napoleonic wars and also during the nineteenth century, mainly to finance military spending. The first appearance of a "progressive" income tax, shortly before World War I, coincided with an expansion in social services (notably pensions). Since that time expenditures by governments everywhere have increased many times, largely due to the costs of modern war and new welfare goals.

Canadian Government Expenditure	1913	1958
	(millions of dollars)	
Defence	11.2	1668.5
Interest on the public debt	12.6	539.2
Social services	0.3	733.0
Total expenditure	112.1	5087.4

Write on the increase in government spending in Canada. Justify the use of the income tax to finance a large proportion of the increased cost.

9. It has been pointed out that Canadians do not have an ideal system of taxation. List some of the shortcomings described in this chapter and some of the reasons why it is difficult to evolve a better system.

10. The typical business man maintains that competition is the lifeblood of the economy. What he dislikes is the "unfair" competition—such as price-cutting, give-aways, etc. — practised by his rivals. Do you think he would prefer to sell, like the farmer, under conditions approaching pure competition? Explain. In what ways have business firms contributed to the decline of the free market system?

11. Write to the Restrictive Trade Practices Commission, Department of Justice, Ottawa, and secure the latest report on an "alleged combine" submitted by the Commission. Write an essay describing the behaviour of the firms investigated. What is the evidence that an illegal price agreement exists? (You may prefer to write for three or four different reports and the class could be divided to prepare essays on several industries.)

Chapter 17

Alternative Economic Systems

1. PRELIMINARY

Among the things that divide our world into two opposing camps is the existence of differing economic systems. This is far from being the only — or even the most important — difference between the two great powers, Russia and the United States. But a textbook on economics cannot venture into history, politics and other social fields. Our task is to discover the points of difference in the economic sphere. Nevertheless, no system can be judged on economic grounds alone. If we are to evaluate the two major systems we cannot ignore political differences. Individual freedom and democratic government are fundamental to the way of life in all Anglo-Saxon countries. For this reason alone the Russian system of dictatorship has little appeal for us.

At the same time Russia does present a formidable challenge. The Russians claim that their economic system is not only superior but will inevitably supersede ours. Moreover, much of the world is uncommitted. In under-developed countries the world over the primary goal is to raise living standards, and we cannot say that they are bound to choose the Anglo-Saxon system which has, on the whole, yielded such impressive results in the West. They may, like the Chinese, pattern their system on the Russian model. We do know that the decision everywhere will be strongly influenced by the performance of the existing economic systems.

As future citizens it is very much our business to discover what the great debate is all about. What are the fundamental differences between our system and the Russians'?

What are the strengths and weaknesses of each? Is there a middle way between the two extremes? These are the questions that are raised in this chapter.

Our own economic system need not detain us long. Throughout this book we have studied our capitalistic system and a brief section to sum up its distinguishing characteristics will suffice. But what do we know about the major alternative — socialism? There are many conflicting interpretations of the term. To some it means revolution and dictatorship on the Russian model; to others the mildest of reforms, such as government health and welfare programmes. In the United States, for example, the Republicans have accused the Democrats of "creeping socialism". In our own country similar charges were levelled at policies of the Liberal government in the period 1944 to 1957. Here we may note that several countries, including Sweden and Britain, have gone further than we have with social legislation yet neither Sweden nor Britain is socialist. We can say, then, that reforms in what is basically a free enterprise system do not constitute socialism. Socialism is a complete economic system, differing in several fundamental respects from our own.

The second thing to note is that there are different "brands" of socialism and they cannot be lumped together under one heading. The Russian brand (which we call communism, although the Russians themselves use the term socialism) must be distinguished from democratic socialism, which may be illustrated by the British Labour Party and the Swedish Socialist Party.

Although the differences are not primarily economic they are fundamental. There is, first of all, the difference between bullets and ballot boxes. In other words, while the communists believe that revolution is the only way to secure socialism, other socialist parties propose to make the change through democratic processes. They would take the economy to socialism by gradual stages — so much after this election, so much after the next. How far and how fast would depend upon the will of the people as expressed on election day. This approach reflects another major difference: a difference in attitude towards dictatorship and democracy. Western socialists believe that a socialist economy can be combined with our democratic system of government. Communism, on the other hand, would put an end to parliamentary government as we know it. All power would belong to a single party which could not be turned out of office. We consider democratic socialism and communism separately because the things that divide them outweigh the things they have in common.

Between the Western democracies and communist Russia the political differences are clear and fundamental. But if we take their economic systems we find the differences are not so sharply defined. The eco-nomic systems of the democracies are basi-cally capitalist and free enterprise but so changed from their nineteenth-century pre-decessors that they are more accurately called "mixed" enterprise economies. In all the Western nations government plays an important economic role. In most cases gov-ernment intervention is aimed at strengthen-ing the existing system; it does not imply a drift to socialism. But in countries with active socialist parties government has a larger role, and many of the major reforms must be attributed to their influence. There is, then, a considerable divergence among the economic systems of the West. The same is true among the members of the Soviet bloc. Russia and China fulfil the essential conditions of communism but the satellite countries of eastern Europe stand in an intermediate position. Although they use some of the techniques of communism they also retain a considerable area of private enterprise.

Another "ism" — fascism — is not con-sidered here because it is a political system with no distinctive economic programme. Like communism it is a one-party system in which the State takes precedence over the individual. In economic affairs, however, the role of the government in a fascist state need not be large.

2. MIXED ECONOMIES OF THE WEST

The Meaning of Capitalism

The kind of economic system we have in Canada goes by a variety of names. To dis-tinguish it from other "isms" we use the term *capitalism*. We may also call it individ-ualism, free enterprise, the profit system or the price system. All these terms are com-monly used and each one gives part of the picture.

Capitalism means that the capital and the natural resources used in production are owned and controlled by individuals or, in the case of corporations, by groups of individuals. This is in sharp contrast to Russian communism where the mines and forests, the machines and factories and funds for investment are owned and con-trolled by the State. Of course, we have state ownership too, but compared with the proportion of resources that is privately owned, public ownership is relatively small. Hence, private property in the means of production is one of the distinguishing char-acteristics of our system.

Free enterprise emphasizes the freedom of the producer. It means that the producer can use his capital or other resources as he himself decides. Whether he wants to run a small business or invest in a large corporation is up to him. The farmer decides what crops he will produce just as the board of a large corporation decides what products it will make. Generally speaking, the government cannot dictate to individual owners or corporations how their resources will be used. Exceptions occur when activities of private owners run contrary to the public interest. Then the government does intervene. For example, it will prohibit the working of a dangerous coal-mine, outlaw combines, or forbid the production of adulterated food and harmful drugs. Within broad limits, however, individual owners control the use of resources.

Freedom of enterprise applies to labour as well as to property. By and large, the individual worker decides freely where he will work. And under the same "freedom of contract" employers decide freely which workers they will hire. Again the government may appear as referee, but most decisions are made by individuals.

Individuals as consumers are also given freedom of choice. A basic tenet of individualism is that each citizen should be free to consume goods and services of his own choice. Again government does intervene — the very young are obliged to attend school, consumption of harmful narcotics is forbidden — but freedom of choice is the accepted ideal in consumption as well as in production.

Another basic feature of our system is the mechanism which determines the pattern of production. As we have seen, every economy must have some method to decide which things are produced and in what quantities. In our economy the method is based on the profit motive and the price system. There is no "master plan" to determine the output of bacon or beef, television sets or automobiles, but individual producers, seeking profits, are led to produce the things that people want. They will produce things that are *profitable* and the wants of consumers, expressed through

prices, determine what is profitable. Thus decisions in production are left to thousands of profit-seeking independent producers, from the farmer on a quarter section to giant corporations in manufacturing and commerce.

In the course of our studies we have seen how the free enterprise system has been modified in Canada by the rise of giant corporations, trade unions and the co-operatives. We have also seen that government has regulated markets, set up publicly-owned corporations and introduced a wide range of social welfare services. Similar modifications and interventions have been mixed with free enterprise in greater or lesser degree in all the Western democracies. But their economic systems remain basically capitalistic.

The Meaning of Socialism

Socialism stands in opposition to capitalism in its basic principles. Socialists would substitute public ownership of the means of production for private ownership. This is called "nationalization". State ownership would not extend to consumer goods such as cars, furniture, houses, and books. These would be owned privately as they are now. Public ownership would apply to the capital and natural resources used in production. The degree of socialism would determine the extent of nationalization: whether or not it would extend only to large production units or to those intermediate and small in size as well. Socialists also strongly support co-operative ownership of the means of production as a complement to public ownership and as a substitute for private ownership.

Socialism would substitute central planning for the capitalist method of the profit and price system. The pattern of production would not be determined by the actions of profit-seeking producers guided by consumer wants. Instead, the general pattern would be set by the government. Within the limits of that pattern individuals would retain freedom of choice in seeking occupations and in consumption. The planned supply of consumer goods could also be rationed among consumers by a price system. But the price system would no longer determine how much of consumer goods and how much of non-consumer goods would be produced. Over-all production goals would be planned by the government.

Nationalization and planning are not ends in themselves. The historic objective of democratic socialism is social equality, including greater equality of income distribution. Socialists believe that nationalization and central-government planning are the appropriate means of achieving this objective. They also believe that a planned economy could eliminate the instability and economic insecurity generated by the business cycle.

Other reformers reject the socialistic solution although they may agree with the socialist criticism of free enterprise. One need not be a socialist to deplore the predatory character of our market culture nor to find a more worthy virtue than profit-seeking self-interest. The individualist and the socialist are as one in condemning the concentration of economic power that accompanied the decline of competition and the unemployment and the inequalities of wealth and income that have been characteristic of a free enterprise system. Economists, whatever their political philosophies may be, accept the same criteria of economic welfare. But they disagree on the political means of achieving the maximum welfare. The liberal reformer and the socialist both want the highest possible national income with as much stability and equality as possible. But the liberal fears that an excess of equality and economic security would destroy incentives and reduce the level of national income. And, having less faith in our ability and desire to control the power of governments, he would limit government intervention in the interest of political freedom. Economics alone cannot resolve these conflicts in political philosophy.

Socialism in the West

Socialism has not yet been a major issue at the polls in North America. The Socialist Party in the United States wins a small fraction of total votes. The Co-operative Commonwealth Federation in Canada, whose platform includes features of socialism, has had greater success but has not won a national election or been the major opposition party. Nevertheless, North Americans generally do support reform in their economic system. Where does reform leave off and socialism begin? And what appeal does socialism make to millions of voters in other countries? To consider these questions we turn to the recent experience of the United Kingdom.

The British Labour Government

When the British people elected the Labour Party in 1945 they elected a party which was committed to bringing about socialism. For the immediate future Labour had promised to nationalize certain industries, to substitute planning in production, and to extend the British social security programme. This did not mean that the United Kingdom would become a socialist economy. The transfer of property from private owners to the State would be confined to a few major industries. Planning would give the government a larger role in determining the pattern of production but still leave most decisions to private industry. Whether or not the British electorate approved of socialism they did endorse the Labour Party's platform and so a socialist party was given the chance to carry out its pledges.

In its first five years in office the Labour government went ahead with the bulk of its programme. It nationalized the Bank of England, the coal industry, overseas wireless and cable services, railways, canals and road transport, civil aviation, gas and electric power and the iron and steel industry. (Nationalization should not be confused with confiscation. Former owners were paid for their shares at prices determined by impartial boards.) The problem of ownership of land received some attention, local authorities being given wider powers to acquire land for public purposes. Some planning was introduced. While there was no attempt to mould the economy with a master plan on the Russian model the Labour government set targets in production for several key industries (including coal, steel, and housing) and did what it could to see that targets were achieved. For example, through its controls over raw materials the government could channel supplies to essential industries; through its controls over foreign trade it could permit certain industries to import while denying foreign supplies to others. A beginning was made in establishing controls over private investment so that the government could influence the amount and direction of investment and, if need be, add to its flow to maintain stability of income and employment.

It should be pointed out that the control of industry was not an innovation. A high degree of control had been found necessary during World War II and, as acute shortages both of goods and foreign exchange persisted for several years after the war, no British government could have dispensed with con-trols. The controls were, however, consistent with Labour's belief that the government should plan the pattern of production.

Other outstanding features of Labour's economic programme were the policies to redistribute income and provide a minimum income for all. They initiated a national insurance scheme which insured the individual against unemployment, sickness and old age. They introduced family allowances, and the National Health Act which provides complete medical and hospital services for all without fee. The Labour government also overhauled the tax structure, reducing income taxes for the poorest income taxpayers and raising death duties, the taxes on estates which the rich pass on to their heirs.

Is This Socialism?

Much, although not all, of Labour's programme could have been implemented by any party in the United Kingdom. Even nationalization is not inconsistent with a free enterprise economy. What Labour did achieve was the establishment of a welfare

United Kingdom Information Service

St. James Hospital in London (shown here is the waiting-room of the out-patients department) is one of nearly 3500 hospitals providing care under Britain's National Health Service. The hospitals include maternity accommodation, tuberculosis sanatoria, mental hospitals, convalescent homes and rehabilitation centres. All forms of specialized treatment are provided.

state which is the objective of some other political parties not only in the United Kingdom but in Canada, the United States and elsewhere. A mixed capitalist enterprise system may have some government ownership, some government planning and an extensive social security programme. Moreover, the bulk of Labour's programme stands today although the Conservatives have been returned to office for three consecutive terms since 1951. On the other hand, Labour's programme cannot be equated with reforming capitalism in view of its ultimate objectives. No reform party could go so far without abandoning the basic economic principles of capitalism.

3. COMMUNISM IN RUSSIA

The system we call communism is a relative newcomer. While modern capitalism evolved in the late eighteenth and early nineteenth centuries, it is only forty years since the Bolsheviks seized power in Russia and even then socialism was not achieved overnight. Through the early years the Russian economy passed through several stages and 1928, the year of the first Five Year Plan, is generally taken to mark the beginnings of the Soviet system in its modern form. Looking at this economic system as it stands today we find the two basic features of socialism: public ownership and centralized planning.

Ownership of the Means of Production

Apart from personal goods private ownership is rare in Russia. By and large, the means of production are owned "collectively". Contrary to popular belief the central government is not the sole owner. Collective ownership includes ownership by state and local governments and by co-operatives, both producers' and consumers'. In fact, as with capitalism, there is considerable variation in the *form* of business enterprise. In retail trade, for example, the cities have chains of government stores while towns and villages have co-operative stores. In agriculture the predominant form is the collective farm which is a kind of producers' co-op. It does not own land (that belongs to the State and cannot be sold) but most of the livestock and machinery are the property of the collective. In addition, individual members of the collective farm may own small plots of land and some livestock. This private ownership does not change the essential nature of the system any more than government ownership of railways changes ours. Individual ownership is the rule in a free enterprise system and collective ownership is the rule in Russia.

Centralized Planning

The Soviet economy is a planned economy. Whether more shoes or cars or television sets are made for consumers, how much is spent on investment, what resources will be used for sputniks or the Red army: these decisions are made at the highest level of government. Successive Five Year Plans set the basic patterns of production.

The techniques of planning are too numerous and complex to be described here, but it is worth knowing more about what planning is — and isn't. For example, there is the widespread belief that Soviet production is planned down to the last nut and bolt, that the only function of management is to carry out orders from above. This is not true. The Plan does set targets in production because the aim of planning is to use resources in a particular way. But the managers of the individual plant (or farm or mill) have essentially the same job of organizing production as managers in our corporations in which over-all policy decisions are made by the board of directors. Management may also have some influence on the targets themselves. Preliminary versions of

U.S.S.R. Embassy, Press Office

Part of the new settlement of the Kalinin Collective Farm in Nesvizh District of Minsk Region, Byelorussia.

the Plan are widely circulated and discussed and targets are frequently revised both before and after the Plan is finally adopted. There is also considerable variation in the degree of authority left to management among different industries. Large industries, such as steel and power, are closely supervised; in most of these industries there is a special government department in charge. Local industries, on the other hand, are controlled locally. The collective farm also has a measure of independence: once it has filled its quota for the government any additional output can be sold — to factories, or co-operatives or in local markets — for the benefit of its members.

Another common misconception is that planning implies the direction of labour. According to this view workers are allocated to particular jobs in the same way as raw materials. In fact, with the exception of wartime, the Soviet worker is free to move. He can choose his job and, although encouraged to stay in one place, he is not prevented from changing jobs. Much moving from job to job has been one of the chief problems in Soviet production. "Forced" labour (by which we mean work done, under duress, by such groups as political prisoners) does exist but observers agree that it is a small part of the whole labour force. The fact of planning, therefore, does not necessarily eliminate labour's freedom to move. But certainly other freedoms are swept away.

Role of Prices in the Plan

Even a planned economy, then, faces the problem of getting labour into the right places. The method used to solve it is essentially the same as our own — higher wages! This is not to say that the two wage systems are identical. There is a great difference in the way in which wages are determined. Consider who decides which jobs are the most essential. In our system, with prices determined in the market, the decision is ultimately made by consumers. In Russia, because it is the government that apportions the working capital (out of which wages are paid) among different industries, the decision is made by the government. The individual firm, if it is efficient and makes profits, can raise wages, offer bonuses or improve working conditions. But it cannot change the basic allocation of resources.

The question of wages raises the question of prices. Would students in the Soviet Union study demand and supply? Whether they do or not prices are used, and, like prices in our system, work to channel resources into particular uses to encourage consumption of this or discourage consumption of that. Again, however, there is a significant difference. In the Soviet system the Plan comes first and prices are a device for putting policy into effect. Prices are controlled by the government. It is the Plan, not the price system, that decides the pattern in production.

The existence of some "free" markets, where prices can fluctuate, does not greatly alter the picture. In local markets for farm products, for example, prices are allowed to find their own level, depending on consumer demand and available supplies. But a high price, indicating strong consumer demand, need not stimulate production. This is a fundamental difference between the Soviet system and our own. In Russia, choices in production are made by the government; and even in the small area where consumers have the opportunity to make their wants known they do not thereby direct production. In our system the job of planning production is actually left to consumers.

It is true that Soviet planning bears the imprint of special circumstances. The Communists seized power in an industrially backward country, where the general level of living was well below Western standards and at a time when World War I had greatly disrupted economic life. To the Communist leaders industrialization was not only the means of raising incomes but also the key to survival in a hostile world. Industrial development, therefore, had to be rapid. And a rapid rate of development without outside aid meant keeping the production of consumer goods to a minimum. In the late thirties, the threat of attack by Nazi Germany added urgency to the twin goals that had already been selected: industrialization and military strength. Nevertheless, while these factors help to explain the neglect of consumers' wishes, it is important to recognize that the consumer would not necessarily get a higher priority, even under the most favourable circumstances, because there is nothing in the system to assure that he will.

Conclusion

All economic systems have their strengths and weaknesses. Our own system is imperfect and we have emphasized its shortcomings. But if we have been zealous in probing weaknesses the reason is that we must understand our problems. Judged on the three criteria of economic welfare — the size of the national income, its distribution and stability — capitalism scores well on the first but not on the second and the third. At the same time solutions are being developed within the framework of a mixed enterprise economy. The goal is to improve the working of our economic system without losing the major advantages it provides: consumer sovereignty and high levels of performance in production.

It is more difficult to judge another system on the basis of a synoptic view. It seems likely that the distribution of income in Russia is less inequitable than ours — although much inequality remains. We may also concede that the Russians have eliminated the business cycle. But these advantages go hand in hand with major disadvantages. The neglect of consumers' wishes is one. More important, in solving economic problems the Communists make use of a political system that we would find intolerable. All power is concentrated in the small group of men who head the Communist Party. On election day the Soviet citizen may vote against the Communist candidate but he cannot vote *for* someone else. There is, then, no possibility of changing the government — by peaceful means — nor any way of influencing the policies of the government. The interests of the individual have been subordinated to the interests of the State and freedom of the individual has been ruthlessly suppressed.

In all the Western democracies such an authoritarian political system is considered insupportable. Whether socialism could solve the economic problems of inequality and instability within the framework of democratic institutions is a question that has not been answered; the evidence is incomplete.

But these are not the major problems in all countries. In a large part of the world interest centres on production, the problem Adam Smith tackled so long ago in his *Wealth of Nations*. How can the nation's wealth be increased and hunger and poverty eliminated? We are accustomed to point to the success of capitalism in the West, but less willing to look for reasons why the methods of Adam Smith, which we followed, have not been copied more extensively. More than a century has passed since the industrial revolution began, yet Asia and Africa record little progress in the age-old war on poverty. Today the poorer nations can see that the Soviet system is also proving efficient in production. These countries would prefer to find their solution within a framework of democracy but their problems are more urgent than ours and the goal inevitably a long way off. Accordingly, they may choose or be driven to follow the communist way of economic organization.

The issues involve all of us. Extreme differences in wealth breed tensions and these tensions are accentuated by the political rivalry of the great powers. Although the world problem goes far beyond the scope of economics an understanding of its economic aspects is essential to intelligent discussion and appraisal of government policies in the democracies.

QUESTIONS FOR DISCUSSION

1. "Nationalization" has long been a magic word for Socialists. Today, however, the British Labour Party is divided on the issue. One faction opposes further nationalization. If this point of view were accepted, would there be any difference between a member of the Labour Party and a liberal who supported the Welfare State? Discuss.

2. Arrange a class debate:

Resolved: that nationalization of key industries (transportation and communications, banks, heavy industries) cannot improve a nation's economic welfare as much as an expanded educational programme at all levels, including primary and secondary schools and the universities as well as adult education.

3. When the National Health Act was introduced in England the reaction in North America—as expressed in newspapers and magazines—was generally unfavourable. Since 1946 the prepaid health schemes offered by private corporations (such as Blue Cross, Physicians Services Inc., Medical Service Inc.) have experienced a great expansion. Co-operatives have also been active in the field of health insurance. Today many Canadians have some form of insurance against hospital and medical bills. Do you think that these schemes fill the need, or do you think that a larger role should be assumed by the State, as in England? List the probable advantages and disadvantages of both.

4. Co-operative stores and farms are found in Russia and state-owned railways and power plants in Canada. Nevertheless, the two economic systems are fundamentally different. List the basic differences under the following headings and, where they occur, the similarities:

        (1)   directing production;
        (2)   management in the individual firm;
        (3)   assigning the labour force to specific jobs;
        (4)   role of prices;
        (5)   fulfilling wants of consumers.

5. One of the first issues raised in this book was the contrast in the wealth and poverty of nations. The differences were explained by differences in land, labour, capital and technology. Did you notice that a fundamental question was not raised: the *reason* for these differences? In other words, why has the development of technology, the accumulation and improvement of capital, and the acquisition of skills been so largely confined to countries of Northwestern Europe and those settled by their immigrants?

Since 1776, which marks both the Declaration of Independence in the United States and the first appearance of the "Wealth of Nations", the rate of economic development has been very high in some countries, negligible in others. As a result, inequalities in wealth have greatly increased. Can you suggest some reasons, not necessarily economic, why the spread of the Western economic system fell short of covering the world? Does this failure help to explain why two great nations, Russia and China, turned to a different economic system? What lesson could the West draw from this concerning aid to underdeveloped countries?

6. As a class project, read Chapter 1 of this book again and then consider what you have learned about the Canadian economy. Have some of your opinions changed as a result of studying economics? Can you think of some beliefs, once firmly held, that proved to be wrong? (For example: to keep all Japanese goods out of Canada is sound economics!) Or can you list events of the past year, reported in the newspapers, that were made more interesting by studying the Canadian economy? Organize a class discussion.

Index